Opera — Front and Back

OPERA
FRONT and BACK

by

H. Howard Taubman

CHARLES SCRIBNER'S SONS · NEW YORK
CHARLES SCRIBNER'S SONS · LTD · LONDON
1938

To
William B. Chase

my old teammate and friend,
whose kindnesses have brightened
countless lives

CONTENTS

Contents

ILLUSTRATIONS

[ix]

Illustrations

The illustrations are reproductions of photographs especially made by the New York Times Studio. The photograph of Arturo Toscanini is reproduced through the courtesy of Foto Rothmaier, Salzburg.

Opera — Front and Back

FORETASTE

OPERA may be a virus. If it gets into the blood, it may have you for life. If it catches you young, the depredations may be severe. A member of the Metropolitan Opera Company frequently exposed his observant five-year-old heir to the performances and mores of the Opera House, and this was the result. At about the time the opera season ended, the father, wishing the boy's experience to be broad, took him to St. Patrick's Cathedral for an Easter Sunday service. The youngster seemed to be fascinated by the splendor of the service. At the close of a tremendous outpouring of song from the chorus, he paid the tribute he knew best. He shouted, at the top of his voice: "Bravo! Bravo!"

Some people achieve a lifelong immunity from the operatic germ. There are the husbands who escort their wives to their seats in the opera house and spend part of the time dozing and the rest at the bar. There are the husbands who do not escort their wives to the opera house. The attendants of the café on the grand tier floor of the Metropolitan reported recently that a young man, who had been sent to the opera by his parents for the good of his culture, spent the entire evening at the bar. Once during the first act of Wagner's four-hour-long "Siegfried" a young couple, in impeccable formal dress, emerged from the theatre hastily, and the young man was heard to say, "We have time enough to make a real show."

Then there is the vast company of middle-of-the-roaders.

Opera: Front and Back

They do not love opera, nor do they despise it. They derive pleasure from a spot of good singing. They respond to a luscious melody carried on the wings of a rounded, resonant voice, and they are properly respectful of the trills and roulades of a showpiece aria, especially when it is warbled by a coloratura soprano of reputation. The links that connect the good tunes are things to be endured patiently, as are the gestures that pass for acting among many opera singers. These people go to the expensive operas like the Metropolitan on occasion if they have money to spare. It does not worry them if they cannot afford a form of entertainment that generally comes higher than any other in the world. For those of modest means the radio and the movies have made the best tunes and the finest voices available for the turn of a dial or a small entrance fee.

Persons of all parties and all operatic persuasions seem to find interest, however, in the chit-chat that pervades the world of the lyric theatre. The opera has a word for it; so have the theatre and the screen. Glamor! It is compounded of great names, fabulous salaries, temperament and gossip. The opera commands a generous share of all of these. Its people have their deeds and their words spread on the record in newspapers and magazines, in films and on the air. Ordinary contretemps are spiced now and then by juicy scandals. The wife of a handsome baritone sues a soprano for alienation of affections. Another soprano spits in the face of a contralto. A tenor hauls off and smacks a soprano. The average man and woman have a healthy appetite for these stories. And even those who detest opera and all its works will deign to chuckle at them.

The inveterate opera fans care for more than sensational tales. They eagerly absorb discussions as to whether Soprano A has a purer high C than Soprano B, whether Conductor A main characters, boy, naturally, loses girl. In the old opera yarns he keeps on losing her for five acts. In the end he wins her, but more often than not the union is achieved in heaven. For operas have a tragic predisposition. The hero or the heroine expires at the end in any of the accepted ways— natural death, suicide, homicide; only it takes some time to depart this mortal coil. The surviving member of the pair follows suit, if death does not come simultaneously. Changes are rung on the theme. But the boy-meets-girl, boy-loses-girl, boy-gets-girl formula applies even—and let the heavens shake at the sacrilege!—to "Tristan und Isolde."

The opera differs from the spoken drama in that there is bound to be less action because music must have time to expand. The protagonists sing long arias, and the listener must adjust himself to giving the song an opportunity to achieve a curve and a climax. That is all right, too, so long as the arias have the power to stir, to purge or to exalt. Opera may—then again it may not—lose something in not having the time to expatiate on its complications, but the music provides compensating advantages. Music can establish a new mood in several measures. It can set the stage for a change in feeling by a simple alteration of tempo or a modulation in harmony. Music may be, as some one said, "nothing else but wild sounds civilized into time and tune," but when the sounds have been ordered by a masterful hand, the origins do not count.

Whether he is aware of these things or not, the opera-goer reacts to them. In this country where the classics of other lands are sung in their original tongues, it takes a linguist to follow the story. But music needs no words. A good melody floated on a sensuous voice above a sympathetic or contending orchestra is its own excuse for being. As W. S. Gilbert put it, "This particularly rapid, unintelligible patter isn't generally heard, and if it is it doesn't matter." The singer may stay in character and address his love, his longing or his despair to the others on the stage or he may step forward to the footlights and sing his high notes at the audience. Most people do not care which so long as they can hear.

3

Visually there may be objections. The singers may not have the "physique du rôle." In the old days this was not a troublesome consideration. No one cared if in "Aïda" the gallant hero was Caruso, a gent with a paunch, and his in-amorata was Emmy Destinn, who had, to be brutally plain about it, the proportions of a barrel. Or if in "Siegfried" the sleeping Brünnhilde was so lavishly upholstered by nature that she dared not stir on her couch lest, as an irreverent critic remarked of one such Wagnerian soprano, she release a cascade of bosom. Distortions of the stage picture were forgiven or ignored when the singing was of overpowering magnificence. Who today would not trade a tenor with a Hollywood façade for a voice like Caruso's?

Time nevertheless has forced changes in the opera picture. Singers are conforming to the demands of a stream-lined age. Only a few hardy souls whose reputations are solidly established have the temerity to indulge their tastes for pastries or beer. It may be that the films, with their standards of slimness, grace and good looks, have made the public less tolerant of the 200-pound Mimi in "La Bohème," who is presumably dying of a wasting disease, of a middle-aged, pot-bellied Don José who is supposed to attract Carmen, or of a Carmen who is inclined to waddle. Singers today are trying to look the part of the people they play, and many are succeeding.

[8]

What the Audience Sees and Hears

Sopranos like Lily Pons, Grace Moore, Rosa Ponselle, Helen Jepson, and Bidu Sayão are slim·and beauteous, as are mezzo-sopranos such as Gertrud Wettergren, Kerstin Thorborg and Gladys Swarthout. Tenors are streamlined; witness Nino Martini, Richard Crooks and Charles Kullmann. And look at the athletic figures of baritones and bassos like Lawrence Tibbett, Ezio Pinza and Nelson Eddy. In the Wagnerian operas we have Kirsten Flagstad, who, though mature in figure, commands a stateliness that is eminently fitting for the goddesses and epic heroines she is called upon to impersonate, and Marjorie Lawrence, who can mount her Grane in the culminating scene of "Götterdämmerung" and gallop into the flames with the aplomb of a lady at the hunt.

There has been no attempt here to call the entire roll of those who make the grade in appearance. And there were honorable exceptions in days gone by—Geraldine Farrar and Mary Garden, to name but two. They were not overstuffed like many of their colleagues. They knew the rudiments of diet, exercise and care. You could not, in all fairness, blame their contemporaries or their predecessors of the Victorian era. Lavish upholstery was the vogue, in furniture, clothes, and human beings. If Lillian Nordica, a great Isolde and Brünnhilde, went on her summer vacation determined to indulge her every whim of appetite for rich food, there were few to say her nay. Today a manager may tell a prospect, as Edward Johnson told a Continental soprano recently, that she must take some weight off if she would come to the Metropolitan. The audience may not sit, with the straight face or the fond forgiveness of the past, through the exciting scene in "Siegfried" when 'the fearless young hero climbed through the fire, ripped the corselet of mail from the sleeping Brünnhilde, disclosing her in a white gown—

[9]

Opera: Front and Back

a Brünnhilde of vast, billowing curves—and cried out in sublime understatement, "Das ist kein Mann!"

Despite these changes, no opera house in the world would reject a glorious voice because of the physical shortcomings of its owner. But it would have to be, beyond question or cavil, a really glorious voice.

4

If the opera pursues its course without mishap, the audience sees the usual components of a theatre-piece and hears the usual recitatives, arias and orchestral commentary of the lyric theatre. Sights and sounds not meant for the customers sometimes obtrude. The prompter's stage whispers may be audible, when the orchestra is muffled. The chorus master, beating time for his minions from some spot in the wings, may stand so close to the open stage that his flailing arms become visible to the occupants of the side seats. These, however, are minor intrusions, noticed by a few. It is the mishaps that occur in full view and hearing of the entire audience that provide the customers with most of their extra-curricular thrills and laughs.

When an artist forgets a phrase or skips one in the course of an opera, the average listener will not be aware of the incident unless he is thoroughly familiar with the music. There was the secondary soprano whose lot was to do all the maids, and once during a performance of "Lucia di Lammermoor" she sang the part of Ines in "Trovatore." How many in the audience were aware of this lapse of memory? Or of what happened to the nervous singer who has to open the door in the second act of "Tosca" and intone several words? He was so anxious to get his poor part right that he kept asking the assistant conductor to repeat the phrase, and when the time came to sing, he could not utter a word. He opened the door, stuck his face through the gap and banged the door shut again.

A handful before the footlights may have realized these minor deficiencies. Possibly as few persons were cognizant of the shame of another singer, a woman who was found to be nervous and was intrusted with parts only in ensemble pages. At long last she received her opportunity to sing solo. In the opening scene of "Louise" she had a part which required her to sing one sentence, beginning with the word "Bas." The woman was so elated at this modest opportunity that she had all her friends and relatives come to hear her. The great moment came. She opened her mouth, enunciated the word "Bas" and no more. Her mouth remained open, but no sound came forth. She confessed later she had suddenly developed a cramp in the jaw.

There was no doubt, however, that the audience—a knowing assemblage at one of the performances of the uncut Wagner matinee cycle at the Metropolitan—knew that something was wrong during a "Walküre" performance some years ago. Frida Leider was the Brünnhilde. At the cue for the anguished passage, "War es so schmälich," in a critical scene of the last act, Leider did not sing. There was a break of a split second. Suddenly a voice, emanating from the wings, took up the music and sang for several measures. Then Leider found her voice and went on with the performance. The duration of the incident was a matter of some moments, but the strain for the audience was intense.

Possibly the listeners forgot the brief crisis in the sweep and majesty of Wotan's matchless farewell and the incandescence of the fire music that end the music-drama. But the newspapermen had a duty to their public. They hurried backstage to discover that Leider had suffered momentary dizziness and that Dorothee Manski, who had sung one of

the Valkyries in the opening scene of the act, had saved
the situation. As the reporters buzzed around, seeking information, a young European assistant conductor, who was
not sympathetic with American news values, cried out that
Americans were impossible: "You have listened to a brilliant
performance," he exclaimed, "and you get excited about a
trifle!"

Another instance of voicelessness of which the audience
was aware occurred during a performance of "Meistersinger"
two decades ago. Hermann Weil, singing Hans Sachs, the
central role, found himself bereft of the power of speech at
the end of the second act. No other baritone was available at
the moment. It was decided to eliminate the first scene of
the third act, wherein Sachs sings almost throughout, and to
give only the closing scene with its celebration of the Jo-
hannesfest and the song contest for the hand of Eva Pogner.
A presentation that ends close to midnight was completed at
about 11 P.M. It was said that some of the boxholders saw
the end of "Die Meistersinger" for the first time.

Going loss of voice one better, the Hippodrome once gave
a performance of "Tannhäuser" for which some one forgot
to hire a Venus. It was a dilemma that Alfredo Salmaggi,
Hippodrome director, could take in stride. A ballet girl was
ordered to recline on the couch in place of Venus, and they
just ignored the music allotted to the lady who sang the
joys of the flesh.

5

Birds and animals used in some operas have managed, on
occasion, to throw monkey wrenches into the proceedings.
In Chicago they once gave a ballet in which occurred a wedding procession. The bride and groom were seated on
donkeys. Some careless person had overlooked checking on

the first principle of animal life on the stage: making sure that both donkeys were female. One animal was male and the other female. The inevitable occurred—in midstage.

Horses, when they are stage broken, are usually well behaved. Yet there was a performance of "Götterdäm-merung" when Flagstad tried to stand close to Grane, her trusted steed, as she completed Brünnhilde's stirring thren-ody. The horse was restive; it moved nervously. Flagstad's voice had anything but a soothing effect on the animal, which seemed to be preparing to lunge at her. The audience held its breath, more concerned with the danger to Flagstad than with Brünnhilde's transcendent music.

A horse that had had no previous stage experience was employed in the last act of "Carmen" in a Metropolitan performance in Philadelphia. The animal was scared by the lights and the noise of chorus and orchestra, and it obeyed that impulse. The evidence of his misbehavior was all over the stage. Margaret Matzenauer was the Carmen, dressed in white. When Don José stabbed her at the end of the opera, she staggered indecisively, looking for a spot where she could die a clean death. She could not delay her end indefinitely and crumbled to the ground, hoping for the best. The spot of her choice was maculate. She took her curtain calls in a dressing gown.

No horse in the annals of opera gave an audience more diversion than a decrepit nag that was recruited for a scene in "Russlan and Ludmilla" in Moscow at the Imperial Opera many years ago. The baritone Georges Baklanoff sat astride the horse as they entered on the stage. His role called on him to seek advice from an old sage who was played by an antiquated tenor. The horse quivered under Baklanoff as they approached, in the center of the stage, the gray-bearded philosopher who had the opening measures in the colloquy.

Opera: Front and Back

The sage's voice shook with age, and it had, moreover, a strange bleating quality. As the tenor finished his phrase, the horse raised his head heavenward and emitted a piercing neigh. The sound, with its high pitch and shake and breathiness, resembled that made by the tenor. That unhappy individual tried to go on with his part of the colloquy. The horse replied in a higher key. The tenor sang again. The horse went him one better.

Baklanoff shook with laughter and did not attempt to sing, and the audience roared with delight. It was clear that, whatever the outcome of the contest between beast and tenor, the scene could not go on, and the curtain brought a merciful end to a historic operatic dialogue.

The goat in "Dinorah" can be a headache to the stage crew and a diversion to the audience. In one performance the animal slipped from a mountain crag and plunged to the floor of the stage in full view of the audience. It broke a leg and had to be destroyed. In a performance of "Dinorah" at the Metropolitan, the goat suddenly became attached to the life on the stage and would not come off when his scene was over. He had to be dragged off by a couple of stage hands who hurriedly threw costumes over themselves borrowed from choristers.

During a presentation of "Turandot," as Giacomo Lauri-Volpi kneeled before the the castle of the Princess, Maria Jeritza, the pet cat of one of the opera staff members strolled out on the stage and rubbed its back against the tenor's leg. As the audience chuckled, he tried to ignore the cat. Finally he picked it up and flung it into the wings.

The geese in Humperdinck's "Königskinder" have been a source of innocent merriment for the audience. At the Metropolitan Geraldine Farrar played the goose girl, one of her finest roles, and the scene in which she fed her flock of geese, enclosed in a wire baby fence, went well. Once, however, the birds were disturbed by something and began a terrific honking. It took some time to pacify them.

At the Chicago Opera the geese turned in a better job in one performance of "Königskinder." The stage force had developed a splendidly disciplined flock which played six performances like good troupers. Just before Christmas the director of the company asserted that there would be no further repeats of "Königskinder." Whereupon the stage manager presented a goose each to a number of stage hands as a Christmas present. Shortly after Christmas a crucial situation necessitated the insertion of "Königskinder" into the week's bill. The stage staff had two days in which to train a new flock of geese. They labored valiantly, recalling, no doubt, succulent Christmas dinners. As the curtain went up on the scene of the goose girl feeding her charges, the birds reacted to the glare of the footlights and the applause of the audience. They let out a raucous explosion of honk-honk-honks and took to the air. One goose landed in the orchestra pit, another in a box, a third in the balcony and the others in the aisles and amid the seatholders in the orchestra chairs.

What price realism in opera? Joseph Addison pondered that question in *The Spectator* of March 6, 1711.

"A little Skill in Criticism would inform us," he wrote, "that Shadows and Realities ought not to be mix'd together in the same Piece; and that Scenes, which are designed as the Representations of Nature, should be filled with Resemblances, and not with the Things themselves. . . . I would recommend what I have here said, to the Directors, as well as to the Admirers, of our Modern Opera.

"As I was walking in the Streets about a Fortnight ago, I saw an ordinary Fellow carrying a Cage full of little Birds upon his Shoulder; and, as I was wondering with my self what Use he would put them to, he was met very luckily by an Acquaintance, who had the same curiosity. Upon his asking him what he had upon his Shoulder, he told him, that he had been buying Sparrows for the Opera. Sparrows for the Opera, says his Friend, licking his lips, what, are they to be roasted? No, no, says the other, they are to enter towards the end of the first Act and to fly about the stage. . . . [Addison went to the opera to see for himself.] I found the Sparrows . . . though they flew in Sight, the Musick proceeded from a Consort of Flagellets and Birdcalls which was planted behind the Scenes. . . . There have been so many Flights of them let loose in this Opera, that it is feared the House will never get rid of them; and that in other Plays they may make their entrance in very wrong and improper Scenes, so as to be seen flying in a Lady's Bed-Chamber, or pearching upon a King's Throne; besides the Inconveniences which the Heads of the Audience may sometimes suffer from them."

6

Human beings are as thoroughly capable of disrupting a scene as any bird or animal. Some years ago a Boston audience, watching the first act of "Madama Butterfly," saw a night watchman, lantern in hand, casually stroll across the stage. The literal-minded watchman, who was unused to opera and this theatre, amiably explained to a wrathful stage manager that the stage was dark and that, by a natural process of logic, he walked across it light in hand.

A Metropolitan audience at a performance of "Aïda" was entertained during the Nile scene by the silhouette of something that looked like a witch out of "Hänsel und Gretel"; the silhouette moved along behind the rear drop. There

What the Audience Sees and Hears

were roars of laughter out front. It turned out that the figure was that of a cleaning woman, on her way home, carrying an umbrella and an old-fashioned shopping net. She happened to cross the stage between the lights and a transparent drop.

A Monte Carlo audience witnessed an incident years ago that would remind old-timers of a piece of business employed by Dixey and Wilson in "Evangeline." The opera was "Aïda," and the management devised a wooden camel to give zest to the triumphal scene. Two men, one for the fore legs and the other for the hind legs, were employed to animate the camel. The invention worked so well that the director ordered the camel placed down front. As the singers joined in the great concerted climax of the scene, some one standing near the camel inadvertently tapped on its side. The man who occupied the fore legs opened a shutter in the neck of the camel, stuck out his head and, with pardonable curiosity, yelled, "Comment!"

Children, when they are required in opera, have a way of distracting the attention of the audience. A Metropolitan gathering once witnessed a child playing the part of Cio-Cio-San's baby in "Madama Butterfly" grow fidgety in the arms of the soprano and begin to cry. The Cio-Cio-San had to pause, carry the child offstage and play the final scene without the infant.

Florence Easton, who frequently sang Cio-Cio-San, had two unanticipated incidents in "Madama Butterfly" because of the need for a child. At one performance a doll was used. Antonio Scotti, the Sharpless, took the hand of the child to say farewell, and the arm came off. Scotti found a dismembered arm dangling gruesomely from his fingers.

On another occasion Miss Easton was fortunate in having a child who played up to her beautifully, returning affectionate caress for caress. At the end of the performance she patted the remarkably precocious child and asked him how old he was. In a surprisingly deep voice, he said, "Twenty-four."

Some months ago the Metropolitan added a group of young children to the ballet in the first scene of the second act of "Aïda." The youngsters amused the audience with their lively, if not wholly accurate or co-ordinated, steps. They were to exit by backing toward the wings, bowing toward Amneris, the daughter of Egypt's king, for whom they had been dancing. One little girl backed from the side to the center of the stage, and several of the other youngsters retreated, instead of into the wings, into a solid set and crouched for some moments in bewildered confusion in full view of the audience.

7

Not all opera accidents are amusing. Operagoers have had unforgettable thrills as witnesses to grave disturbances on the stage. There was the time at the Metropolitan when the bridge in "Carmen" gave way in the first five minutes and crashed a number of persons to the ground, inflicting serious injuries. More recently, a weight detached itself from on high and plunged to the stage, barely missing Queena Mario who was singing Gretel. The fights in "Carmen" between the Carmen and Don José have sometimes been so realistic that one of the singers was injured. Jeritza and Martinelli put on such a fight, and Rosa Ponselle suffered a broken arm from a fall caused by a violent push from René Maison, the José.

In her first season at the Metropolitan, Flagstad developed a nosebleed in the first act of "Lohengrin." As she kneeled praying for the advent of a defender, her maids in waiting encircled her as she dabbed at her nose with a handkerchief and attempted to quell the flow of blood. In the final moment of a scene in "Thaïs," Jeritza tumbled down a long flight of stairs, incurring a severe shaking up. The curtain for the next scene had to be held for twenty minutes.

No audience, however, saw a more throbbing incident than was vouchsafed a gathering in Brooklyn on December 11, 1920. The visiting Metropolitan troupe was playing "L'Elisir d'Amore." In the middle of the first act, Enrico Caruso began to bleed at the mouth. He sang with difficulty but finished the act. Gatti-Casazza at his Manhattan hotel had been notified the moment the trouble began and when he was called again at the end of the first act, he ordered the performance halted. The audience, which could see clearly Caruso's distress, was in a state of tense excitement. No opera could have wrought it up in this fashion. Gatti-Casazza, who, in his four decades as an opera director, never failed to complete a performance, ordered this one cut short, because he felt that the audience was too unstrung to relish continuance with a substitute for Caruso. The admission price was refunded.

It was not Caruso's last performance. He sang several times that December at the Metropolitan Opera House. In his last appearance on any stage on the night of December 24, 1920, he gave his magnificent portrayal of Eleazar in "La Juive" without any suggestion to the audience that he was suffering severe pain. The Brooklyn audience had received the most racking thrill.

8

Most opera accidents, at least those to which the audience is privy, end more happily. There was the performance of

Opera: Front and Back

Montemezzi's "L'Amore dei tre Re" where Lucrezia Bori, playing the principal female role, had died. Leon Rothier, who wore the make-up of an elderly man with an impressive beard, picked up the dead girl in his arms and placed the body on a bench to the rear. This manœuvre was executed with his back to the audience. When he faced the footlights once more, the audience tittered. The beard had become detached and Rothier was now a clean-shaven gentleman.

The loss of parts of make-up and costume is a recurrent operatic sidelight with varying capacities for tickling the audience. There was the time when Gertrud Wettergren, singing Carmen, kicked with hoydenish vigor, and sent one of her shoes flying into the wings. Result: she played the rest of the scene while hobbling around in one stockinged foot.

There was another occasion when a young soprano found her freedom of action impeded by the fact that the pantaloons that she was wearing under a bustle came loose. It took a great deal of resourcefulness to keep the garment up until the end of her scene.

In a performance of "Carmen" many decades ago, Emma Calvé bent down and a powder puff fell from her décolletage. The tenor Salignac picked up the offending object and, in an effort to be helpful, he attempted to replace it whence it emerged. Apparently Calvé thought that he was trying to get fresh. She snatched the puff from his hands and brought it in a vigorous sideswipe against his face. He was enveloped by a cloud of powder and looked more like a baker than a soldier.

Whether some persons in the audience regarded this incident as a legitimate piece of stage business is not recorded. There is no question that a more recent "Carmen" audience was aware of the unprepared quality of a last-act incident.

What the Audience Sees and Hears

The American mezzo-soprano, Jeanne Gordon, was the Carmen and she wore a wide hoop skirt of Spanish style in the final act. Armand Tokatyan was the José. He stabbed Miss Gordon, and Carmen fell dead, feet first to the audience, with the hoop skirt high in the air. There were titters from the auditorium, and Tokatyan hastily stepped on the skirt and gave the dead Carmen's body a modicum of modesty. He kept his foot on the skirt as he sang the closing apostrophe to Carmen, but, to give his last notes all the zip he could muster, he stepped forward and up bounced the skirt. "Carmen," wrote one reporter, "with a hoop-la finish!"

Perhaps the most notorious fall from grace occurred in a Calvé performance. On that memorable occasion her—shall we give them the name of the period?—bloomers dropped to her ankles in full view of the audience. In those days such an occurrence was scandalous. It caused horrified whispers. One distinguished dowager accepted the incident calmly and pronounced judgment on Calvé and the bloomers.

Said the dowager, "If they were clean, it was intentional."

III

WHAT THE AUDIENCE DOES
NOT SEE AND HEAR

WHAT is visible and audible to the audience is but a fraction of the activity involved in any opera production. The lyric theatre has all the problems of the spoken drama, and dozens of others thrown in for good measure. An opera is not like a Broadway production; a show cannot be set and allowed to run its course, six evenings and two matinees a week, with every manipulation neatly grooved. A theatre like the Metropolitan puts on a different opera each day of the week but Sunday, and while any work may be repeated as many as six or seven times a season, it requires long memories and careful training to make everything function according to schedule backstage.

Add to the problems of a repertory theatre the complications thrust on the opera by the music, which permits no latitude for lapses. Music is an exigent taskmaster. Every movement—walking across the stage, sheathing a sword, sitting down or rising—and every stage effect must be on time. It takes a veritable corps of lieutenants to synchronize the diverse elements of an opera. The more lavish the opera, the more complex the backstage machinery.

A music-drama like "Die Walküre" is comparatively simple to mount. Save for the opening scene of the third act, which demands a contingent of eight women to sing the Valkyries, the work relies on six principals. It has no chorus, no ballet, no stage band, no supernumeraries. All that is required is that the singers have their cues and that they know their business. For the rest, there are stage effects such as the magic fire at the end of the opera and some tricky lighting.

But take an opera like "Die Meistersinger" with its opulent panoply of a medieval feast day in the closing scene, or "La Bohème" with its colorful bohemian café scene in the second act, or "Carmen" with its turbulent life in a Seville street in the first act, its second act inn and its final act outside the bull ring. Hundreds of persons must be marshalled for these operas. And it takes some doing.

Opera has no luxury such as a "single set" production. It is true that some short works, especially one-acters, have only one mise-en-scène, but it takes two or more short works to fill out an evening. The full-length opera is almost never confined to a single set. Presumably it wouldn't be either opera or grand if a story could be told in three or more acts with no change of scene.

Once the performance is on, two men are in command. They control every aspect of it. They may be likened unto generals, and they have their adjutants. These men are the conductor and the stage director. The former is responsible for every musical phase of the performance; the stage director, for the mise-en-scène.

The conductor is seated on his perch in the pit, back to the audience. Directing the orchestra, in itself, is no problem. The men see the conductor and he them. It is also a simple matter for the conductor to make known his wishes to the artists on the stage. They can follow his beat and his cues. But that is not enough; that, in fact, is only where the fun begins.

2

At a theatre like the Metropolitan there is a group of assistant conductors, known also as répétiteurs. Each one has his own score, with notations of cues, tempi and cuts carefully indicated to correspond with the conductor's conception. The assistant conductors perform a variety of functions backstage. One man is stationed at the call board on the Thirty-ninth Street side of the stage. There is a long rectangular opening in the call board, so fixed that the répétiteur can see the conductor and his every movement clearly. The répétiteur who is stationed at this point is charged with the duty of watching the stage hand who operates the great golden curtains. If the overture leads into the opening of the opera, he must warn the stage hand of the imminence of the curtain and must give him the signal to raise it. At the end of a scene his score is marked to show whether the curtain is to be lowered slowly, rapidly, or at a moderate speed. As the scene nears its end, he calls out "Slow curtain," "Fast curtain," "Medium slow curtain," "Medium fast curtain." Then he holds his hand poised and at the down beat the stage hand lowers the curtain as instructed.

Years ago the master of the curtain's ascent and descent was a retired basso named Viviani. He had survived a notable career in secondary roles among which were Monterone in Victor Maurel's "Rigoletto." He had been in the cast of the memorable performance in which Jean de Reszke sang a tenor role for the first time and was roundly hissed for his efforts. Viviani, in short, was a man of and for the opera, and he liked to discourse of its past and its traditions.

During a performance of "Bohème," Viviani was chatting with friends backstage. He knew the opera, of course. Suddenly he became aware of the music of the final duet of the third act. What he heard was the statement of the melody in the orchestra, which is followed by about thirty-two measures of singing by Mimi and Rodolfo. Viviani acted as if in a dream. He shouted, "Fast curtain!" The great golden drapes swooped down. The conductor, Gennaro Papi, stared in amazement, then thought rapidly. He whispered an order, gestured with his baton, and the orchestra answered with the closing chords of the act. Backstage the Mimi, Frances Alda, stormed at Viviani and assorted authorities.

Whatever else can be done backstage at the opera, you cannot recall a curtain. Did more than a handful of persons in the audience realize that they were cheated out of the final duet of the act? They did not, judging by the applause.

No artist, whatever his or her prominence or dependability, makes an entrance without the sanction of an assistant conductor. The singer takes his place at whatever point he must make his entrance, and a répétiteur stands at his side. Often the répétiteur holds the artist's hand. Sometimes he will count the measures. On the required beat, the répétiteur gives the artist the signal and on he goes.

When an artist has some backstage singing to do, a répétiteur stands beside him and beats time for him. If the singer's part during a scene requires him to work at the rear of the stage, beyond the reach of the voice of the prompter down front, the répétiteur acts as a prompter. When Nedda sings in the teatrino of "Pagliacci," her prompter is at the rear, not the assistant conductor who prompts from under the hood at the footlights.

The theory of opera is that the members of the company have many roles to learn and that the most conscientious of artists may forget a line or a bar of music. Caruso, an excellent musician and an artist who never trusted to chance, once forgot a phrase in "Le Prophète" and it required quick thinking on the part of the conductor, Artur Bodanzky, and the orchestra to cover up the slip. Kirsten Flagstad is another artist who combines conscientiousness with consummate musicianship, and yet in a performance of "Tristan und Isolde" she

Opera: Front and Back

began a phrase in the last scene before the Liebestod on the wrong note. Since she has absolute pitch she sang the next few bars with the correct intervals between notes, but her singing was at odds, in pitch, with the orchestra. She recalls that the eyes of the dead Tristan, Lauritz Melchior, flew open, and there were signs of dismay from the conductor. But she caught and corrected herself.

The opera's system of prompting is designed to provide double and triple insurance. The prompter gives the singer the first word, or more, if necessary, of every line, and the note as well. "You'd be surprised," one conductor said, "how many of them and what famous ones perpetrate bulls." The audience has so much to follow that it rarely is aware of bungling unless it is done on a grandiose scale.

In a performance of "I Puritani" a long scene, assigned to baritone and basso, was being sung by Giuseppe DeLuca and José Mardones. The late basso, who was beginning to suffer from the inexplicable lapses of memory that caused his ultimate resignation from the company, found himself stumped. DeLuca, being a veteran of the stage and an excellent musician as well, sang both parts.

On another occasion—the opera was "The Barber of Seville" —a basso was waiting offstage for his cue to enter and to sing an aria. The singer who was to utter the cue phrase inadvertently skipped to a passage further along in the opera. The bewildered conductor followed, and the poor basso waited in the wings for a cue that never came.

A blunder that was redeemed in part so that the audience did not realize what had happened occurred at the Metropolitan in a performance of "La Juive." There is a scene in which the old Jew, Eleazar, discovers his daughter, Rachel, in rendezvous with Prince Leopold. The three artists sing a trio, and then Eleazar demands that Leopold marry his daughter. Leopold replies, "I cannot, I am a Christian." Then he turns and runs to the rear and escapes by hopping through a window.

It may have been that the tenor who sang Leopold in this performance had been discovered in compromising situations before. When Eleazar entered, Leopold's actions were almost like reflexes. He bolted and leaped through the window the moment he saw Eleazar.

The Eleazar and Rachel stared at the departing Leopold and wondered what they would do about the trio. The assistant conductor who was standing backstage near the window was aghast. He inquired acidly where the tenor was going. The latter looked sheepish. But in opera you can get away with murder. The tenor turned, went back to the window, climbed onto the stage again and calmly joined in the trio.

3

Before going on, the artist is given his pitch by a répétiteur. For this purpose the Metropolitan has pitch pipes that look like sawed-off pianos, or better still, like the side of a piano accordion without the rest of the instrument. There are two such instruments, one for the higher voices and one for the lower, and the range of each is two octaves. They are called pipe organs. A curved pipe attaches to one end of the keyboard. The répétiteur blows into it, and presses the note or the chord on the keyboard. It is amusing to watch a répétiteur, trailed by a singer backstage, puffing into this pipe organ and looking like a screwy edition of the Pied Piper of Hamelin.

When a répétiteur is not able to use the rectangular cut-out passage in the call board to watch the conductor, he will watch a colleague who is stationed there. The chief electrician at the Metropolitan has invented a device called a time-beater, which can be placed anywhere backstage to guide singer or répétiteur. It works electrically, clicking as rapidly or as slowly as desired. It is operated by a répétiteur who presses the clicker. Thus a répétiteur can get the beat by following the clicking. In the Nile scene of "Aïda" an offstage chorus of priests is located in the scene dock way off to the rear. The singers get their tempo from the time beater.

Holes are made in the sets to facilitate a direct view of the conductor. There are angles in sets which make it impossible to keep the assistant conductor at the call board within the line of vision; the simplest thing in that case is to keep an eye on the conductor out front. The audience is usually not aware of these holes. They are small and there are not many of them; at least there should not be many. But répétiteurs are short, tall and medium-sized, and they make holes at different eye levels. Sometimes a property on the stage stands above the eye level and the répétiteur must climb a ladder; he proceeds to cut a hole at the new height. Some canvases begin to look perforated even to the audience, and patches have to be sewed into them. But, as one stage director observed wistfully, "no matter how many holes there are in a set, the répétiteurs have to make new ones." Maybe it gives them something to do.

The chorusmaster acts as the assistant conductor backstage during a performance for the choristers. He is behind the scenes at all times when the chorus is working, and he places himself where they can watch him and he leads them, always making sure that he is following the conductor's beat out front. The chorusmaster, since he has a large group of men and women to direct, usually perches himself on a stepladder or some lofty spot where they can all see him. In the first act of "Gioconda" he stands on a great balcony that is part of the scene, just out of range of the audience's vision. He is constantly shouting admonitions: allegro, andante, presto; sometimes they are wrathful invectives like "Basta!" and "Per Bacco" and "Dummköpfe."

4

For a picture of how offstage and onstage singing is synchronized, let us stand by during the temple scene in the first act of "Aïda." The audience sees the priests—members of the chorus—lined up at each side of the stage. A large idol squats on a pedestal in the rear center, and before it stands Ramfis, the high priest. The members of the ballet do a sacred dance as the priests intone the music of their order. The audience hears the voice of a priestess, and it seems to float out from above the idol in the rear center. Twined around the song of the priestess is a chorus of women's voices, that sounds almost like an angelic choir.

Actually the singer who is chanting the music of the priestess stands on the Fortieth Street side of the stage, surrounded by the chorus of women. A harpist sits beside her. The chorusmaster, who is directing the singer and the chorus, stands aloft on a ladder, beating time. He is taking the beat from a répétiteur, also perched on a ladder, on the Thirty-ninth Street side of the set, and the latter is watching the conductor out front through a hole in the set or taking the lead from the assistant conductor stationed at the call board. So remarkable are the acoustics of the Metropolitan that a voice projected from the sides sounds out front as if it were coming from dead center. The soprano who is the unseen Voice of the Forest Bird in "Siegfried" is placed on a high platform—always with a répétiteur beside her—because in this scene the music must seem to come from the tops of the trees.

The scheme by which offstage and onstage voices and movements are harmonized is vividly exemplified by a subterfuge practiced in the bridal chorus of "Lohengrin," a subterfuge of which the audience is wholly unaware. It is difficult for marching singers to keep in time with music that may not have the exact pace of their steps, especially when, in transit, they may not see the beat of conductor or chorusmaster. While the chorus marches on, the bridal hymn is sung by another section of choristers behind the scenes. As soon as the marchers are all on the stage, they take up the music, and the backstage unit desists.

Involved in this sleight of hand transference of the singing from one group to another are not only the conductor, the chorusmaster and répétiteurs backstage, but also a small behind-the-scenes orchestra of about twenty men.

The triumphal return of Radames in the second act of "Aïda" is one of the most difficult to put together without a slip, both from the point of view of the music and the staging. As many as half a dozen répétiteurs are stationed at strategic points behind the scenes. Singers must be given their cues. The chorus and ballet and supers must be told when to enter.

Getting these forces on the stage before the audience is the job of the stage director. He sees to it that the three hundred or more persons who take part in the scene are called from their dressing rooms in good season. Before the curtain goes up he casts a final glance at the choristers who are on the stage as the scene begins. Then he walks down the line of the supers who are drawn up in file, with a full time super at the head of each division. They are dressed in costumes of the great Egyptian populace. Seen close at hand they look as if they had emerged in their winter underwear. The stage director examines the costumes. If he is sensitive, he is pained. It is an unusual super whose wig is not askew and who does not look like the morning after the night before, instead of like a citizen worthy to stand before his king. It gets hot backstage and supers have a habit of removing their wigs to massage bald pates, and when they restore the wigs they usually put them on at a drunken angle. Possibly the audience does not descry individual peculiarities, but the stage director suffers for them.

The grand march of "Aïda" begins. Several musicians playing long trumpets take their places in the van of supers and choristers. They, too, are dressed as Egyptians and some of them carry it off with as little grace as their silent comrades, the supers. One of them wears a pince-nez, another tortoise-shell spectacles, the better to see their music. Each musician has a card with the notation of his music stuck on the end of his instrument, and that distresses the stage director almost as much as any other failing in the picture. "Every singer and chorister knows his music by heart," the stage director complains, "but the musicians, who have been playing it for ten, twenty, thirty years, haven't yet memorized their parts."

As the grand march burgeons in splendor, the squadrons of choristers, supers and musicians march on and form part of the assemblage. They are togged out as ordinary citizens or as soldiers. As they walk out on the stage, in full view of the audience, the veteran at the head of the line barks out the count in what is meant to be sotto voce, so that the marchers will keep in step. The orchestra in the pit is going full blast and the audience does not hear these warnings. Several lines of soldiers march on and off the stage, re-form at the rear and march on again.

Then come the supers who carry the sacred bull and the heavy spoils of gold that Radames has brought back. There are four supers, strong, husky fellows, to tote the sacred bull. They hoist the animal on their shoulders, and just at that moment a toothless old bird who holds the end at the rear left gets the giggles. The bull shakes precariously. The stage director swears a horrible oath. But it is too late to do anything about it. The cue sounds for the entrance of the sacred bull. The supers march on. The bull shimmies and steadies. The stage director breathes deeply.

Then come the Negro supers. They have been standing around wearing jackets and overcoats. The coverings are flung off. The men wear nothing but loin cloths. The women have on skin tights. They scurry on and crawl on the ground, as captives and slaves may be expected to do.

The ballet enters. The men in the ballet, also made up as Ethiopian captives, run on and off at the side. They start to dash to their dressing rooms. The stage director yells at them to return. Some of them keep running and the stage director shouts he will fine them $5 apiece. Those who have heard this threat return and they are pushed onto the stage to give it a more crowded look. Those who have not heard are gone, and the stage director is much too busy with other matters to take note of the identity of the delinquents or to carry out his threat.

The girls of the ballet enter and dance for the edification of the King and his daughter. The King happens to be sung by a young American artist. He looks tall and imposing in his black beard. As the girls dance, he whispers at them—but the audience does not hear him—"Swing it, girls, swing it!"

Now comes the moment for the entry of Radames, the hero himself. He takes his place in the chariot behind the scenes. The chariot is drawn by two white horses. Standing at the head of each horse is a man from the stables. These men are also in Egyptian costume. They look no worse and no better than others of the populace. They walk on, grasping the bridles of the animals. The Metropolitan is taking no chances of an accident. As it is, the tenor who sings Radames seldom

What the Audience Does Not See and Hear

looks comfortable in his chariot, although it is doubtful if he has heard the tale of the Moscow horse and tenor.

The tenor need have no fears. The horses used in "Aïda" at the Metropolitan are veterans of the opera. The current pair, both white animals, are about twenty-seven years old, and have been acting in the triumphal scene of "Aïda," man and boy, for twenty-five years. Believe it or not, they even know their cues. I refused to believe it. But I have watched the horses as the grand march began and have seen them rear up as the music soared upward.

When all the participants are on the stage, the stage director relaxes for a moment. The stage hands look as if they have been relaxed for days. They sit and lie around as the voices and instruments build climax upon climax. Some of them even catch a nap.

In the wings nearest the footlights sit the curtain boys. There is one for each side. They wear black breeches, stockings and pumps, purple tail coats, white shirts and black bow ties. The get-up is traditional. It also has a purpose. The stage director explains: "If the curtain should suddenly become snagged and fail to close, leaving the curtain boys visible to the audience, they will look theatrical."

Standing beside the répétiteur at the call board is one of the Metropolitan office boys. He is used for special errands, but when he has no job to do, he follows the score with the assistant conductor. He has aspirations to become a singer.

5

No one but those who are taking part in the performance or in its handling is permitted on the stage of the Metropolitan. That has become an ironclad rule in recent years. It used to be permissible for the wives and secretaries of singers to congregate backstage. That was not a serious impediment in a scene that required the co-operation of merely a handful of leading singers. But where hundreds of individuals had to be gotten on and off the stage, visitors were a problem.

The general manager of the company or the assistant general manager may, of course, come backstage during a performance. Giulio Gatti-Casazza was a frequent visitor. He was fond of seating himself on a chair near the call board and watching the proceedings. Edward Johnson likes to visit backstage.

When the scene is over, the curtain drops and the call boys bring the ends of it together in the center. Then the call curtain is suspended behind the great golden curtain, permitting the latter to be drawn aside partly, as the singers take their bows. Thus the stage hands can prepare the next scene while the artists are acknowledging the applause of the audience.

The curtain calls are carefully regulated by the stage director. He tells the singers when to go out. If he decides on individual curtain calls, he suggests the order. When solo calls are taken, each leading singer receives one. The management knows from experience that there must be the utmost impartiality in the awarding of curtain calls. There are artists who are indifferent to them. But they are indeed exceptional. The stage director allows the singers to take as many curtain calls as the audience's applause warrants. If an important debut or première is involved, the general manager himself will come backstage and supervise the disposition of curtain calls. Occasionally the calls are kept going until the conductor has had time to come backstage, and he is given an opportunity to join the artists in a call.

If something should go wrong backstage the stage director is responsible. He sees to it that the costumes of principals and others are correct. A Nedda in "Pagliacci" who is wearing no stockings and the wrong shoes gets a sweet bawling out. The stage director will rehearse certain movements up to the final moment. He will spend a brief interval instructing a singer, of whom he is uncertain, how to pick up a knife from the floor in time to the music. And he will stand in the wings and whisper instructions as to where the singer is to stand or what he is to do even during the performance.

In the event of an emergency, the stage can communicate with the conductor in the pit. There is a hand phone at the call board that connects to a receiver at the maestro's desk. Usually a button is pressed throwing on a light at the conductor's seat to tell him that all is ready on the stage. The phone is rarely used. But it can be, and has been.

The stage director must see to it that the singers are on the stage in time for their entrances. His chief call boy, who is also entrusted with the job of leading the supers, visits the dressing rooms of the leading singers himself to notify them when they are due on the stage. And yet there have been slips betwixt the call and the arrival.

Elisabeth Rethberg, for instance, has a habit of departing for her dressing room directly she is finished with a scene on the stage. In a performance of "Tosca" at Ravinia Park some years ago she completed her opening scene of the first act and, although she was due to appear in the latter part of the act, she went off. Just before her entrance they went looking for her. She was in her dressing room; she had changed into her second-act costume. In the first act Tosca is in street garb and in the second she wears evening clothes for the famous dinner party with Baron Scarpia.

They rushed the soprano to the wings. Her cue came to sing, and sing she did. But she did not go on until her first-act costume was thrown over the evening gown while she stood singing in the wings.

Opera: Front and Back

On another occasion Miss Rethberg strolled off to her dressing room, unbeknown to the stage manager, to vocalize a bit. She did not estimate the time correctly, and the stage director, assuming that she was still on the stage, did not bother to have her called. The cue for Leonore—the opera was "Il Trovatore"—was sounded in the orchestra: there was no Leonore. The conductor looked up in bewilderment, but kept on conducting. Some one dashed off to call Rethberg and returned with her on the run. She made her entrance two minutes late.

A more serious delayed entrance occurred at the Metropolitan some seasons ago in a performance of "La Bohème." In the intermission between the third and last act a photographer took Claudia Muzio, the soprano who was singing the role of Mimi, to the roof stage to make some pictures of her in costume. The curtain went up but Mimi did not appear. Fortunately, the soprano who had the role of Musetta knew the music of Mimi and she hastened on and began to sing it. In due time the photographer finished taking his pictures and Mimi returned to the stage, to hear another voice singing her music. She made an entrance that Puccini had never imagined. She got onto the stage just in time to take over from Musetta and, in the final poignant pages, to do her own dying.

The stage director determines the length of the intermissions, save in the case of one or two prima donnas—notably Rosa Ponselle—who insist on being the arbiter in this matter. He must allow enough time to set the stage and yet must not permit too much time. He must remember that the stage hands are paid overtime after three and a half hours of work, and the musicians after four. No operas except certain of the Wagner music-dramas run more than three and a half hours these days, and the Wagner works are managed in less than four. Only when the "Ring" is performed uncut in the annual Wagner matinee cycle or during the special productions of "Parsifal" does the time run over four hours.

6

So far as the mechanics of the mise-en-scène is concerned, the repertory opera house, especially the Metropolitan, is forced to develop a technique of its own. Because there is so little space backstage, the new lighting system installed recently had to be specially designed. All the proscenium lights were made movable so that they could swing out to a point midstage and back into the gridiron against the top of the proscenium. The control board is down under the stage floor and a telephone connects the light man on the stage, placed near the call board, with another electrician below, who operates the switches at the controls. When a scene requires exact timing the electrician below will climb up a narrow stairway near the one that leads to the prompter's box and seat himself under an aperture in the footlights; the electrician's box is smaller than the hood over the prompter. A smaller control board connecting with the large one is rigged up under the electrician's box, and the electrician can watch the action and operate the lights. In the first act of "Siegfried," when the young hero forges his sword he pulls a cord that causes flames to leap up at his work table. The cord is just a stage prop. The leaping flames are red ribbons which fly up at the behest of a blower underneath the work table. The electrician under the prompter's hood controls the blower. He must give it the juice in exact time with the movements and singing of the Siegfried.

The stage hands cannot be expected to remember exactly where every set goes in every opera. The Metropolitan has several floor cloths which cover the entire area of the stage in use. On these are written the abbreviations of the various operas: Cav. & Pag., Trov., Trav., Tr. & I., etc. There is a separate floor cloth for the Wagner operas, and several for the others. An independent floor cloth had to be worked out for the repertory of the Spring season. One floor cloth averages about ten operas.

The properties are another problem, and the stage director must be ever on the alert that they are in order. It happens that the property men, as well as the other stage hands at a theatre like the Metropolitan, have been working in that house for an average of twenty years or more. Some have been there as many as forty years. They know where a helmet and spear should be placed in "Walküre," where to have an easel set in "Tosca," where to have a manuscript ready in "Bohème," and a thousand other details.

Make no mistake about it. Stage effects that seem perfectly simple to the audience are come by with a great deal of careful preparation. Others that seem difficult are easily achieved. The swan that hauls in Lohengrin in the first act is run on rails as is Lohengrin's chariot, and a couple of husky stage hands pull the swan with ropes. Wind, thunder and rain are unleashed by pressing buttons on the call board. Erda disappears and appears in "Rheingold" and "Siegfried" through a trapdoor which ascends and descends like an elevator. There was a performance of "Siegfried" some years ago in which the tenor who played Siegfried disappeared during the dark-scene change in the last act. Some one had forgotten to have the movable part of the floor in place, and the tenor, Curt Taucher, plunged some twenty feet through a labyrinth steel framework to the rocky floor of the basement. By some miracle, he was not killed. In fact, although he was badly shaken up and incurred a severely strained back and broken fingers, he climbed back in two minutes to finish the performance of the hero's love duet.

What the Audience Does Not See and Hear

One of the most evocative stage pictures in opera is the first scene of Wagner's "Das Rheingold" in which the three Rhine-maidens are seen swimming and floating under water. The undersea effect is easily achieved. A thin transparent curtain is suspended in the forefront. It has patches of gauze which look like ripples and waves when light is thrown on them. A couple of small spots are leveled on this curtain from the stage, but the most important light comes from the orchestra pit. The Metropolitan has no spotlights in the rear of the auditorium. Therefore the light for this scene is attached to the railing that circles the orchestra pit. It is hung inside the railing, between the conductor and the woodwind section, where the audience cannot see it. Since there are lights above the music stands in the pit, the rays of the spot are not visible.

But the lights are only a fragment of the problem. The handling of the Rhine-maidens is more important. For them the Metropolitan has flying machines that resemble overgrown corsets. They have little floors to stand on and they reach up to the waist. Suspended from a track overhead that connects between the flies, they ride like cable cars. They are manipulated by hand, and it takes four stage hands to control the swinging and rising and falling of each Rhine-maiden. So far as the audience is concerned the naiads float through the water with the greatest of ease.

It used to be a practice at the Metropolitan to have the artists who sang the Rhine-maidens ensconced in the flying machines. But some complained that they did not like the sensation of soaring and that they could not sing to the best advantage under these conditions. One or two even became seasick. Now the Rhine-maidens the audience sees are three ballet girls who have been trained to gesture and to move their lips as singers would. The singers are hidden on the

[39]

stage under the platform over which Alberich moves. They can watch the conductor through an aperture. The scene is synchronized perfectly. The singers are happy to devote themselves exclusively to singing, the ballet girls in the flying machines enjoy the ride and the stage hands who tug the ropes that operate the machines are tickled that they do not have to split a gut to keep aloft a ponderous soprano.

In the second act of "Faust" Mephistopheles strikes the sign of the inn—a carved image of Bacchus astride a keg—his sword cleaving the spout of the keg. Wine flows like a stream of fire, and Mephistopheles fills his goblet. Is it really wine or flowing fire? Of course not. A property man releases, at the instant that the sword strikes the keg, a dribble of salt or rice. On the floor directly under the sign of the inn stands an upended barrel. A small spot is fixed in it, and as the salt or rice is released, the light is turned on, providing the audience with its illusion.

One of the most impressive effects ever used at the opera was achieved in homely fashion. In Respighi's "La Campana Sommersa" one scene required the appearance of two figures with halos. Two ballet girls were aureoled in this manner: Ordinary rounded metal lamp reflectors were painted black, with rims of white. They were strapped to the necks of the girls. The stage was dark and when the tiny lights inside the reflectors were switched on, the white rims gleamed like celestial orbs. They looked like halos, and were, in fact, more like halters.

Foods are often real. For "Marouf" a pie was ordered from Voisin's. Even the incense in the temple scene of "Aïda" is the McCoy. Most people in the audience can smell the aroma. Only experts know what flavor it is. For the benefit of the non-experts, the Metropolitan uses rose-geranium. Other operas, "Samson et Dalila," "Turandot" and "Iris," call for incense and get it. Having found that rose-geranium is satisfactory, the Metropolitan uses it for them all.

7

There are a host of other things that the audience does not see, hear or realize. There are the speed and movement with which scenes are shifted in pauses, with the stage manager casting a final appraising glance on the set-up before the signal is broadcast that the curtain is ready to go up. There are the quick costume changes, when the artist has no time to repair to a dressing room and a screen is set up backstage to serve as a temporary dressing room. There is the small organ on wheels; it has thirteen stops and one manual; its tones are not cathedral-like, but they serve—in "Meistersinger," "Parsifal" and many others.

There are animals, as I have indicated, who know their cues and those who feel that they have cues to follow natural processes on the stage. Animals are never fed before performance time, yet they forget that they must comport themselves on the stage like ladies and gentlemen. For emergencies like these there is the brush and shovel brigade, stable attendants who work so rapidly that the audience may not be aware of what has happened.

There are the illnesses and accidents, news of which never percolates to the world outside. Karin Branzell, the opulent-voiced Swedish contralto, sang through a performance shortly after an enervating illness. She became faint while she was on the stage. She leaned on a stage prop, sang several measures weakly but pulled herself together to complete the performance.

Paul Althouse was the victim of a serious accident that was not publicized. In "Boris Godunoff" he exited through a window. His long cloak tangled around his foot and he fell heavily, his foot smashing against the sill. He completed the performance, and afterwards his high boot had to be cut off. It was found that several small bones had been fractured.

There are occasions when even the composer and conductor may not be aware of an unanticipated stage development, so rapidly does it occur. A composer conducted his own opera. A singer in a minor role became ill and could not go on at the last moment. The stage manager donned the disabled singer's costume, entered for him and went through the part in action but not in song. It was a short role and the composer-conductor never mentioned the failure of the character to sing.

There are the superstitions of the stage folk. Some singers wear or carry with them special charms. Antonio Scotti always had on his dressing table a little rag doll that his mother had given him when he was a boy. Just before her first entrance in an opera Gertrud Wettergren begs a stage hand to kick her in the rear. Singers who are devout Catholics may be seen crossing themselves before they go on. Giovanni Martinelli brings pictures of his family to his dressing room and kisses each one before he goes on. Once, when he thought he had forgotten one, he hurried back to kiss the entire gallery over again.

IV

PREPARING A PERFORMANCE

AN OPERA is but black marks on white paper until it is clothed in flesh and blood and sinews on the stage and in the orchestra pit. Even then it may be only a shadow of itself if it is brought to life inappropriately or ineffectively, for it requires a superb production to make it stand forth with the fullest vitality. These observations may seem self-evident, but they are important to bear in mind in considering the activity that precedes a performance of opera. For the preparations make the difference between a slovenly show and a stirring realization of a lyric work. There are singers and conductors who, under the stress of playing to a responsive audience, will add something to the performance that was not prepared in rehearsal. Call it inspirational lift. Whatever it is, it occurs rarely. The rule of thumb may well be that the audience sees and hears what has been worked out in rehearsal. Artur Bodanzky has said that he considers it more important that he should direct all the rehearsals than that he should lead the actual performance.

The time needed to prepare a production depends on many things: the knottiness of the work, the character of the conductor, the experience of the singers, the quality of the orchestra and the demands of the audience. I have heard of a performance of "Rigoletto" at the New York Hippodrome, where opera is put on sporadically at prices up to 99 cents, for which there were no rehearsals at all. In fact, the soprano who sang Gilda had never met some of her colleagues, and when she emerged from her dressing room for her first entrance she was formally introduced to her fellow singers.

On the other hand, in some of the subsidized theatres of Europe months of study and labor are lavished on an opera. In Soviet Russia some productions have taken almost a year to prepare. And there is the story about Toscanini at Bayreuth. The tale has it that twenty-one rehearsals were set for orchestra, and that these were to be employed to prepare "Tristan und Isolde" and "Parsifal." Toscanini was doing "Tristan," and Karl Muck "Parsifal." The Italian maestro used twenty of the twenty-one rehearsals, and one was left for Muck. So goes the story. Whatever its truth, Muck departed from Bayreuth.

In fairness to Toscanini, this was his first contact with the orchestra in Bayreuth. When he knows his men and they him, he is likely to require less time. There is on record the famous occasion at the Scala in Milan when Richard Strauss's "Salome" was being put on for the first time in that theatre. Toscanini had carefully rehearsed all the elements—chorus, orchestra, principals—independently. He had done his job so well that, at the ensemble rehearsal when these components were brought together for the first time, Toscanini went through the opera without a pause.

Even today "Salome" is nobody's plaything. It is a difficult opera for any theatre and for any company, no matter what their experience. An eye-witness of this rehearsal was amazed that Toscanini did not stop once. He asked whether it had really gone smoothly. Toscanini replied: "If there had been a single mistake, I would have stopped." And when Richard Strauss arrived in Milan some days later and was told of Toscanini's feat, he insisted that they were pulling his leg.

A new opera or a revival of one that has not been in the

repertory for many years takes a great deal more time than
a work that recurs year after year. A theatre of reputation and
standards lets no opera come before the public unless it has had
some attention. But it naturally devotes the largest portion
of its available time to preparing for the novelties or revivals.
Let us examine the procedure at the Metropolitan when a
work in one of these categories is being prepared.

2

Months before the production the general manager desig-
nates the conductor, stage director and principal singers for
the opera. Each one obtains a copy of the score for private
study during the summer. Before intensive rehearsals begin,
the conductor, assistant conductors, stage director, chorus and
ballet masters and scenic designer may confer on broad problems and procedure and a general approach may be laid down.

The singers begin their preparations on their own. If they
are prosperous and can afford the luxury of employing a
full-time accompanist, as a few can, they have their own
pianist at their elbows. Some singers are versatile musicians,
and prefer to work out a new role by themselves. The amount
of time and concentration devoted by the individual artist to
a new part in the off-season often may determine the quality
of a performance six months later.

Caruso and Chaliapin may be cited from the honor roll
of those who spared no effort to develop a role. Caruso
worked on a new character for six months. He studied the
libretto and made his own sketches of the mise-en-scène. He
went to authorities for advice as to costumes. He began to
study score and text months in advance, and by the time the
first formal rehearsals were called he knew his part by heart.
It was rare in those days, and it is perhaps rarer now, for a
singer to have a new role memorized completely by the time

group rehearsals commenced. Habitués of the Metropolitan recall only one novelty for which Caruso used a score during the initial ensemble rehearsals. That was "The Girl of the Golden West." Caruso knew his role. But David Belasco was directing the staging and Caruso had his score on hand to make notations of Belasco's suggestions.

Chaliapin immersed himself in the plotting out of a new character weeks before the performance. Some nights he could not sleep because his mind was so wrought up by the blossoming conception. The Russian basso tells a story that concerns his concentrated preparation. He was in Paris, studying a new role, and in the middle of the night, being unable to sleep, he arose, dressed and went out for a stroll. The streets were dark and he was alone. Suddenly he heard a voice beside him.

"Monsieur is lonesome?"

It was "une fille de joie." Chaliapin saw that she smiled invitingly.

"I am not lonesome," Chaliapin said.

"But monsieur wants companionship?" She took his arm.

"I am busy. I want nothing."

"But what does monsieur do here at this hour?"

"I, I," Chaliapin hesitated—"I walk the streets, and I work."

The girl paused, held out her hand and said, with an understanding smile: "Comrade."

As the date for the performance approaches, the conductor prefers that one of his assistants take over the guidance of the principal singers, since the répétiteur knows the conductor's conception and the private accompanist may not. The services of the répétiteurs are available at the opera house with no charge to the singer. The répétiteur will also work with the artist at the latter's home, but the management requires that the artist pay him a small fee for these services. Most artists would do so on their own; the rule is set up for the tiny minority who are inclined to be frugal. The Metropolitan pays its assistant conductors modest salaries, and they can use the little extra. The majority of the leading artists have the répétiteurs come to their homes.

Some conductors prefer to work with their singers even during the preliminary period. Toscanini is one; Tullio Serafin another. It appears to be a characteristic of the Italian school of conductors. Germans depend largely on their assistants for the spade work. Some years ago Toscanini decided to revive "Falstaff" at La Scala in Milan. He chose Mariano Stabile for the title role, and worked with him at his own home the entire summer.

When he was at the Metropolitan, Toscanini would labor endlessly with the principals. He would leave nothing to chance or to other hands. Other conductors would cheerfully do likewise, no doubt, if they could match the exhaustless fund of energy of the little Italian. There were weeks, during those years, when Toscanini would rehearse singers, orchestra and even the chorus unceasingly, besides directing as many as five performances a week. Despite these tremendous labors, his freshness and resiliency continued unabated; they were the envy of those who knew him. And many years later, when he directed the Philharmonic-Symphony for eleven seasons, he never sat down during a rehearsal and was always drenched with perspiration at the end.

Toscanini's methods have not altered as the years have gone by. In preparing the production of "Die Meistersinger" for the Salzburg festival of 1936, he worked the principals unlimited hours. He did not spare himself, and he did not spare the others. The breathing spells between rehearsals did not come often, and the drilling was not diminished as the day for the performance approached. At the première there was a suggestion of weariness in the singing, although it was clear that the conception of Wagner's joyous and mellow comedy was on Toscanini's unapproachable level. It was not until the second performance that the artists, having had time to rest, did justice to their voices and to their maestro.

3

The conductor himself takes charge of the orchestra. The instrumentalists are expected to familiarize themselves with their parts at home, and their collective meetings with the conductor are meant for the establishment of tempo, nuance of tone-color and shading, balance of the choirs and other details of a rounded interpretation. What fearful imbroglios these rehearsals can be! The ninety members of the ensemble have not the same intelligence, keenness and precision, and conductors, on occasion, fail to state their requirements in the simplest terms. Clashes of temperament occur in the best regulated of symphony orchestras. Consider how much more likely they are to develop in the opera house where the orchestra is commanded by different conductors with different ideas and peculiarities at each performance and rehearsal.

Probably the most fearsome encounters between orchestra and conductor in the history of the Metropolitan occurred during Toscanini's tenure. It may be that Toscanini achieved more epic clashes in other theatres, but it is not probable that his feats have been surpassed by other maestros.

Gatti-Casazza, who knew Toscanini from their common labors at La Scala, urged him to make his acquaintance with the Metropolitan Opera orchestra in 1908 in a rehearsal of "Götterdämmerung." Gatti insisted, moreover, that Toscanini should not use a score, and he prevailed. Shortly after this initial rehearsal began, Toscanini stopped a 'cellist and said that he wanted a B-flat in a certain phrase. The musician demurred. He pointed to his score, said it called for an A-natural, added he had always played an A-natural, and ended that he was going to continue playing A-natural. Toscanini replied that the musician's part was wrong and had always been wrong. The musician looked doubtful and Toscanini asked: "Would you like to see the score?" The master score was sent for. The note proved to be B-flat. A sensation among the players and loud applause! Toscanini had won their respect.

It was not long, however, before a committee of instrumentalists visited Gatti-Casazza to complain that Toscanini was calling them unendurable names. In those days, possibly today as well, Toscanini's vocabulary, especially in Italian, was so lurid that it would have won the envy of a seaman with a genius for cussing. Gatti requested the men to give him an example of Toscanini's language. They did. Gatti smiled. "Gentlemen," he said, "what can I do about it? You should hear what he calls me."

What does Toscanini call the players? I knew of one sample. When he seeks to draw more sonority and greater intensity from his men and they do not respond, he will use one word, speaking it fiercely between clenched teeth: "Castrade!"

Before rehearsals begin the conductor estimates how many he will need with orchestra. He usually receives what he wants. If he has underestimated his requirements or if some new problem crops up that demands further work, the management will give him what rehearsals he considers essential.

When he is not working with orchestra, the conductor brings the principals together in ensemble rehearsals. Only the piano is used. Virtually all these meetings occur at the opera house. In some instances the conductor has the artists come to his house. But this is a matter to be decided by mutual agreement.

Some conductors will outline a general plan of procedure or summarize their conception of the opera under scrutiny. Most chefs d'orchestre, at least in the major opera houses, assume that the singers, artists of reputation, know what it is all about. Occasionally a leader will insist that the singers mold their interpretations to conform with his untraditional point of view. At the first rehearsal of a performance of "Meistersinger," Toscanini stated briefly his approach to the opera.

"I do it," he said, "as a symphony."

There can be tension at a rehearsal in the home of an artist even if a fiery conductor is not present to do the initial erupting. When "Carmen" was restudied for Geraldine Farrar, she invited the cast to her apartment to rehearse certain scenes. This was before America's entry into the war, in a period when Miss Farrar was criticized in some quarters for evincing sympathy with the German cause. On her piano stood an elaborately framed photograph of the German Crown Prince, a memento of the years when the young American soprano was the toast of Berlin, not only in operatic but even in royal circles.

Among the rehearsing singers was a Frenchman who made no effort to conceal his annoyance with the conspicuous position allotted to the Crown Prince. In an exciting scene that justified sweeping gestures, the Frenchman swung, with mock clumsiness, and caught the Crown Prince squarely on the nose, hurtling photograph and frame across the room, where they landed in shreds and splinters.

There was no apology and no comment from any of the group. Miss Farrar, it was said, appeared not to have noticed the incident.

Preparing a Performance

4

Shortly after a decision to present a novelty has been taken, the designing of the sets is entrusted to some artist. The Metropolitan used to depend largely on European artists for the plans, and the job of painting and building was done here. Then artists who worked and lived in this country were called in. Joseph Urban was a frequent contributor. Among contemporary scene designers who have been represented at the Metropolitan are Robert Edmond Jones, Jo Mielziner, Donald Oenslager, Frederick Kiesler and Jonel Jorgulesco.

To design sets for the opera, especially the Metropolitan, is to confront hazards not found in any Broadway theatre. There are few auditoriums so high, from ceiling to floor, as the Metropolitan Opera House, and few with so lofty a proscenium. The distance from floor to dome is seventy-six feet five inches, and the proscenium is fifty feet high. A major poser is how high to raise the curtain: If it is lifted most of the way up, the customers sitting on the parquet floor will have an unobstructed view of the mechanism—the flies, the swinging lights, etc.—above the stage. If the curtain is kept too low, the customers in the topmost gallery will see only the footlights.

This problem is a serious one for the scene designer. He begins with the limitation that the curtain must go so high and no higher. Then he must consider the essential narrowness and lack of depth in the stage. He cannot let his décors run too far to the rear at the sides because the patrons in the side seats will not be able to see anything.

If the artist is not aware of these considerations, he is speedily educated. The working out of a batch of sets requires many conferences between the management, stage director and artist. Sketches are made first; then models; then the sets are built and drops are painted. Even after they are painted and built, changes may be necessary. The size of the cast, the rapidity with which supers, ballet and chorus must be brought on and off, will affect the sets. For opera normally deals with large masses, and there must be ample space to plant them on stage and sufficient opening for them to get on and off.

There have been some riotous conflicts during the creations of sets. I have heard that Jo Mielziner was forced, in spite of his protests, to change his plans for "The Emperor Jones" because he envisioned a forest with long, drooping fantastic leaves, and he was told that the Metropolitan audience would not understand such a forest. Once when Robert Edmond Jones, who is sensitive and easily wrought up, encountered a strong opposition front, he was driven to tears.

Designers of opera sets, for the Metropolitan or elsewhere, must realize that the artist has to sing as well as act, and in singing he must glance repeatedly at the conductor. He cannot always watch his step. Complicated sets can thus be impracticable or downright dangerous. Friedrich Schorr recalls a set for "Walküre," designed by "an original fellow" for the Berlin Opera. Every bit of floor space sloped in varying degrees. Remember, Wotan carries a patch over one eye, wears a bushy beard, a heavy helmet, a trailing tunic and wields a spear. When Schorr tried to ascend and descend the precipitous rock with its tortuous, narrow, uneven approach —at risk of life and limb—he was profoundly irked. He grabbed the designer by the hand, led him to the height, and demanded that he descend without looking down. The designer tried and after two steps tumbled from on high. The sets were changed.

When the sets are completed, there are rehearsals for

them alone. The stage crew puts them together and shifts the scenes. At the same time the lighting is worked out, and a score is marked up for the men in this department.

5

The stage director who has been sitting in on the décor conferences has begun the charting of the action. If he is conscientious, he has made diagrams and outlines of the movement of the play, with an analysis of what is required in the way of actions, entrances and exits for principals, chorus, supers, et al., for every measure of the music. For these purposes he has conferred with the conductor, the property men, the electricians, the wardrobe department, the wigmaker.

The stage director has also taken over the chorus for rehearsals of its share in the action. These workouts are conducted with piano in the preliminary stages, as are the action rehearsals with the principals. The stage director meets with the principals in groups. He tries to impart to singers of different backgrounds and nationalities a homogeneous style of acting. He tries to keep wild gestures down to a minimum. He succeeds with some; others will never learn.

When he fails and when the conductor cannot whip his charges into a coherent ensemble, then we see and hear the kind of performance which caused a James Huneker to write with burning indignation:

"Like the rich we shall always have 'grand opera' with us. It is the pabulum of the unmusical, the unthinking, the tasteless. Its theatricalisms are more depressing than Sardou's. . . . There is a growing public that craves, demands, something different from the huge paraphernalia of crudely colored music, scenery, costume, lath and plaster, and vociferous singing. Oh, the dulness, the staleness, the brutal obviousness of it all. Every cadence with its semaphoric signaling, every phrase and its accompanying gesture. Poetry is slain at a stroke, the ear promise-crammed, but imagination goes hungry."

Operatic acting, however, must vary of necessity from the conventions of screen and stage. The singer cannot use his face as freely as the actor on the speaking stage. The production of the voice in a sustained melodic curve limits the use of the facial muscles for other purposes. Other parts of the body may be constrained in similar fashion, for the singer breathes from the diaphragm, and the chest, stomach and throat muscles are called into play. The stage director must understand the singer's problem and must design his action so that it will not, at any cost, interfere with the singing. The music, moreover, limits the time allotted to any movement or series of movements. Tosca must kill Scarpia in certain given measures, and she must place the lighted candles at his head in a certain number of musical phrases. Wolfram and Tannhäuser must stroke their harps in time. Exits and entrances must be cued in with vocal attacks and pauses.

A conductor like Toscanini will insist on a rhythm of movement as well as of song. When he was directing the rehearsals of "Madame Sans-Gêne" at the Metropolitan, he caused Farrar to repeat one scene endlessly until he was satisfied that she had it right. She had to do some ironing on the stage and sing at the same time. Toscanini demanded that the iron move to a fixed rhythm which was not the same as the pace of the music. There is no need to expatiate on the difficulty of doing two things at the same time in widely varying rhythms. Farrar mastered the requirement, and it made, of course, a more effective stage picture.

Preparing a Performance

6

Then come the full ensemble rehearsals on the stage. Orchestra, chorus, ballet and principals are joined. The conductor is on the alert for weak spots in the musical interpretation. The stage director tries to whip the mise-en-scène into shape. Frequent stops are the order of the day. Passages are repeated. Movements are done over again. It does not go well with those who have not retained the instructions that were given them during the preliminary rehearsals.

The stage people of the Metropolitan tell the story of Maria Jeritza rehearsing for the "Jewels of the Madonna." As she knelt to sing a prayer in one scene, her long skirt began to creep up, revealing her shapely leg. The stage director, Wilhelm von Wymetal, Sr., tiptoed over and returned the hem of the dress to its erstwhile place at the ankle. Several moments later the skirt seemed to creep upward again. Wymetal again provided the leg with its chaste covering. A third time the skirt moved up. Wymetal stopped the scene.

"That skirt," he thundered, "remains where it belongs! We'll take the leg for granted this time!"

Artur Bodanzky kept stopping an ensemble rehearsal on another occasion because the prima donna was consistently and painfully off pitch. Each time a passage was repeated, but always the prima donna and the orchestra moved, with splendid individualism, along different tonalities. The conductor lost patience. He paused and addressed the soprano with piercing politeness.

"Madame," he said, "will you be good enough to give the orchestra your A?"

The first full ensemble rehearsals are run off without the

sets. These are not used until the dress rehearsal. Nor do the principals get into their costumes and make-up until the dress rehearsal. But the chorus and ballet are sometimes asked to wear their costumes for earlier ensemble rehearsals, so that the costume and wig departments and the stage director may concentrate on the principals when the dress rehearsal takes place.

7

The period of preparation, although it follows the general outlines sketched in, varies according to individual needs. Singers who are quick studies can smooth out difficulties and hasten preparations. Singers who are slow, forgetful or plain stupid try the souls of men. There are such singers at the leading opera houses of the world. They may even have glorious voices, which is more to be pitied, since a singer without intelligence, power of concentration, will to work and a gift for music, will not amount to much as an artist.

Some singers are superb soldiers. They absorb instantaneously. Kirsten Flagstad prepared the three Brünnhildes in German, a language with which she was largely unfamiliar, in the space of a few weeks and sang two of them at the Metropolitan immediately to resounding success. Only illness prevented her from revealing the "Siegfried" Brünnhilde during her first season.

Margaret Matzenauer was a joy and delight to a hard-pressed director. She had a photographic memory and was, in addition, an excellent musician. The Metropolitan had a performance of "Parsifal" scheduled for New Year's Day many years ago, and Olive Fremstad, who was to sing Kundry, became ill two days before the performance. There was no other Kundry in the company, and it looked as if the production would have to be postponed. Some one suggested

Matzenauer, a contralto, who had begun to sing the soprano repertory in the Wagner music-dramas. They called her on the telephone and she reported that she had studied Kundry years ago but had never sung the role on any stage. She asked for a couple of hours to look over the score before making a decision. Then she agreed to sing the role. She had only one rehearsal with piano. But she went through Kundry, one of the most difficult parts in all opera, with the assurance and ease of a veteran of one hundred repetitions.

To the average operagoer it is sometimes a mystery why some artists are retained in the company. Their voices appear to have lost their lustre, if they ever had any, and their acting may be as stilted as that of well-meaning amateurs performing at a church social in a small town. The explanation may well be that such singers are good musicians. The conductor knows he can depend on them to follow his baton. He knows that they will make their entrances on time, that they will keep in tune during a difficult duet, that they will remember their words, that they will sing the notes as they are written, instead of holding high ones for the delectation of the gallery. Their singing, as Bill Nye said of Wagner's music, is better than it sounds.

Rudolf Laubenthal who used to sing leading tenor roles in the German wing of the Metropolitan's repertory was an artist upon whose head was heaped unabated vilification. The public complained about the peculiar whiteness of his voice and laughed at the stiffness of his stage postures. Yet he was kept in the company—because he was a dependable musician. The conductor did not have to sweat blood with him at rehearsals; he could be confident that Laubenthal would follow the musical line with fidelity.

It might be added in passing, now that Mr. Laubenthal has left for other pastures, that his undoing with press and public in New York may have been chargeable to the fact that he was too self-conscious in his portrayal of the great Wagnerian heroes. His movements lacked fluency, and it seemed that he forced his voice in an attempt to achieve heroic lines. In the comic operas "Schwanda" and "Boccaccio," where he assumed lighter roles, Laubenthal suddenly and gracefully seemed at ease and there was more opportunity for the listener to become aware of his honest musicianship.

8

Once an opera house like the Metropolitan undertakes to prepare a production, it rarely turns back. There is not on record, in recent annals, an occasion when rehearsals were begun on a work and when it was decided to abandon the opera midway in the preparations. The expense of rehearsals, the time of the artists, the difficulty of finding a fresh novelty or revival for substitution at the last moment, make sudden changes difficult, if not impossible. There is no such practice as that indigenous to the spoken drama on Broadway: booking a show out of town for a tryout and never bringing it into New York. The Metropolitan, once it has launched a work, takes its beating as best it can.

In his forty-two years as director of opera Giulio Gatti-Casazza was obliged to abandon a work only once. That was at the Scala in Milan. The opera was "Norma" and the conductor was Toscanini. Preparations were carried forward almost up to the dress rehearsal. Then Toscanini decided he would not go on. Gatti never would discuss the reasons—evidently the memory of that occasion rankled three decades later—but it was said that the soprano who took the title part did not develop as had been hoped and Toscanini would not go on with her. Another Norma could not be found overnight.

Preparing a Performance

All the elements of a production must work in harmony if it is to be prepared expeditiously. If the conductor establishes himself, beyond doubt or dispute, as the boss, he may be able to control his forces, drawing the best from them and keeping them from flying at his throat or squabbling with one another. There is no intention here to give the impression that all artists are constantly creating difficulties. Productions have been prepared in which the conductor comported himself like a gentleman and the singers behaved with due regard for each other's feelings. But temperament has not yet been banished from the lyric theatre, and as long as it retains a foothold, it will confound managers and directors. Occasionally it will snarl preparations and will add to the cost in money and time and sheer physical exhaustion.

When Toscanini was in command in the Metropolitan pit, he was the principal prima donna during rehearsals. There was a clash once with Geraldine Farrar, who had come to the Metropolitan several years before Toscanini and who had firmly secured her reputation in her native America. It seems that the little Italian told her, with no little plainness, what he thought of a scene in a certain rehearsal and what he expected from her. Miss Farrar, fiery in her own right, stepped to the footlights and reminded Mr. Toscanini that she was, after all, a star. The records have it that Toscanini lifted his eyes upward and said, "I know only the stars in heaven."

There is another story, a pretty one if true, concerning Toscanini and rehearsals at the Metropolitan. It seems that one member of the orchestra had won his extreme displeasure that morning and, try as he might, he could not carry out the maestro's wishes. Toscanini, so the tale goes, berated him and, finally, in a burst of anger, told the fellow to get out.

The orchestra player arose slowly and strolled to the exit.

Apparently he had a temper of his own. As he reached the exit, he turned and yelled, in English, "Maestro, you can go straight to the devil!"

Toscanini turned on him indignantly and motioned him to go.

"It's too late," he said in Italian, "to apologize."

During the seasons in the Twenties, when Feodor Chaliapin made guest appearances at the Metropolitan, there were occasional ructions during rehearsals. Chaliapin had a way of taking command of the proceedings. He would beat time, not merely for himself, but for his colleagues and the conductor as well. On one occasion his beating of time irritated the conductor, Vincenzo Bellezza, to a point where he could no longer remain silent. He extended his baton in one hand and lifted the score in another.

"Here, Mr. Chaliapin," he said, "you conduct!"

Chaliapin undertook to advise his fellow artists on their stage deportment, their acting and even their singing. It may be that his experience and his genius for the stage warranted his proffer of counsel and it may well be that his colleagues would have benefited from accepting it. But it is one thing to whisper a piece of friendly advice and it is another to announce it publicly so that every one on the stage and in the pit can hear. Chaliapin achieved his high point when he tried to tell Giuseppe DeLuca, the Italian baritone, who was considered one of the world's finest exponents of the art of bel canto, how to produce his voice.

Chaliapin was one of those artists who would not listen to conductor or stage director. He was a law unto himself both in rehearsal and in performance. He got away with it because some of his impersonations were creations of indisputable genius. There have been other artists whose knowledge of the stage was a good deal less dependable than Chaliapin's and who attempted nevertheless to improvise their own action and to add or detract from the score as the composer had written it. Their attempts were fruitless if the conductor and stage director were men of power and with minds of their own.

In her first season at the Metropolitan, Jeritza scored her wildest tribute as a result of a tour de force of acting that was her own contribution. The stage director did not dispute her idea. In fact, the intelligent stage director will permit an experienced artist a great deal of leeway in his stage movements. Jeritza, at any rate, decided to sing the aria, "Vissi d'Arte," in the second act of "Tosca," while lying prone on the ground. She sang the aria effectively, but it was the fact that she was able to sing it at all while lying prone that won the tremendous enthusiasm of the audience.

Needless to say, the well-prepared production is the one that moves smoothly through its preliminary phases and that holds the stage without fuss or fervor. When such a production occurs, the only news about it is its music, its acting, its singing and its staging. It develops no incidents that become the delight of gossips. It is an opera manager's dream. Unhappily for him and happily for those who traffic in the mischances and humors of the opera house, the perfect rehearsals are as rare as genius.

V

PREPARING A SEASON

A SEASON such as the Metropolitan Opera Association or any major company presents is not brought into being overnight. It is not and cannot be an improvisation. It requires reflection, study, travels to scout for talent and ideas, awareness of what the audience wants and innumerable compromises. In the old days when the Metropolitan gave a peak season of twenty-four weeks at home and several weeks on tour, the repertory exceeded forty, often approached fifty, operas. In recent years, with a low of fourteen weeks, the total ran up to thirty operas.

In the days of prosperity the management of the Metropolitan did not have to worry about the fundamental question of the theatre's continuance. It was able to begin thinking of the next season in the middle of the current one. February was the month when the season under way seemed capable of running on its own momentum, and the manager and his aides began to prepare for the ensuing year.

But in recent years the first question to be dealt with was the establishment of a guarantee fund for the coming season. Before that could be fixed, it had to be clear that the season in hand would be carried through, without further difficulty, to its conclusion. The manager could not make contracts with artists, he could not consider novelties and revivals, he could not, in short, prepare for the next season's program without being assured that there would be a season and without knowing how much money there would be at his disposal. As a result, the full list of artists was not com-

[62]

pleted until a few days before the season and several times newcomers were introduced into the company at midseason, an unprecedented occurrence in the days when everything worked smoothly. The program could not be established until the last minute, which means, in the opera house, at least two months before the beginning of a season.

Once the length of the season is determined, a date is set for the opening night. The period when Holy Week occurs the following spring is a prime consideration. For an opera company cannot hazard visits out of town during Holy Week; there will not be as complete a response as in another week. Therefore if a three-week tour is scheduled the opening is set to bring the local season to an end three weeks before Holy Week. Then the company can travel into the provinces and return in time to observe the holy days with a couple of performances of the "sacred festival play"—"Parsifal."

In the days when the season ran for twenty-four weeks, the opening was fixed so that the local span took in Holy Week. Thereafter it was possible to brave the road.

One of the difficulties engendered by the uncertainty of the season's dates in recent years has been the engagement of the stars for recitals. Thus Kirsten Flagstad was booked last year for concerts in December before the management decided to open the season on November 29. Obviously the Metropolitan could not begin a new season without its foremost soprano in some of the opening performances. Concert managers were besought to make changes, dates were shifted and the thing was done—but at a cost of energy that might have served a better purpose.

Opera: Front and Back

In working out a season's repertory, a manager does not give precedence either to his personnel or his program. The operas are planned with artists in mind, and artists are engaged with operas in mind. Certain operas are performed because the singers are available. Others are not done because the singers are not to be had. There is, of course, a fundamental repertory which the pretentious lyric theatre must give, and it must turn heaven and earth to find the singers for them. If great artists are not to be found, the best that are available must be used. Can you picture a season at a major opera house without "Aïda" or "Traviata" or "Bohème" or even "Der Ring des Nibelungen"?

There have been seasons and there will be seasons, alas, without works like "Pelléas et Mélisande," "Norma," "Don Giovanni," "The Marriage of Figaro," "The Magic Flute," "Tosca," and, believe it or not, "Carmen." Gatti-Casazza maintained that he had always wished to add Debussy's unique opera to the repertory but could not do so until he had the cast. He waited more than fifteen years before he found the singers he wanted, Lucrezia Bori for Mélisande and Edward Johnson for Pelléas. And now that Miss Bori has retired and Mr. Johnson has exchanged the simple joys of a singer for the extravagant trials and sorrows of a manager, "Pelléas et Mélisande" is no more. It takes a woman of outstanding gifts as an actress and singer to do "Carmen" excitingly. Therefore, "Carmen" has languished away from the Metropolitan in certain years.

On the other hand, operas are done especially for artists who need new vehicles. "Coq d'Or" is revived because Lily Pons is sick unto weariness of the endless flutings and tragic endings that composers have written for coloratura sopranos. In "Coq d'Or" she has a comic role for a change, and so has Ezio Pinza. "Norma" was revived because the Metropolitan had, first, Rosa Ponselle, a soprano with the breadth of vocal equipment for the title role, and, more recently, because Gina Cigna, another well-endowed singer, turned up. "The Tales of Hoffmann" was restored to the repertory because the management wished to give its foremost singing actor among the baritones, Lawrence Tibbett, a juicy evening's work.

The management, in preparing a season, assumes that the standard works of the repertory will be heard with favor once again, and its attention, so far as they are concerned, is restricted to finding fresh talent for them. The emphasis in the working out of the repertory is on the new works and revivals. Here the management must provide new vehicles for its leading artists and it must attempt to give its audience something different. There is also the element of prestige to be considered. An opera house must do some operas because they are great works, even if the public does not respond to them. The critics and the elect in the audience clamor for them. And the sensitive manager tries to satisfy these claims. Gatti's production of "Pelléas" was a prestige gesture. The opera developed an audience of a sort, but one that, at best, remained small. At its first performance of the season it had a good house. The second invariably was poorly attended.

When novelties and revivals are set, an attempt is made to select one for each division of the repertory—that is, one opera in German, one in French, one in Italian and possibly one or more in English. Thus all the leading singers and the first-line conductors will have something new to do. For novelties and revivals receive more attention from the press and the public than the run-of-the-mill productions. Who ever heard of a singer or a conductor who did not like to be, at least artistically, in the public eye? The management will try not to give one principal artist a greater share in the novelties and revivals than the next. In the first place, artists are busy people these days, what with commitments for the concert stage, the radio and the movies; one new role, or two at the most, is all they have time to study. In the second place, the management seeks to avoid jealousies, accusations of partiality and internecine strife.

The opera in English, at least in Mr. Gatti-Casazza's day, was usually a new work by an American. He made an intensive search for a native work year after year. Edward Johnson is also on the alert for compositions by American artists, but he has begun, in a modest way, the development of a repertory of certain classics translated into English.

When the novelties and revivals are determined upon and the casts fixed for them, the musical secretary sees to it that the conductors and artists receive copies of the score for study during the off-season. For all the major roles there is not only one full cast, but a full list of replacements, and sometimes a third line of substitutes. A theatre like the Metropolitan cannot afford to leave a major production to chance. It must always have two or three individuals ready for each role. There has been only a handful of occasions when an opera had to be changed because the company could not depend on a capable replacement. Several seasons ago a performance of Puccini's "La Rondine" was shifted for another opera when Lucrezia Bori fell ill. There were extenuating circumstances. It was Miss Bori's last season in opera; "La Rondine" had been revived expressly for her, and the management felt that the audience would prefer no "Rondine" at all if Miss Bori were not to be in it.

Preparing a Season

There was also, several years ago, a sudden change of program when "Carmen" was replaced by another opera. "Carmen" had been revived the previous week with Rosa Ponselle in the title role. Her impersonation had taken a fearful beating from the press. Miss Ponselle, the announcement said at the time, was ill and could not appear in the scheduled repeat. The management had another Carmen available in Gertrud Wettergren. But it chose to permit Miss Ponselle to recover from her ailment and to let her have the first repeat. The theory was, no doubt, that a show of faith in Miss Ponselle when she had taken a terrific critical drubbing was better policy.

Once the program is devised, the manager departs on a scouting jaunt. He has hopes of meeting up with a lively new opera, but he knows from experience that the lively new operas are as rare in Europe as a stable government, possibly rarer. He is on the lookout for new singers. The hunt for the artist is such an unpredictable, contradictory, depressing and exciting saga that a separate chapter will be devoted to it hereafter.

While the manager is gone, sets are refurbished, new ones are designed. Other details are attended to. Although the season is less than half the year, the opera house transacts business the twelve months.

3

The manager returns and begins to lay out the exact schedule for the coming season. These plans are usually worked out two months in advance. The first matter to be decided is the identity of the opening night opera. That is a delicate and difficult matter in itself; it involves a number of considerations. The management wishes, naturally enough, to make a splash. It wishes to put on a work that has broad popular appeal. It requires a work that can be cast with a handful of the foremost singers.

Gatti-Casazza began with the singers and chose the opera that would suit the foremost artists. From his first year in command, in 1908, until 1920, the opening night had Enrico Caruso in the leading tenor role virtually every season. That was a natural selection. He was the world's most famous singer. He was a must for the opening. The sopranos, contraltos and baritones were rotated to give all the leaders a crack at first-night honors within a period of years. After Caruso was gone, Gatti-Casazza attempted to alternate the glory among his leading singers. Toward the end Lawrence Tibbett occupied the place of honor and an opera was usually chosen that had a fat role for him. Mr. Gatti made what he liked to consider the beau geste when he commenced his penultimate season with an American opera, Deems Taylor's "Peter Ibbetson."

Otherwise Mr. Gatti's opening nights were given over to Italian and French operas, however. He felt perhaps that a gala audience which arrived late and spent its time being photographed and promenading had no need of weighty musical fare. Only once did he undertake to begin the season with an important novelty or revival. That was in his second year, when he launched the proceedings with Gluck's "Armide." He never ceased to regret that choice. There was so much time and attention devoted to the social aspects of the opening that the artistic revival took on the importance of an also-ran.

Newcomers were rarely introduced to the public on the first night. A first-line conductor, possibly. But singers hardly ever. Only in his first season at the Metropolitan did Mr. Gatti begin with a squad of new artists, plus a new conductor, one Arturo Toscanini. But the management itself was then new, and it wished to prove that it had endeavored to bring in a host of new faces.

Edward Johnson went against tradition in his opening nights of 1936 and 1937. He began his second and third seasons with Wagner, a thing that had not been done for three decades. His reason was the presence in the company of Kirsten Flagstad, who had become the most potent drawing-card in the operatic world. It was the management's tribute to her rank in the company and to the ascendancy of the Wagnerian wing among the international stars of the company.

Once the opening night opera is selected, the next step is to space the novelties and revivals. Their dates are fixed to prevent conflicts and to draw the maximum good from their anticipation by the public. At least a week intervenes between novelties and revivals; more often, a fortnight. Then the remaining operas are sketched in. These depend in part on the spacing of new singers, which is another vital ingredient. You can't run too many together.

The opera in which a new singer will make his debut must be selected with care. Some managers will give an experienced singer the choice of a debut role. The artist may be presumed to know what part he does most effectively. There are some singers, of course, who fancy that a heroic role is their best, ask for it and receive it, only to find that they were gravely mistaken. It is not always possible to give a singer what he wants. For example, a Wagnerian soprano can make a more effective debut as Sieglinde in "Die Walküre" than as Brünnhilde. The latter role demands that she begin a new career with the glittering and taxing Valkyr's cry, while the Sieglinde has smooth, graceful music to begin with and the singer has time to control and overcome nervousness and uncertainty. But the exigencies of other commitments, of public demand and of rehearsals may necessitate the soprano's appearance as Brünnhilde.

There was the history of a Wagnerian tenor who was assigned to Siegfried in "Götterdämmerung," an enormously difficult role, for his debut. He was not a bad tenor, but he was inclined to be deliberate in his singing. The conductor followed his careful pace for a couple of acts, but the performance was moving slowly and might run over the four-hour limit, which would mean overtime for the orchestra players and hell from the management. The tempi were whipped up. The poor tenor could scarcely follow; he stumbled, skipped and puffed like a cross-country runner. The debut was not a world-shaking success.

Where a young, comparatively green artist is involved, the management with the advice of the conductors may be able to make a wiser choice for an initial role. It may wish to nurse a bright prospect along, placing him only in the right spots. It may make all the difference in the world in a career if it is launched smoothly, if not brilliantly. I know of several artists with good voices, convincing stage bearing and adequate training who cracked up in a tough debut and never came back.

4

In the uncomplicated days before leading artists were turning up with conflicting and overlapping outside engagements, the arrangement of the season's program was comparatively simple. Mr. Gatti-Casazza used to arrive from Europe about two months before the opening of the season with the first six weeks plotted out. By the opening night he had twelve weeks, or half the season, scheduled. By midseason the full program was mapped in detail, and it was rarely altered. Only a cataclysmic plague of colds, sore throats and downright failures of new operas or new singers forced changes in the schedule. It is true that Mr. Gatti consulted with Edward Ziegler, the assistant manager, and with Earle R. Lewis, the box-office treasurer, now also assistant manager, before fixing his program finally. But once he was persuaded that it was right, it remained fixed.

Nowadays plotting the season is an agonizing affair. It causes men of poise and experience to grow gray-haired overnight. The schedule is never finished in the sense that it used to be in Mr. Gatti's heyday. It cannot be. Only a limited number of the leading artists are engaged for the full length or for half of the season, as almost every one was before 1929. Some contracts call for two weeks or a month off in midseason so that the artist may go off to concertize. Some artists are engaged only for a few guest appearances, say three, four, six or eight. Others have radio contracts that necessitate their appearance on the air on the same evening each week. Lawrence Tibbett, who was broadcasting on Mondays, once had to wear his costume for "Aïda" to the radio studio and hurry directly to the Metropolitan and onto the stage in the second act after his broadcast. Lily Pons and Nino Martini had Wednesday and Friday broadcasts for thirteen weeks. The Sunday night symphonies draw heavily on the Metropolitan artists.

Actually the Metropolitan contract with a singer forbids outside appearances during its term without the consent of the management. But the management must grant concessions if it is to receive them. And in the depression years the artists made many concessions. They took large reductions in salaries. They agreed to shortened seasons. They helped the Metropolitan to go on. The management has no choice but to return kindness and generosity with an equal amount of consideration.

[71]

Opera: Front and Back

When an impasse develops, the management can prevail on some artists to postpone concerts and to switch radio engagements. Occasionally there is no apparent solution. In the season of 1936–37, one week's bills became hopelessly snarled. There seemed to be no way out. It was suggested, with fear and trembling, that the only solution would be to ask Kirsten Flagstad to sing three performances on successive days. The official who had the temerity to make the proposal was laughed at by the others. It was impossible for any artist to undertake a task of this kind, especially in the difficult Wagnerian repertory. Nevertheless, they asked Miss Flagstad. Without the slightest suggestion of dismay or displeasure, she agreed. The week was saved.

5

In mapping out a long season the management must consider the vertical and horizontal lines. In other words, there must be no repetition of operas in the same weekly subscription evening or matinee during the season. In the early days of the Metropolitan Opera House's existence, subscribers did not mind repeats. In one season, in fact, "Faust" was given seventeen times, and the late W. J. Henderson called the Metropolitan the Faustspielhaus. Some years ago one subscription night had "Cavalleria Rusticana" twice during a twenty-four week season. The other half of the bill was different. And the cast of each "Cavalleria" was completely changed. One was headed by Rosa Ponselle, the other by Maria Jeritza. You would think that listeners would welcome the opportunity to make comparisons of famous prima donnas in similar roles. Perhaps a handful were interested. The majority were indignant. They swamped the management with protests.

An attempt is made to give each subscription equal treatment. Each has allotted to it, as far as it is possible, the same number of novelties and revivals and an equal distribution of the most-sought-after artists and conductors. The offerings cannot be identical, and the management is pleased if it can strike what seems to be a happy balance. But to the operagoer the far-off hills are greener. The other subscription groups complain that Monday nights are favored. They argue that the Monday audience is traditionally the swankiest social gathering of the week, and that the management plays up to this gathering. The first count in the indictment is true; the second, the management swears, is not. Try to make a subscriber believe.

Today a new charge of favoritism is being leveled against the management: the Saturday matinee crowd is getting the best casts and shows because that performance is broadcast. Since the Metropolitan receives extra money from the radio rights and since it wishes the millions of listeners throughout the world to hear its productions at their best, the accusers say, the Saturday matinees have the cream of the week's bills.

The present Metropolitan management, under current conditions, does not attempt to plot the season comprehensively more than a fortnight in advance. It lays out the general scheme of novelties and revivals and trusts to developments to suggest the operas in between. Mr. Johnson and Mr. Ziegler work out the plans together. Then they call in Mr. Lewis. From his vantage of thirty years' experience in the box-office, he recommends changes. He may suggest that a new opera, which looks as if it were going to click, be repeated sooner than planned, in order to make capital of its success. He may advise that a new star is waxing or an old one waning and may suggest alterations accordingly. When all is said and done, the manager of the Metropolitan has to be a showman as well as an artistic director. He must gauge public reaction and public trends. He must play up to the requirements of each day if he is to keep attracting the customer.

The planning of the season depends not only on the availability of singers and on the exigencies of the audience but also on rehearsal requirements. Before the première of each novelty and revival three or four days must be left clear. The management calculates that there will be a full-dress rehearsal two days before the première, and a general ensemble workout the day before the dress rehearsal. You cannot work singers too hard up to the last minute of the performance. Their voices and their carriage will show the effects of the strain and the performance will be anticlimactic. It is the normal procedure, then, to fill in the three or four days before the novelty or revival with standard works of the repertory and with casts of experienced singers so that no rehearsals will be necessary. Naturally the artists who are to appear in the novelty or revival are not called upon to sing in the performances that precede.

6

Having decided on the general layout of the season, the management must work out a rehearsal schedule. The contracts call for singers to be on hand two weeks before the season begins, or two weeks before their first appearance. Even this provision is flexible, and there have been occasions when foreign artists arrived from abroad a day or two before their scheduled appearances and have gone on with no more than a piano rehearsal. This procedure is permitted to veterans. The management will take no such chance with a youngster.

The chorus and ballet begin rehearsals a month before

the opening night, and the orchestra begins three weeks in advance. The Metropolitan boasts of the fact that it gives a complete rehearsal to every work, new or old, that reaches its stage. It does not trust to luck or to individual memories. Each opera has a full rehearsal on the stage with chorus, orchestra and principals, besides preliminaries with piano. This happens before the first performance of the season, and if further rehearsals are needed for later presentations because of the addition of new singers, such rehearsals are held.

Once the total amount of rehearsals is worked out and his due portion is distributed to each conductor, it is difficult to make changes. If a conductor insists he must have another rehearsal, he is sent to his colleague to ask whether the latter can spare some of his time. Sometimes a dress rehearsal to which the press is to be invited is called off because that is the only way for the conductor to have another complete workout.

Occasionally overtime and extra rehearsals are unavoidable. At the beginning of the season of 1936–37 the Metropolitan had refurbished its orchestra and chorus, changing perhaps 30 per cent of the first and 10 or 15 per cent of the latter. A new conductor, a new stage director and a number of new artists had been engaged. These unfamiliar elements meant that more time was needed to oil the cogs in the machine, and more than $15,000 was expended on extra rehearsals.

During the first two weeks of rehearsals an effort is made to get the staples of the repertory out of the way. As many of the standard works as possible are scheduled and rehearsed. If a good many of the standard works can be prepared during this time, the midseason rehearsals can be devoted largely to the preparation of the novelties and revivals.

[75]

Opera: Front and Back

The chorus begins its rehearsals before the orchestra because it must learn its music and text by heart as well as master stage business for a number of operas. Rehearsals take place twice daily. The various divisions—soprano, alto, tenor, and bass—are taken separately at first; then the ensemble is fused.

When the orchestra swings into action, it rehearses twice a day, three hours at each session. The new scores are read through quickly, each under the direction of the maestro who will take charge of the performance. The choirs of the orchestra are rehearsed separately if the conductor thinks that is necessary. It is often necessary. From time to time individual musicians, especially those who play solo passages, will receive attention by themselves.

Then the principals arrive, working singly and in groups with the assistant conductors as well as with the principal leaders. The stage director eats into their rehearsal time. Then the principals are joined by the chorus, and finally these elements meet with the orchestra.

The ten days that precede the opening of the season produce the most concentrated activity of the entire year. Every available room in the opera house is in use. Sounds that may merge later into sweet and noble harmonies mingle in wild discord. On the stage a scene and light rehearsal may be taking place. The orchestra is going full blast on one of the two roof stages that Gatti built because he found insufficient rehearsal space on his arrival in 1908. The ballet is prancing and pirouetting on the other. In the grand tier foyer the chorus is going through its paces. In the ladies' parlor on the grand tier floor several principals are working on a scene under the eye of an assistant conductor. In other rooms other singers are rehearsing. And the stage directors take the remaining space and the unoccupied artists for intensive work.

While the house is ringing with the assorted sounds, a general rehearsal may begin on the stage. Assistant conductors are still at work in rooms at the sides with singers for other operas. But the stage itself is crowded with several hundred persons: perhaps one hundred choristers, sixty dancers, fifty supernumeraries and anything up to fifteen principals. The coatless conductor pauses to plead with the orchestra seated before him in the pit. The people on the stage stand by in groups and chat. The stage director suddenly calls a halt to correct or alter a piece of business. Again chatter fills the air. Some one is always yelling, "Silenzio! Silenzio!" And still the rehearsals go on in the little side rooms.

7

Once the opening night has been successfully negotiated, the management has nothing to do but keep subscribers happy, plan for the coming weeks, manage to fulfill its contracts with the singers by giving each his stipulated share of work, and take care of several hundred other odds and ends. As for the subscribers, Gatti-Casazza came close to dealing with them with scientific precision. He gave each subscription an Italian, French, and German opera every third week. This rotation was scrupulously and almost undeviatingly observed. Nowadays the management is not so meticulous. It will give two German operas on successive weeks to the same subscription, add a French opera for the third week's bill and come back with a German for the fourth. The reason for such unorthodox arrangements is that the Wagner operas and their casts are the strongest and most in demand in the entire repertory. The Metropolitan tries to give the public what it wants. It knows the Italian wing of the company is not up to the strength of other years, and that phase of the repertory is reserved for future conquests.

During the season of 1936–37 the operas of Puccini did not turn up until the final three weeks of the season, and rumors were rife that the Metropolitan was feuding with Ricordi's, publisher of the Puccini operas. But the management insists that an opera would not be kept out of the repertory for such a childish reason. The Puccini works were held off because the Metropolitan was waiting for the singers engaged for these works to arrive.

Generally a theatre like the Metropolitan cannot afford to hold out its standard works for the arrival of special singers. It tries to have several complete sets of singers for each section of the repertory, and to space their presence so that that section of the repertory will have continuous representation throughout the season. Thus if Lawrence Tibbett's contract calls for a four-week break in midseason to permit him to go off concertizing, it may be arranged that John Charles Thomas, adept at phases of Mr. Tibbett's repertory, will be on hand while Mr. Tibbett is gone. If Kirsten Flagstad needs a two-week absence in midseason, the management must have another dramatic soprano to take over her roles.

Like the operas, the stars must be rotated through subscriptions. Unfair play will bring outbursts of displeasure and abuse. If one subscription gets Flagstad twice, the others will howl to high heaven for the same treatment. If Lily Pons is skipped in one series, those subscribers will make the life of the management miserable with their complaints and threats.

In making its programs for the week, the management must think of everything. It cannot, for example, put on a big Wagner work in the afternoon and hope to get by with an opera of similar proportions in the evening. The members of the orchestra will not be equal to the strain. Nor will the conductor.

Preparing a Season

But assuming there are two Wagner conductors available, the secondary principals are the same and they will raise the roof if requested to sing twice in the same day. Thus the management must balance easy works beside difficult ones. It must not schedule wearisome rehearsals on days when there are four-hour operas to negotiate.

The last two years have thrust an additional complication into the seasonal planning. That is the annual spring season of popular opera. In the off-season it used to be possible to concentrate on the coming season. Now the energies and time of a number of executives must be addressed to the spring program. Its problems are not unlike those of the major season, except that they are on a smaller scale. They are also more concentrated and more intense.

No wonder the job of managing an opera house is a twelve-month affair. It is impossible to say which is the more exacting aspect: the actual running of the season or planning it. Friends of Gatti-Casazza used to say that in the last years of his tenure he referred to occasional nightmares he had: they consisted of planning a season's repertory, especially with Toscanini.

VI

THE HUNT FOR THE GOLDEN VOICE

THE search for the gifted singing actor is the most arduous, and perhaps the most important of all aspects of running an opera house. It is like prospecting for gold. The hazards are inestimable. The failures outnumber the successes overwhelmingly. But when you strike pure gold, your finances may be secure for years to come.

For the singer is the principal stock in trade of the opera house. You may dilate at length about the enduring genius of Wagner and Verdi, Mozart and Rossini, Gounod and Bizet, Puccini and Massenet, Debussy and Gluck and all the other immortals and near immortals of the composers' firmament. Experience has proved, time after time, that a great voice will rocket into prominence and with it will come a group of operas that have been languishing for want of public interest.

The giants in the days of Grau and Conried were the de Reszke brothers, Lilli Lehmann, Milka Ternina, Lillian Nordica, Schumann-Heink, Olive Fremstad, and the music-dramas of the master of Bayreuth were in the ascendant. If the Italian and French operas shared the spotlight, it was because these singers appeared in them as well, and they were abetted by such artists as Nellie Melba, Emma Eames, Marcella Sembrich. Later on, when the Italian and French wings achieved indisputable leadership, it was because figures like Enrico Caruso, Geraldine Farrar, Lucrezia Bori, Rosa Ponselle, Emmy Destinn, Scotti, Amato, DeLuca, Giovanni Martinelli and Beniamino Gigli attracted the public. An incandescent singing actress like Mary Garden focused attention on a new repertory that embraced "Pelléas et Mélisande" and "Louise." Chaliapin brought to life works like "Boris." The disclosure of Kirsten Flagstad skyrocketed the Wagnerian operas into the first flight once more in recent years.

The idealist who would prefer to stress the score, the ensemble, the coherence and unity and justness of the interpretation may despair at this state of affairs. He may take courage, however, from the knowledge that a great popular figure may also be an artist of perception and conscience. But he must face the fact that distortions and lack of comprehension get by, so long as they are floated on large pealing voices. He must realize that, save in rare cases, music of nobility and grandeur plays to sparsely filled houses if the singers have not resounding popularity.

The manager must face the facts. He may prefer sensitive, refined singing to the detonating clamors of a leather-lunged tenor, but he must engage the powerful gent if the public likes ear-splitting high notes. It may gall him to do so, and he may have to pay higher fees and give longer engagements to the loud-mouthed personage. In addition he may have to put up with innumerable displays of temperament.

2

Those who are in the perpetual hunt for fine voices look first for the singer who is endowed generously, not only with a voice, but with the other qualities—intelligence, musicianship, discipline—that go to make a real artist. But the searchers will take what they can find. Great artists appear rarely.

The hunt is shot through with contradictions. You may think you have discovered the voice of the ages when you hear a new soprano in a small theatre. Place the lady on the stage of the Metropolitan Opera and she sings with a still, small voice. A booming baritone in the provinces may sound like a crooner in New York. A tenor gives a tremendous audition, but he quails before a crowded house like a nervous old lady. A singer hired with qualms scores a stunning success. Some voices thrive for a day or a month, then fade like morning-glories. Some that have given no signs of improvement suddenly take on a brilliant refulgence. The hunt for baseball talent in the major league produces no greater quota of contrarieties.

The emergence of Kirsten Flagstad three years ago is the most recent shining example. In the summer of 1934, Giulio Gatti-Casazza was preparing what proved to be his final season as director of the Metropolitan Opera. His leading Wagnerian soprano in the past few years had been Frida Leider. During the spring he engaged a new leading lady for the Wagner repertory. She was Anna Konetzni and he counted heavily on her. Frida Leider was offered a contract for half the season, and the story has it that she balked at sharing the limelight with Konetzni. She demanded a contract for the entire season. She was not re-engaged at all. That left the Metropolitan with a gaping void in the German wing of the company.

Some one thought of Flagstad. Outside of her native Norway and the other Scandinavian countries she was virtually unknown. Otto Kahn had heard her in Oslo in 1929 and had recommended her to Gatti. At that time she had not answered letters from the Metropolitan agent at first and then, when she did, she declined an invitation to come to New York. As she explained it later, she had just remarried and did not want to leave her husband. Several years later Oscar Thompson, then on *The New York Post*, heard her and

The Hunt for the Golden Voice

wrote approvingly of her. In the summer of 1933 Bayreuth had used her as one of the three Rhinemaidens and in 1934 the Wagner shrine was giving her a crack at Sieglinde.

Flagstad was invited for an audition to St. Moritz where Gatti was staying. Artur Bodanzky came down to hear her. She sang in a hotel room that was covered with rugs and drapes, and she made a pleasing, if not exciting, impression. The time was late, the emergency had to be solved, and she was engaged. Gatti anticipated a smashing success for Konetzni and passable returns for Flagstad.

The season began and Konetzni, who was on hand for the first half, was indifferently received. It was learned later that she sang her debut with a sore throat. Her standing in New York improved only slightly in succeeding weeks, and the management was roundly cursed for its stupidity in letting Leider go.

Flagstad's debut was completely unheralded. Those whose business it is to poke around the Metropolitan Opera House heard from confiding friends that this newcomer from Norway had revealed startling gifts in her initial rehearsal with orchestra when she sang a scene from "Götterdämmerung." It was rumored that the men of the orchestra had risen at the end of the rehearsal and shouted their approval. But old hands at poking around had heard such stories before, and took them with a ladle of salt.

Flagstad made her debut as Sieglinde. She was good, no doubt of that, but other debutantes had succeeded with Sieglinde surpassingly well. Next came Isolde. Then there was no longer any doubt. The rest is history.

Call it an unadulterated fluke. But it meant perhaps the life of the Metropolitan. For Flagstad packed them in. A season that seemed to be a financial disaster was saved. The losses were mounting so that they seemed to exceed the entire guarantee fund, but Flagstad's success brought them down under the fixed margin.

Persons with hindsight could point out that Flagstad was not a raw, inexperienced artist. Subsequent investigation developed that her training had been sound and that she had sung every kind of role in every kind of theatre for twenty years in Scandinavia. Why had she not been discovered by the Metropolitan before, the censorious demanded to know. Certainly the scouts of America's ranking opera house should leave no spot untouched in the hunt for great singers. But the Metropolitan could reply, with some justice: Why had she not been found by the impresarios of the operas in Berlin, Vienna, Paris, London? For them she was nearer home. They could have used her as effectively. They have, in fact, engaged her since for limited performances at fancy prices. There is no explaining it. Chance, pure chance.

The history of Lawrence Tibbett is another case in point. When the Metropolitan engaged him he was a gangling young man, with some limited experience in operetta but none whatever in opera. He had no repertory to speak of. When he was asked to sing Valentin in "Faust," a good role for a baritone and a short one, he had to slave to master it at short notice. He spent a year as one of the secondary artists, hanging around, filling in here and there in the smallest parts, learning, but, on the whole, being discouraged and unhappy.

In his second season a piece of luck brought him a crack at the role of Ford in "Falstaff," the secondary baritone part which had a fat aria at the end of one scene. It was partly chance that gave Tibbett this role. Another baritone had been selected for it, but he fell ill. Gatti decided to give the young American a try. Tullio Serafin worked with Tibbett himself. There were some doubts about the outcome. What happened?

[84]

The Hunt for the Golden Voice

Tibbett sang his big scene with the emotional power of a man who knew that his career depended on it. He poured into it the fullness of his growing voice and the intensity of his feeling. At the end of the scene he came out for a curtain call with Antonio Scotti, who was singing Falstaff. Repeatedly he was sent out with Scotti. Gatti had taken command of curtain calls himself. He would not let the youngster take a solo because it had taken much persuasion to induce Scotti to do Falstaff and he did not wish to hurt Scotti's feelings by letting an unknown steal the show.

The house lights darkened. Serafin poised his baton. The next scene was to go on, at Gatti's orders. The audience ignored the signal. The tumult of cheering and applause increased in intensity. The demonstration was unprecedented, unbelievable, for the Metropolitan, citadel of good breeding; at least it had that reputation.

The demonstration did not have its origin in the claque, but came from every part of the house. Holders of stalls in the orchestra were of one mind with those who were perched a few inches from the ceiling in the aerial family circle. And the ladies and gentlemen of the parterre boxes, whose ardor seldom manifests itself in more than a few polite handclaps, were on their feet, waving their handkerchiefs, pounding hands together vehemently and shouting.

The conductor lowered his baton. Gatti shrugged his shoulders and gave the order. The curtain parted, and Tibbett came forward alone. The outburst mounted to a terrific crescendo. It was not merely a tribute to a deserving artist, but the crowd's cry of victory. Tibbett, a tall young man costumed and made up as a substantial middle-aged citizen of sixteenth-century England, bowed, dazed and elated. He slid behind the curtain. The excitement subsided, and the performance went on.

[85]

Opera: Front and Back

As one dignified subscriber put it, "If they think we can't get that American boy out here, we'll have to show them!" An American audience had shown them. That was news! The next day the story was carried on the front pages.

It was a felicitous event for both the Metropolitan and Tibbett. The opera company had uncovered a new and rising star in its ranks and Tibbett had found himself. He never wavered from that point on. He assumed an impressive succession of major roles and filled them with authority.

It may be argued, and, in fact, it has been, that an artist of Tibbett's sheer natural gifts would have arrived at his present position as a ranking singer without the break of that performance of "Falstaff." Possibly. Even probably. But who knows how long it would have taken? Who knows what another year or two of disappointment would have meant to the morale of a young man who had a family to support?

The rise of Rosa Ponselle is another overnight success story. She jumped from vaudeville to the top of the operatic heap in one leap. She had the voice for the amazing transformation, and the management of the Metropolitan was willing to gamble on her. She was given an audition, and she was a bundle of nerves. It was clear, however, that she possessed a remarkable vocal instrument, and another audition was arranged. This time she did better, and was engaged. What is more, she was allowed to make her debut—this nervous, easily wrought-up youngster in her early twenties —in the difficult leading role of "Forza del Destino" in the first week of the season, with Enrico Caruso singing opposite her. She made good, of course. Despite her artistic limitations which were owing to inexperience and incomplete training, her marvellous voice was immediately acclaimed.

Was it a singing teacher who created these young vocalists? An adroit master can show the way, but he cannot manufacture voices. Gatti-Casazza used to say, "The great singing teacher is the man who is lucky enough to have great voices come to him." And Basil Ruysdael, who was Tibbett's teacher for a time, observed, "The only thing I could teach that boy was how to hold his arms."

3

The success of Flagstad, Tibbett, Ponselle stands out in such high relief because they are the exceptions that prove the rule that a theatre like the Metropolitan must depend for its personnel on singers of established repute. Think of the thousands of youngsters throughout the nation and throughout the world who aim and struggle for an operatic career, and consider how many of them reach the top. The major opera companies cannot play around with the inexperienced boy or girl. They charge high prices for their tickets and their audiences expect, not experiments, but recognized achievements.

Thus it is that the management of the Metropolitan, in its search for the singer, looks first at the other opera houses of the world. Most of them are in Europe, and eyes are turned across the Atlantic. Gatti-Casazza in his long regime, and his predecessors in office before him, did this; and Edward Johnson in his turn must roam the European cities during the off-season. And traveling with them is one of the principal conductors—at least part of the summer.

The great artists that America has known arrived with some experience obtained in European theatres. Caruso had been the rounds of the Italian theatres. Farrar had made her mark in Germany. Fremstad had sung in Europe. Mary Garden had conquered Paris. These people and their contemporaries came with solid reputations. They pleased their

American audiences immediately. There was little or no romance in their American triumphs.

Not that a reputation won elsewhere—whether in the opera houses of Europe or in the concert halls—will guarantee a success at a theatre like the Metropolitan. There have been artists who arrived with all the auspices in their favor. But the audience would not cotton to them.

Take the case of John McCormack. No singer has ever had a larger or more faithful following. His concerts, especially at the height of his career, were always sellouts. He had a tenor of beautiful quality and he used it, judging from his concert work, with style and distinction. Here was a natural for the opera. He had everything, even an audience. John McCormack's debut at the Metropolitan attracted a large crowd. His second performance attracted a handful; scores of seats remained unsold. The explanation may have been that his special audience loved the Irish songs and could not pay Metropolitan Opera prices. Or it may have been that McCormack was a singer first and foremost, and not a singing actor. At any rate, his engagement, which looked to the naked eye like a ten-strike, proved to be a fizzle for the opera. But McCormack went on packing them in in the concert hall.

The Metropolitan has had other disappointments of this kind. There were the cases of Alessandro Bonci, the little Italian tenor, and Luisa Tetrazzini, the coloratura soprano. Both singers had won generous plaudits abroad, and had scored signal successes at Oscar Hammerstein's Manhattan Opera House. What would be more natural than for them to become firmly established leaders of the Metropolitan personnel? The box-office records show that neither artist caught on at the Metropolitan.

In extenuation of Bonci's lack of success, it should be

pointed out that he had the misfortune to come along during the years of Caruso's ascendancy. That was tough competition for the French and Italian tenors of the time. Only one of them is still on hand who survived the years of Caruso's glory; he is Giovanni Martinelli.

As for Tetrazzini, she was not, even though it is ungallant to say so, a dazzling figure on the stage. She was short and heavy. But that was not why she failed at the Metropolitan. Coloratura sopranos seem to be in a class by themselves, anyhow. Why they succeed or fail will probably never be charted by mortals. The very qualities that mean success in one house will spell failure in another. The very attributes that mean success for one soprano will cause a hurricane of abuse for the next.

The career of Amelita Galli-Curci may serve as a text. She came over from Europe about two decades ago with a modest reputation. The Metropolitan was accorded the first chance to obtain her services. Mr. Gatti-Casazza and his staff of conductors listened to her in an audition and were not impressed. The girl could emit brilliant high tones, they realized, but they were not regularly on pitch. They decided that her singing was uneven, and turned her down, although they could have had her services for a pittance.

The Chicago Opera Company engaged her, and she was an immediate sensation. The Chicago troupe came to New York on tour and Galli-Curci was the prize draw. People poured into the Lexington Theatre to hear her. They mobbed the streets around, till women in satin slippers walked through blocks of mud to reach the theatre. And the anvil chorus began. The Metropolitan was damned for its complacence, for its failure to get out and find new talent, for letting the Chicago Opera Company discover Galli-Curci. The clamor and criticism were so acrid and recurrent that

Mr. Gatti, by his own account, bowed to his better judgment and engaged Galli-Curci. Saddest of sagas! Galli-Curci became but an ordinary drawing card at the Metropolitan.

Galli-Curci was aware of the constant criticism that she did not sing on pitch. She dismissed it once with a simple observation:

"I have made a million dollars singing off-pitch," she said, "and I won't spoil it now."

Coloratura sopranos! There was Marion Talley, the little girl from Kansas City. She bowled over the Metropolitan authorities in an audition. She was engaged. Her debut was accomplished to greater public furore than perhaps any other at the Metropolitan. It was more like a première at Grauman's Chinese Theatre in Hollywood. Two special trains—they had cost $50,000, it was said—brought Miss Talley's fellow townsmen and family from her native Kansas City. Her father, a telegrapher, sat backstage and tapped out the story of her debut to the natives back home. The newspapers devoted columns of space to the event. So great was the tumult that Miss Talley's succeeding performances drew large audiences; some thought that people came out of curiosity. The Kansas City girl made money in a concert tour. After several years she retired from the opera. The reason, to be honest, was that her career there was over. After the first fine careless rapture, her audiences dwindled. It was impossible for an inexperienced young singer to live up to all that had been promised for her.

The Talley affair taught the Metropolitan a lesson. When a singing teacher brought in a little unknown named Lily Pons for an audition, no word of it was allowed to seep out. The girl was engaged for the following year. She remained in New York for a time and studied. She went back to Europe, and returned many weeks before her debut. But still the press carried no advance laudations of her talents. In fact, no one could learn anything about her. She was merely one of a dozen newcomers who make their debuts each season. She might be given a minor role, and never graduate from the secondary class. Her first role was announced as Lucia, a leading part, but still there were no premature rumblings. Only the day before her debut did one newspaper carry a short account of a remarkable dress rehearsal. The story had it that the newcomer's singing had caused old hands to shed tears, and the net result of this intelligence was that the hard-boiled critics were out for blood.

It was later revealed that William J. Guard, the dominie of press relations for the Metropolitan, got the lecture of his life from Mr. Gatti when the news account appeared. Gatti had ordered that no word be permitted to leak out concerning Lily Pons. He wanted the press and the public to discover her after her performance. He did not want a repetition of the Marion Talley affair.

There is no need to dilate on Miss Pons's success. One writer observed that she would do as a coloratura soprano even though he did not notice that she caused people to weep. The manner of her introduction proved to be sounder than Miss Talley's. She consolidated her first triumph with successive accomplishments, and her career at the Metropolitan may turn out to be one of the longest for a coloratura soprano. The public for this type of singing is, in the last analysis, capricious. It takes a real personality to cling to it over a stretch of years, as Miss Pons has done.

4

Artists of rare distinction crop up on occasion in the most unexpected places. For example, there were a series of visits after the war by a troupe known as the German Opera Company. It presented the Wagner works at popular prices through the country. It was led, and some said financed, by Johanna Gadski, former Metropolitan soprano, who wished to make a comeback. The small touring companies are usually sorrowful affairs. The casts are made up of antiquated singers, youngsters who know next to nothing and incompetents. But this company had capable casts. It had also at least two fine artists. The Metropolitan snatched them up. They were Editha Fleischer, a charming lyric soprano of versatile attainments, who is now, unhappily, gone from the Broadway opera house, and Friedrich Schorr, who, fortunately, is still there. Mr. Schorr belongs to that rare company of singing actors who join head and heart to glorious voices. For many years he has been a pillar of strength in the Wagnerian operas. His Wotan, his Hans Sachs, his Amfortas, his Kurvenal have been among the company's most glittering adornments.

A theatre like the Metropolitan fails, from time to time, to obtain the services of distinguished singers. It is duly criticized for this neglect; sometimes unfairly, on occasion deservedly. Just before the war there blazed into Europe's opera heavens a bright new personality—Maria Jeritza. The Metropolitan did not get her until the early Nineteen Twenties. The criticism for this delay was not just, for Mr. Gatti had engaged Jeritza in 1915. She declined to come over during the war, and it was not until a number of years later that she finally arrived.

When Samuel Insull was the patron spirit of the Chicago Opera—not to mention thousands of unfortunate security holders—he assembled a brilliant company. There were Lotte Lehmann, Frida Leider, Rudolf Böckelmann, Maria Olszewska, Alexander Kipnis, Hermann Nissen, Vanni-Mar-

coux, Mary Garden. Why, it was demanded, had not the
Metropolitan engaged some of them?

Insull paid them more than the Metropolitan chose to
offer. But, it was said, others would have come cheerfully to
the Metropolitan. Was there any truth in the gossip that
Lotte Lehmann was not engaged in those years when she
was at the height of her powers because Jeritza did not wish
to have her around? I don't know. I do know that Lehmann
had much the same repertory and that she was engaged
directly Jeritza left.

There is no doubt that all the famous names of the opera
are not congregated at a house like the Metropolitan. Politics may play a part in who shall be engaged. There is also
the practical element. The Metropolitan can use only a certain quota of each type of voice. If there is a preponderance
of competent artists in a certain class, some must be left out.
The tendency these days is to engage singers for a limited
number of performances so that there will be room for more.

5

There are two ways in which a theatre like the Metropolitan samples vocal talent. One is to hear it in its own environment in a performance. The second is to hear it in an
audition. In his annual scouting trip through Europe the
manager travels through many countries and sits through
performances at a dozen opera houses, and one member of
the conducting staff may do likewise.

The directors of the foreign theatres are wary of the manager from America. They fear that their ablest artists will be
singled out and carried off. They know that most artists are
only too happy to come to this country. Johnson was unable
recently to obtain the services of several Italians because
their government appeared to be unwilling to let them go.

Opera: Front and Back

There may be some private auditions in Europe, but these are avoided wherever possible. A better judgment can be formed from watching an artist in action before an audience. Furthermore, certain well-established singers consider it an indignity to be asked to stand up for a private audition like the veriest tyro. There have been instances where such artists refused to give auditions. The Metropolitan, they contended, could engage them on their reputation, or it could do without them.

The audition is the method used in America. There are only a handful of opera companies in this country and their outstanding stars are drawn from the Metropolitan personnel. The management therefore must hear the new prospects without benefit of a production or an audience.

What happens at an audition? The singer steps out on the stage of the Metropolitan. He brings his own accompanist, or the Metropolitan provides one. A piano stands at the side of the stage. The accompanist begins playing, and the singer sings. Out front he sees only dark, empty spaces. If he is concerned about the identity of his listeners, he will strain to see in the gloom, but he will be lucky to make out the few figures seated in chairs in various parts of the orchestra. The faces will be shrouded in darkness and will be indistinguishable. If the singer is wise, he will forget about the void out front, and will attend strictly to his singing. When he has finished—he has sung an aria of his own selection—a voice below may call out to ask for a different type of aria. When that is done, the singer walks off with the accompanist. And the next prospect comes forth.

The listeners are usually the manager, some of his assistants and a representation of conductors and assistant conductors. They have years of experience in listening to young voices. They can tell a good vocal prospect instantly. They

The Hunt for the Golden Voice

may be favorably impressed by the young man or woman who walks down to the footlights and sings with ease and with poise. But they will not hold it against a singer if he or she is nervous. They have seen too many of these youngsters. They have seen them tear open their collars; they have seen them tug at their dresses; they have seen them twist and fidget and tremble; they have heard them cough and they have observed that many break down in the first effort and must begin all over.

If the audition impresses, the singer is, perhaps, engaged. Gatti adopted a policy of making an offer, signing and sealing a contract, and no more. No fanfare. No burst of publicity. No compliments. Let us see what the singer does publicly.

Almost any one can have an audition. The Metropolitan has learned only to ask that the singer have some vocal training. There was the time when a Swede turned up with a letter of recommendation from a prominent person. The Swede wanted an audition. The Metropolitan official who spoke to him said that they would be glad to give him one. He asked the Swede where he had sung before. The Swede said he had not sung anywhere. With whom had he studied? He hadn't ever studied. What arias did he know? The Swede wanted to know what was an aria. The Metropolitan official had met some queer ducks in his time, but this fellow took the prize. What songs did the Swede propose to sing? The prospect was prepared for that one. He smiled broadly, like one who knows the ropes, and said wisely, "O Sole Mio."

The world is full of crackpots, and the Metropolitan has learned that a good share of them think they are unappreciated opera stars. Therefore, it now demands that a person who wishes to have an audition show some kind of credentials. Usually training with a vocal teacher is enough. Previous experience in the theatre or on the radio is acceptable. Some singers like Grace Moore have come up from the musical comedy stage, and several have made their beginnings in night clubs.

The number of individuals who receive auditions each year runs into the hundreds. Persons who have been heard one year will be given another chance the next year, and the judges assume that they have had additional training. The hordes of prospects have increased since the instituting of the Metropolitan Opera auditions of the air two years ago. More people have learned about the auditions and more have asked for them. The scheme has its virtues, however. A committee of musicians listens to all the prospects and sorts out the most promising. The best are heard on the air. The manager and his aides can hear them under the strain of an actual performance.

The prize for the winners is, of course, a debut at the Metropolitan. The inception of the spring season during the same year that the auditions of the air began has meant that other promising youngsters, besides the winners, have received debuts.

The auditions are not confined to Americans. The candidates come from every part of the globe. They know that the Metropolitan is the most cosmopolitan of theatres. A fine voice whatever its origin will receive a hearing. There is no regard for race, creed, nationality or previous condition of servitude.

The color line, however, seems to prevail. There has never been a Negro singer at the Metropolitan, nor, for that matter, in most of the opera houses of the world. There have been honorable exceptions. The New York Hippodrome, to its credit, has not hesitated to give Negro singers a chance. It has had at least two colored Aïdas.

The Hunt for the Golden Voice

Whether the Metropolitan has ever consciously set up a color line I do not know. It may be that the audience would not approve of a Negro in a cast of white singers. The Metropolitan audience takes for granted, however, Negro supernumeraries in "Aïda," and it approved a cast of Negro dancers in Gruenberg's setting of O'Neill's "The Emperor Jones."

It may be that the Metropolitan is needlessly timid. At any rate, it would be worth a trial. The artist who would be an obvious choice for the honor is Marian Anderson. Here, if ever, is a voice of opera dimensions, of warm color and vivid personality. Here is an artist who carries herself with dignity and who uses her matchless gifts with superb art. If the opera companies of America are looking for great voices, here is one they have ignored. If she is not suitable to many roles, Marian Anderson would certainly make a magnificent Erda. Dare the Metropolitan, the Chicago, the San Francisco operas accept the challenge? Dare they flout prejudice and unenlightened conventions?

VII

ARTISTS AND PRIMA DONNAS

WHEN a flock of singers of all shapes, sizes and sexes has been assembled and herded into a single corral, the fun has only begun. Now that you have them, what will you do with them? Or, to put it more accurately, what will they do with you? The opera house is notoriously the sum and summit of the artistic temperament. It may be that Hollywood can hold its own in a fair and equal contest. But it couldn't be fair or equal, since the film stars are distributed through a number of studios, while the opera harbors its galaxy under one roof.

The majority of singers are sensible, kindly, well-ordered human beings, on the testimony of Giulio Gatti-Casazza, who spent forty-two years with them. A few of these may have harmless little idiosyncrasies, but they are minor in scope and sphere of influence. A few can be troublesome. Just a minority. But oh! that minority!

The head and fount of a healthy segment of temperament in opera is jealousy. What quarrels have been generated, what outbursts of anger have spilled over, what acts of meanness have been committed in the name of jealousy! The kind of jealousy for which Cupid is responsible is a mild, soothing emotion compared to passions unloosed by the envy of one singer for another.

A theatre like the Metropolitan knows from experience how strongly the green bile flows in the veins of some artists. It has rigid rules that no singer will receive prominence over another in billing, advertising or publicity, insofar as the management is concerned. The singers are listed in the roster in alphabetical order; no name is in larger type in the programs. The company cannot prevent a singer from hiring his own agent to trumpet his mastery to the world at large. Consider what happened after Caruso died. Each leading tenor tried to establish himself as the sole pretender to the crown of world's greatest tenor. Blast was followed by counterblast. The claims of one contender became more lurid than the next. Beniamino Gigli's cohorts argued with those of Giovanni Martinelli, and Lauri-Volpi's representatives fought with both.

It can now be told that Lauri-Volpi would not sign a contract with the Metropolitan unless he received more for each performance than Gigli. He did not care how much more. If the rate for each was $1500 a performance, Lauri-Volpi would ask for $1501. He would settle for $1500.10. His vanity would be assuaged by a differential of even a nickel.

There was the time when a soprano who was tall and blonde and reckoned beautiful heard that the Metropolitan had engaged another soprano who was tall and blonde and comely. The first soprano was firmly established with the public and the management. She had a juicy contract and she sang some of the fattest roles. Nevertheless, she did not like the engagement of the other soprano. When the newcomer made her debut in a role that the established star sometimes sang, the latter was not at the theatre. But she was adequately represented. Eyewitnesses swear that her two maids were stationed at the rear of the house. At the end of an affectingly rendered aria, when the audience applauded and shouted its approval, the two maids set up a counter-demonstration. They hissed as insistently as they could.

The preparation of a revival of "Carmen" some years ago was vivid proof of the lengths to which some prima donnas will go to argue their importance. The revival was planned for one of the leading sopranos of the company. The Metropolitan, however, always assigns double casts for each opera, to fend against possible accidents or disabilities. In this case a well-thought-of singer who had sung Carmen considerably abroad was also asked to prepare the role for the New York stage.

There were difficulties with the leading soprano during the rehearsal period, but that was nothing new. The première was scheduled for two days after Christmas. Normally the dress rehearsal would be set for forty-eight hours before the performance, but it was decided to give the staff the morning and afternoon off on Christmas Day. The dress rehearsal was scheduled for the day before Christmas.

Some time before the dress rehearsal the leading lady notified the management that she was not well and that she could not possibly sing through the dress rehearsal. The schedule was upset, and the management was obliged to cancel the partial holiday for several hundred persons—orchestra, chorus, ballet, stage crew and the other principals—and to call the dress rehearsal for Christmas Day after all. Several hours before the postponed dress rehearsal the leading soprano again notified the management that she was not well enough to go through with the dress rehearsal.

No purpose would be served by calling off the dress rehearsal entirely. Even if the leading lady's health should mend in time for the première and even if she could go through her part without benefit of a dress rehearsal, the rest of the company needed the workout. The management hastily telephoned the substitute Carmen, who had been too busy with other duties to take part in the ensemble rehearsals, and asked her whether she could go through the dress rehearsal. Being an agreeable person, she offered to try. She hurried down to the opera house and went through the role in mufti while the rest of the cast sang in costume. She gave a lively account of herself as Carmen and the management breathed more easily.

Perhaps fifteen minutes after the end of the dress rehearsal the manager and his aides were exchanging the greetings of the season over a glass of champagne. The rehearsal had gone well, and the second Carmen could be depended on to do a fine job. The phone rang. It was a message from the leading lady. She reported that she had spent a restful day and that she felt certain she would be ready for the public performance. The manager thanked her. He gave no hint that he knew—if he really did know—that friends of the leading lady had been in the theatre and witnessed the dress rehearsal with the secondary Carmen and that they had undoubtedly reported back immediately that the substitute was altogether too good.

Rivalries are not confined to singers who have the same type of voices and sing the same roles. Not at all. Artists in the same show will try to steal the limelight from each other. They will step out of character to dazzle the audience with a thunderous high note or they will add new business to the action that will center attention on them. When two singers have a simultaneous exit at different points of the stage, it is a hoary trick for one to stumble and to be the last off and, therefore, the recipient of the most applause.

2

Disputes over curtain calls may create a furious disturbance. The Metropolitan enforces certain rules for curtain calls to mitigate difficulties. If one leading artist receives a solo call, then the others get one too. Otherwise, they take their bows together. If you think that this arrangement leaves no margin for differences of opinion, glance at the famous Jeritza-Gigli incident of some years ago. Some of the facts of the row became public property because part of it erupted in the view of the audience. Here is the whole story. It should be added in passing that because of this incident Jeritza and Gigli were never again placed in the same cast.

It seemed that Jeritza thought that Gigli was trying to steal the curtain calls. She charged that when they came forward for a bow at the end of an act of "Tosca," he would leave her to her own devices and step nearer the footlights than she. It may be that Gigli, who had recently come from Italy, was accustomed to being the kingpin in any opera. In his native land he was, in effect, the prima donna, and it was natural for him to step out in front of his colleagues. In New York the rule of equality was followed. Perhaps Jeritza expected the rule of chivalry as well.

When they got behind the curtain after one bow, Jeritza, who was smoldering at Gigli, planted a sharply pointed toe in the tenor's slats. Gigli howled with pain and lunged at Jeritza. His open palm lashed across her face. In the meantime, the audience was applauding, demanding another curtain call for the singers. Jeritza was sent out for a solo bow. She came out before the audience, holding her hand against her face and weeping. In sobbing tones she confided in the three-thousand-odd persons in the auditorium.

"Gigli," she said. "He has not been nice to me."

3

The jealousies of love can also thrust themselves into the opera house to make things lively. There was a German basso in the company who had the physique of a god and the strength of a Hercules. He was an excellent athlete. No one knew him to have suffered any ailment beyond the occasional sore throat that is the blight of every singer. Yet one season he began to develop a variety of symptoms. He had pains in the chest, pains in the back, pains in the head. In midseason he decided that his health was so bad that he had to have his contract canceled at once. He wished to sail for home, and one night the management caught him just as he was really packing to leave. It took some fine persuasion to induce him to finish his season. The troubles were caused by a girl in Berlin. The basso was wildly in love with her. He telephoned to her overseas almost every night. He wanted to hurry home because he "thought she was being unfaithful to him."

In any group of highly strung men there is likely to be one fellow who wishes to be a Don Juan or who plays the part in fact. And in a contingent of nervous, emotional women there may be a potential DuBarry. The atmosphere of the opera house is certainly tense and sultry and it can be depended upon to produce its recurrent Don Juans and DuBarrys with their attendant scenes and complications.

The wife of a baritone who had philandering tendencies used to make miserable the life of the Metropolitan officials with her constant accusations and suspicions. To be fair to the lady, she certainly fancied she had sufficient excuse and provocation. But how could the management interfere in the couple's private lives? Nevertheless, she continued to complain. One day it was a ballet girl that fell under her suspicion; the next it was a leading singer. She told one singer whom she suspected that her husband suffered from a venereal disease. What thanks did she get? He left her to live openly with another singer.

How did all this affect the opera company? The management could not cast the husband in the same role with a woman whom the wife suspected without eliciting protests from her. Innocent women of the company found themselves being trailed by snoopers and they screamed imprecations at the powers that be.

[103]

Opera: Front and Back

In one performance a gentleman who had a roving fancy was singing the role of an elderly dignified personage to whom the heroine came to confide in her hour of need. The heroine was sung by an attractive newcomer. When she placed her hand on his shoulder and sang of her troubles, he whispered in her ear.

"You are beautiful," he said, as she tried to keep her mind on the opera. Then he sang a consoling phrase. And as she answered with her passage in the opera, he murmured: "Let's go to Baltimore [the first stop on the forthcoming tour] together. We will take adjoining rooms." He smiled dashingly and wholly out of character. "We will have fun."

The opera house has produced all kinds of relationship. There have been marriages of people in the company, divorces, remarriages, triangles, extracurricular affairs. Marriages are simple enough to handle. An unattached male weds an unattached female. Every one is happy. You can put the two into the same cast and get a sentimental reaction from a romantically inclined world. You can even put into the same cast a pair who are carrying the torch for one another and get a sophisticated response, provided Walter Winchell or one of his fellows has spread the news of the alliance abroad. But try and bring together a rowing couple or a rowing trio! And throw in a wife or a husband for good measure! Then you have a fine brew!

The gossips have always contended that a famous conductor left an opera company because of the complicated relationships among a female singer, a male singer, the conductor and a wife. The gossips have also retailed the yarn about the flighty soprano who made a shambles of a company's discipline by changing off tenors, baritones and bassos with awesome frequency.

There was a soprano in an American opera company—it

was not the Metropolitan—who had a fine natural voice but who used it coldly, unimaginatively, uncommunicatively. She was a good prospect, and the officials of that company decided that the girl needed a love affair to add character, color and variety to her singing. The poor beggars plotted to throw the soprano into the company of various attractive men, in and out of the company. The girl seemed not to be interested. The plotters learned at the end of the season that their diagnosis was all wrong; the soprano had been married all the time.

There was the French baritone whose affair with the wife of a prominent Western man was causing the town to talk, and the management forbade him to see her. The baritone obeyed for a time, but then his resolution began to waver. He pleaded with an official for a partial lifting of the ban.

"I promise," he said, "to see her with my clothes on."

4

Some singers will stir up troubles because it is their nature. They wish always to have flattery. They like to get their own way. Cross them and you barge into a hornet's nest. Play up to them and they will purr like satisfied felines, provided you are not also playing up to a hated rival.

One day a soprano dashed into the office of the director of an opera company. She was wearing a dressing gown. She had just been rehearsing.

"Look how devoted I am," she cried. "Even when I am sick, I continue to sing for you. Just now I hurt myself in a fall. But I went on with the rehearsal. Look!"

She flung open her dressing gown and pointed to what appeared to be a deep red gash on the leg.

The manager glanced at it, murmured a commiserating comment and thanked her for her fidelity and heroism.

When the prima donna had gone, the manager turned to his secretary.

Opera: Front and Back

"Did you see that horrible wound?" he said. "I know her. She painted it on herself with rouge."

Some artists insist that they must have special temperatures prevailing on the stages and the dressing rooms of the theatres in which they sing. Rosa Ponselle likes it cold. Her preference has brought her into violent conflict with various elements in the opera house. She used to quarrel with Rosina Galli about the temperature on the stage. The latter in her capacity as ballet mistress would not stand by and let her girls shiver in their thin gauze costumes on a stage that was frigid.

Once, during a cold wave in New York, the voice of Gatti-Casazza was heard thundering behind the closed doors of his office to a stage worker: "No matter what Rosa Ponselle says, I say there shall be heat on the stage!"

Giovanni Martinelli contends that he must have warm surroundings to protect his voice. After singing a performance with Rosa Ponselle at the Brooklyn Academy of Music several years ago he caught a cold. He insisted that it was caused by the lack of heat backstage. The next season he balked when it was proposed that he sing in "Gioconda" with Rosa. The management insisted, and he submitted. He caught hold of Ponselle before the performance and demanded that they have sufficient heat on the stage. The story has it that a lively dispute took place. It ended with a threat from Martinelli.

"If I catch cold and lose any performances," he shouted, "I'll sue you!"

One evening when Ponselle was singing in Philadelphia at the Academy of Music it was unseasonably warm and humid. She demanded of an attendant that the heat be turned off. He assured her that the heat was not on. She was in her dressing room at the moment. The attendant pointed to a closed window and asked whether she wanted it opened.

"Yes, let's open it," she cried, and she picked up a shoe and flung it at the window. The glass shattered, and the shoe bounced off a brick wall and back into the room. The window was a fraud.

5

The distribution of dressing rooms can stir up the cauldron of furies. There have been violent disputes at the Metropolitan on days when matinee and evening performances were billed. The prima donna who occupied the star's dressing room at a matinee once did not leave the theatre until more than two hours after her performance had ended. She took her own sweet time in removing costume and make-up, and then she held court for a number of friends. The prima donna who was to sing the evening lead arrived early to prepare at her leisure, and she angrily demanded the dressing room. The afternoon prima donna blandly took her time. A high official was called in to act as judge and jury. Out of this incident grew a ruling that singers must vacate dressing rooms within a certain reasonable period after a performance.

When a double bill is presented in the same evening there are further opportunities for dispute, and the management must assign dressing rooms, at the hazard to its subsequent peace of mind. In Chicago a tense situation arose because of the disposition of the star's dressing room in a double bill. The lady who was to sing in the second half of the bill arrived early and took possession of the dressing room. When the leading lady of the opening opera arrived, she would accept no other dressing room but the star's. In this dispute possession was better than nine-tenths of the law; it was a full 100 per cent. The occupant would not leave. Stage managers reasoned with the pair, argued, implored, but neither would budge an inch from her declared position. Suddenly the prima donna who was to sing in the first opera turned and left the theatre entirely. The stage people were terrified. They thought that she was walking out on the performance. Not at all! She returned to the Congress Hotel where she was staying, got into her costume there and taxied back to the opera house ready to go on the stage.

At a gala performance at the Metropolitan some years ago virtually all the prima donnas were scheduled to sing. It was a matter of first come, first served for the star dressing rooms. One young contralto, who was conscious of her importance, made an appearance at 6 P.M., thinking that her early arrival would insure her occupancy of the leading contralto's dressing room. But another contralto had had the same idea and had arrived earlier. The young contralto accepted another dressing room. But she was so bitterly disappointed that she broke down and wept.

Not all the artists in opera attach importance to their dressing rooms. Some apparently have the quaint notion that one room is as good as another, and that the singer's principal business is to sing. One of these is Kirsten Flagstad. She actually turned down the star's dressing room. She decided that an adjoining chamber was much pleasanter and asked whether she could have it. Seasoned stage officials almost swooned from the shock. But they have learned that Flagstad is one of those simple, unaffected persons who put on no airs. She is concerned with her work, not with extraneous trifles.

Geraldine Farrar dealt with the dressing-room question after her own fashion. She chose a dark, windowless little room that served as an occasional storage chamber and asked for permission to turn it into a dressing room. She had it decorated cheerfully and she had a lock placed on the door, keeping the key for herself. At best it was not a dressing room to be compared with the star's chamber, but it was Farrar's own, while the other had to be forfeited when one did not sing.

Ay, there was the rub! Other leading sopranos objected to Farrar having a private dressing room. It did not matter what kind of a room it was. There were squawks galore, and the loudest came from Frances Alda, who happened to be the wife of the general manager. Farrar was not moved by complaints. She held on to her dressing room and maintained it as her private retreat.

Ecclesiastes coined the phrase for it: All is vanity and vexation of spirit. Not quite all, in the opera house, but enough, enough. Some singers surround themselves with idolaters—secretaries, maids and valets, managers and assistant managers, accompanists, coaches, press agents and assorted hangers-on. In some cases the following develops because an artist is genial and generous. Caruso was always followed around by a small army. While he did not need this adulation —here, if ever, was a man who had universal esteem—he liked it. Some of the people who attached themselves to him were just leeches. Caruso, however, endured them, fed and wined them and often supplied them with sizable sums of money. The tenors who followed in his wake tried to ape his way of life outside the opera house and created entourages of their own.

6

The large sums earned by opera singers of the first rank make them the happy hunting ground of those who like easy money. Caruso was a shining mark. He derived immense pleasure from giving, and he gave with gusto. His beneficence fell on rotters; often it helped worthy souls. Typical of his generosity was his kindness to the late William Punzel, who was the wig-maker at the Metropolitan Opera House for many decades.

Opera: Front and Back

Toward the end of the season of 1909–10, just before the company's departure for a season in Paris, Punzel was in Caruso's dressing room before a performance of "Aïda." Punzel was curling the tenor's hair, for Caruso used his own mop of black hair for the role of Radames. At that moment the paymaster entered the dressing room and placed on the table before Caruso a packet of money. It was Caruso's salary for the week. The tenor picked it up and idly thumbed through the roll. Caruso liked to be paid in cash, and his roll contained about $5000. As Caruso fingered through the package, Punzel's eyes, straying from the curling job, literally popped. Caruso noticed Punzel's dazed expression.

"What's the matter, Punzel?" Caruso asked.

The wig-maker gasped. "So much money!"

Caruso laughed in great good-nature.

"If I had money like that," Punzel said witsfully, "I'd, I'd . . ."

"You'd what?"

Punzel breathed deeply. "I'd take my wife and child to Paris."

"Oh!" Caruso fingered through his week's salary and calmly handed Punzel a bill. As the wig-maker took it, his hands trembled. He could scarcely finish curling the tenor's hair. Then he rushed out to tell his friends backstage. He gathered them around him. He repeated his conversation with Caruso. Then he let the others peep into his wallet at a bill marked $500.

Caruso's giving has become almost legendary today at the Metropolitan Opera House. He would give money, gifts, personal possessions whenever the whim struck him, and it struck him frequently. If a stage hand admired a watch, Caruso insisted that he take it. His Christmas giving had a baronial sweep. Caruso remembered every one in the opera house. For the administrative staff there were gold pieces, $20 coins many of them. There were boxes of cigars for every member of the orchestra. There were gifts for the chorus, the ballet, the stage hands. Some one estimated that the illustrious tenor gave away at least $5000, possibly more, at Christmas time in the opera house alone, and his largesse to his own circle was equally princely.

The tradition of Christmas giving was valiantly carried on by people like Gigli. Nowadays, however, the giving is small and sporadic, according to old hands. They look back on former days with regret. Then the Christmas take was something to which one could look forward. It helped out a man whose wage was modest. The Metropolitan does not permit the practice prevalent in Europe: The factotums of the opera line up at the end of the season, as if on dress parade, and the artists pass by with their offerings.

There have been some singers who carried their regard for money to the other extreme. Francesco Tamagno, the great dramatic tenor for whom Verdi wrote "Otello" and who occupied the position of pre-eminence in the days before Caruso's advent, had a reputation of being miserly. He was brought over to the Metropolitan by Maurice Grau, the general manager at the time. Grau sailed with Tamagno on the same boat, but gave the tenor the money for his passage. On the second day out, Grau made a search for his tenor but could not find him. He was alarmed, and caused the ship's officials to make a minute study of the passenger list. It turned out that Tamagno was travelling second class, and Grau had looked for him in first class, for he had provided the tenor with enough funds to cover the best room available on board the vessel. He asked Tamagno for an explanation. The latter replied that he preferred second class because there were no airs, no dressing, no fuss. In short, he was "a democrat." He forgot to discuss the fact that he had pocketed the difference between first and second class.

Grau protested. "I paid you for first class. I cannot have my most famous tenor arrive in New York traveling in second class."

Tamagno held firmly to his position.

"What kind of an impression will it make?" Grau persisted.

Tamagno intimated that he did not care.

Grau was ultimately obliged to make up again the difference in the cost of passage and Tamagno made himself comfortable in first class, where he suffered the airs, the dressing and the fuss with the calmness befitting "a democrat."

The height of frugality was achieved, however, by several French singers in Chicago, if the story told about them has foundation in fact. It seems that they lived in a hotel overlooking a park, and pigeons used to pause in flight on their windowsill. An eyewitness swears that he saw the singers catch the pigeons with improvised lassoes and cook them for inexpensive dinners.

The singer whose thriftiness bespoke a way of life in the profoundest sense was perhaps Fernand Ansseau, the Belgian tenor. Habitués of the Metropolitan Opera may not even have heard of him, for Ansseau's few seasons in America were spent at the Chicago Opera. Artists who sang with Caruso and Ansseau characterize the Belgian's voice as second only to the great Neapolitan's. It was described by Charles Hackett, a tenor of parts in his own right and a perceptive student of voice, as "a big, round, luscious instrument; it was all meat, like a fine, bulky tender steak." The only quality that Ansseau lacked was excitement. There was a touch of lethargy in his singing, native to his temperament. He sang in Chicago for about five years, earning large sums of money. He had also drawn fat fees in the European opera houses. Then he decided to retire. He told friends that he had accumulated several million Belgian francs which, invested in the safest securities, brought him an annual income of about 150,000 francs.

"Why should I sing any more?" Ansseau said. "I have more than I can spend in any year. I can live my life quietly with my wife."

He has not sung again. He had offers, after his retirement, to return to Chicago for fabulous fees. His laconic reply was, "Let me alone with my fishing."

Ansseau's way of life was simple. He had a large farm, a comfortable home, a brook in which he could fish the whole day long. What indeed could a man want of life? He had a fine Minerva car, for an occasional trip. His one extravagance, so far as his friends know, was connected with that car. He built a special garage for it with a turnable floor. He did not like backing out.

Ansseau knew what he wanted. One may quarrel over his right to silence a voice such as his. At least he used it enough to make himself comfortable. His colleagues who remained in Chicago through the crash were left with badly battered fortunes. Virtually every one in the company speculated in stocks and bonds, and most of them lost their shirts on Insull securities. It is said that one married couple, both members of the company, saw a nest egg of about $1,000,000 turn into worthless certificates. In the days before 1929 almost every one, in the opera house and out of it, speculated in securities. The Chicago crowd, I understand, was not solicited to buy the Insull issues. But virtually every one in the Mississippi Valley got in on what looked like a good thing and watched paper profits mount at a fantastic speed. The Chicago singers were harder hit than opera people elsewhere who had speculated, because the Insull securities never came back. Rosa Raisa said, "Mr. Insull called us his children and said he wanted to help us."

One singer got out with his profits intact and he, naturally enough, was a Frenchman. He was the baritone, Vanni-Marcoux. He, too, had bought Insull securities and watched in bewilderment as they soared upward. Some months before the crash he sat down and figured out that his profits, plus his capital, had reached a point where he could be assured of all the things he wanted for the rest of his life. Acting on irrefutable logic, he sold out.

Vanni-Marcoux was shrewd. There was another baritone in Chicago, a lesser one, who was lucky where money was concerned. He drew a salary of $500 a week for about twenty weeks, totaling $10,000, and worked in only one act of one opera during the entire season. Even his one appearance was the result of a break. It is worth telling because it throws light on the ways of singers as well as managers.

Another baritone named Schwarz was singing the role of Rigoletto. In the intermission before the last act he told Désiré Defrere, the stage director, that his voice was weakening. The stage director replied that not much voice was needed for the last act of "Rigoletto." The baritone said he wouldn't have any. This baritone had a gesture of sounding a note on his fingers and bringing them to his ears, as if they were a tuning fork. He sounded a note in this fashion. He shook his head sadly and went to his dressing room. At the end of the intermission the leading singers came forth for the final act, but not the Rigoletto. The stage director rushed to his dressing room. The baritone was not there. He had left a note: "My voice is going, I am going."

While the curtain was held, the company made a frantic search for another Rigoletto. A baritone who had not worked all season was found at the rear of the auditorium. He was hauled backstage and tossed into a costume. He sang the last act. That was his work for twenty weeks' salary.

7

Some singers perpetrate deeds on the stage for which they are not paid. One prima donna, who was feuding with a tenor, found him singing José opposite her Carmen one evening. She felt that he had played her dirt on a previous occasion and she decided to even the score. In the last act, when José must kill Carmen, the prima donna would not stand still. She moved around the stage rapidly, and the tenor chased after her. The cue had come to kill Carmen, but José could not lay hands on her. The prompter barked an admonition. The stage director howled imprecations from the wings. Carmen let herself be slain, but measures late. The tenor ended the performance in a sweat.

One of the most vicious acts in the calendar of prima donna cattiness occurred once in a performance of "Tristan und Isolde." The contralto who sang Brangäne was a capricious, egocentric woman. The Isolde was a singer who had not achieved a great reputation or wide experience, but she was a competent artist. The faithful, understanding Brangäne turned out to be a serpent in this performance. She kept whispering to Isolde throughout the first act as the latter sang. She asked, sotto voce: "Have you ever sung Isolde before?" "Where do you come from?" "How is it we never heard of you before?" "Have you sung anywhere else?"

On another occasion this same contralto, also playing Brangäne, did about everything imaginable to distort the action on the stage. In the first act she stalked around the stage, drawing attention away from Isolde who is, after all, the principal character. When Isolde was attempting to confide in her, this Brangäne, instead of sitting humbly at her feet, strode back and forth, hands on hips. She behaved as if she were playing Carmen. At the end of the second act, Brangäne prowled around the rear of the stage hovering in and out, instead of standing by Isolde.

In a Chicago performance of "Tosca," a baritone avenged himself for a fancied slight from Mary Garden. In the casting of the opera the soprano, it was whispered, had objected to the choice of this baritone for Scarpia on the ground that he was too short for the role. Although her point was well taken, the baritone had to be used as Scarpia in the end. During the singing of the "Vissi d'Arte" in the second act, Mary had a way of reclining on a couch, her head resting on its back and her eyes looking heavenward. It was an effective manner of singing this prayer. But during the performance the baritone proceeded to improvise new action. Although it is customary for the soprano to sing this aria undisturbed, he sat beside her. His hands moved over her figure. He bent over her. A Will Hays of the opera would have placed this scene on the index expurgatorius without a second thought.

In a performance at the Metropolitan, Michael Bohnen chose to enter on the stage in a novel, and uninstructed, fashion. On the whim of the moment he walked in on his hands.

These unprepared acts are not always induced by meanness or jocosity. Occasionally they stem from kindness. Farrar once saved a performance of "Tosca" and a young tenor to boot by whispering on stage during a performance. The tenor was Paul Althouse, and he had prepared Cavaradossi at the last moment when Riccardo Martin became ill. The performance took place at the Brooklyn Academy of Music, and Farrar did not know that Althouse would sing with her until a half hour before curtain time. They had had no rehearsal together, and there was only time for a word of advice.

"Take my hand when you're in doubt," Farrar warned the young Althouse, "and I'll tell you what to do."

All through the performance Farrar not only sang and acted her part but whispered instructions to Althouse as to where he should stand and how she should move in good season for him to be ready. She did not miss a single cue, either her own or Cavaradossi's.

There was a tenor who suffered from hay fever, and he had the temerity to take an engagement in Ravinia Park for the summer. As he was standing in the wings waiting for his cue, a practical joker began to simulate an attack of sneezing. It was a good performance, and it stimulated the hay fever victim to the real thing. His cue came, and he finished his fit of sneezing on the stage. He opened his mouth to sing, but no sound came forth. The conductor stared at him. It was some minutes before the tenor recovered his voice.

8

Tenors! Why is it that they are the symbol of opera madness? The only answer must be that great tenors appear less often than outstanding artists in the other categories, and those who do achieve a reputation are zealous to maintain it. Those who have little or no reputation like to think that they have and act as if they were indispensable.

No artist is indispensable in any theatre. The loss may be felt for a few weeks, even several seasons. But the opera goes on. When Gigli departed from the Metropolitan because of his difference with Gatti-Casazza over a salary cut—and I recall his tears as he explained the principle of the thing to a group of us—Toscanini sent a message to a friend which summed up the whole story: "Caruso died, the Metropolitan went on. Farrar retired, the Metropolitan went on. Toscanini left, the Metropolitan went on. Tell Gatti to have courage."

Courage, of course! But an opera house cannot be run without tenors, much as such a consummation would please the management. A tenor like Caruso, whatever his playfulness outside the theatre, was all seriousness in his work. A tenor like Martinelli, who did not raise the roof over salary differences and who did not make a general nuisance of himself as others did, has remained at the Metropolitan for a quarter of a century, where men whose voices were as dependable but whose brains were not, have passed on. A tenor like Lauritz Melchior goes on year after year without creating disturbances. Is it because he began life as a baritone?

Melchior is endowed with a remarkable physique and incomparable vitality. Who remembers his missing a performance because of illness? Then consider how many times casts are scrambled in the course of a season because of sore throats and other ailments. Melchior has been known to sit up all night at a party, take his share of food and drink and turn up the next day to sing a magnificent performance of "Götterdämmerung."

He has one distinctive characteristic. He likes to keep a record of what he is doing. He has a little notebook in which he sets down, at the beginning of the season, a careful schedule of all his engagements. He lists the date, the place, the fee. As he fills each engagement, he carefully checks them off.

If baseball players watch their batting averages, why shouldn't a tenor do likewise?

There was the French tenor who arrived full of eagerness for his debut at the Metropolitan. He gave a hint of his capacities several days before his debut when he accosted an official of the company and asked him for some advice.

"I have three voices," the tenor began.

"You have what?"

"Three voices," the tenor replied. "I want you to listen to them and advise me which to use."

The dazed official listened as the tenor exhibited his three voices. One was full voice, natural in production. The second was falsetto. The third was a throaty monstrosity.

The official suggested that he sing as he always had. The tenor used all three of his voices. He lasted one season.

There was another tenor, who stayed at the Metropolitan only one year. He had a German accent as thick as Herman Bing's. The day before his debut he confided to an opera executive that he was not well and did not expect to do his best. The executive wanted to know why. The tenor explained that he had a pain in the leg.

"How will that affect your voice?" he was asked.

"Like dis," he answered. He began a series of gestures that are characteristic of the worst kind of Wagnerian "acting." First he stuck his chest out. Then he flung his arms outward and upward. Finally he thrust his right foot forward emphatically, bringing it down to earth with a bang. He clutched his right leg at the spot where the pain was. He did not sing a note.

"See?" he said.

One tenor who remained at the Metropolitan for a number of years was a storm center a good deal of the time, but he had a magnificent voice. He was kept on until his trouble-making became unendurable. In his early days as a singer this tenor had not been content with a pitch-pipe to give him the tone before he went on for a scene. He used to have a chamber orchestra playing for him backstage. As he grew more experienced he stopped using the orchestra, but he never became accustomed to criticism. If the New York press roasted him, he complained to the management. If another tenor received what he thought was a better assignment, he complained to the management. There was no end to his complaints.

Caruso, when he was not singing, was a child of nature. He loved a practical joke. There was the time that he was giving lessons to Edward McNamara, the singing cop from Paterson, N. J. The manner in which Caruso became Mc-Namara's teacher is a story in itself, since Caruso never had pupils. A group of proud civic spirits discovered McNamara at a local festival in Paterson—he was dragooned to sing—and they made a bet that their protégé could lick any one at singing. They matched him with Caruso, and the latter entered into the game with zest. But when Caruso heard McNamara sing, he refused to take further part in the jest. He insisted that the copper from Paterson had a voice and offered to instruct him.

During the period that Caruso was teaching McNamara, he had his pupil come to his suite at the Vanderbilt Hotel. His old friend and boon companion, Antonio Scotti, had a suite on the floor below. One day Caruso led McNamara from the studio into a small dark room at the far end of the apartment and instructed McNamara to sing. The reformed cop obeyed.

Caruso yelled, "Louder!"

McNamara sang louder.

Caruso shouted, "Louder still!"

McNamara went into fortissimo.

Caruso aggrievedly demanded whether McNamara could not sing any louder.

McNamara gave it all he had, and he was a healthy, powerful young man who could pour forth voice with the volume of an expert hog-caller.

Caruso smiled, satisfied. He told McNamara to stop and

led him back to the studio. There he ordered his pupil to sing, and when McNamara resumed fortissimo, Caruso bawled him out.

"Here," he said, "you sing like a human being."

"What was the idea in there?" demanded McNamara.

"That?" Caruso roared with glee. "That room is over Scotti's bedroom. The son-of-a-bitch is sick!"

Caruso and Scotti had quarreled, in jest and in earnest, innumerable times during their careers. The first time, when they were both youngsters, it was over a girl. On another occasion Scotti urged Caruso to accept an offer from Covent Garden, even though the price was not higher than what Caruso could obtain in Italy. Caruso refused to go to London. But Scotti argued with him.

"Take it this time," he said. "Until you have sung at Covent Garden, you have not arrived. Sing for this sum. Make a success. Then you will get anything."

Caruso finally agreed, went to Covent Garden and, of course, scored a smashing success. But the small salary continued to irk him. One day he told Scotti what he thought of him.

"You low Neapolitan," Caruso thundered—and remember, he was himself a Neapolitan—"you persuade me to come to Covent Garden for this salary. The salary of a baritone!"

Caruso and Scotti were fast friends to the end. But that did not prevent the tenor from playing practical jokes on his pal. In a performance of "Gioconda," Caruso took Scotti's hand in his and placed an egg in it. Then he watched the baritone's discomfiture. Scotti did not know what to do with the egg. He dared not deposit it into a pocket for fear that Caruso would pound him heartily where the egg rested. So Scotti sang, his hand clutching the egg. He looked around eagerly for some way to get rid of it. But Caruso, with a diabolical gleam in his eye, stood by him through the scene, ready to upset any plan. When Scotti finally got off the stage, the régisseur observed acidly that the distinguished baritone was as nervous as a debutante, while Caruso roared with joy.

Temperament is not the exclusive property of the tenor, nor the prima donna. It is to be found in every vocal category. As Gatti-Casazza used to say: "Prima donnas there are in every walk of life, and you will find persons with false pride and fine airs in every occupation."

Chaliapin could be temperamental or genial offstage as the humor moved him. His capacity for food and drink is wonderful. After a performance he has put away a heaping serving platter of spaghetti. And I have seen him prelude his breakfast with a trio of Scotch and sodas. An artist once made a caricature of him and showed it to the basso, asking him to place his signature under it. He cocked an eye at it, and shook his head.

"Let me have your pencil," he said.

The artist handed it to him. Chaliapin began to sketch, commenting at the same time on the deficiencies of the other caricature. In several moments he was done. He held up his work.

"Is this not better?"

It was.

9

Singers may themselves be well-disciplined members of an opera company, but they sometimes have husbands and wives who can make more trouble than a dozen prima donnas. There are the spouses who believe that their mates are being poorly used. They complain about salaries, about assignment of roles, about length of contracts.

Artists and Prima Donnas

There have been several wives who managed to talk their husbands out of good jobs as Metropolitan singers. The wife of a baritone fought so hard against a wage cut which every one was being asked to take that she succeeded in having her husband eliminated from the company. The noisier half of a tenor squealed that her husband was not receiving the top price for tenors. To be sure, he was not; he was not a top-flight draw. Nevertheless, he was earning a respectable sum each week and receiving a fair share of appearances. She squawked so loudly that the management, in order to rid itself of the wife, did not renew its contract with the tenor. One opera wife started a feud between her husband, a tenor, and the soprano with whom he often sang because the latter had more attention from the press.

An opera wife is likely to be more troublesome than an opera husband, for the simple reason that she usually has no other occupation. Most opera husbands, being self-respecting citizens, continue with their jobs or their businesses when their wives score successes. They interfere only when they believe injustice is being wrought on their wives. A woman whose occupation is her husband's career has her peer only in the man whose sole occupation is his wife's career. Some husbands try to fill the role of manager, public tub-thumper and buffet between colleagues and the wife.

Some husbands are useful to the management. They act as shock-absorbers. They smooth out the ruffles of the lady's tempers. They know from experience what is likely to cause the next outburst and can hoist storm-signals. Some have even a sense of humor, and observe the tinsel world with which they are associated by affinity with a quizzical eye. One of the mellower group of husbands visited Gatti-Casazza one day, after the New York newspaper critics had hailed the latest Wagnerian soprano as the ultimate interpreter of certain of the master's greatest roles. It happened that this husband's wife was a veteran interpreter of these roles. But he had not come to complain.

"I wish to congratulate you, Mr. Gatti," the husband said, and his eyes twinkled, "on the magnificent success this season of your 'Tristan' and 'Walküre' and 'Götterdämmerung.' I only wonder that you have managed to find adequate casts and to give all these operas in so many past seasons."

10

When singers grow old, they are likely to become anxious about their careers and create difficulties. A few know how to step out of the picture gracefully. There are two charming ladies, still in the public eye, who withdrew from the theatre of their own choosing. They are Geraldine Farrar and Lucrezia Bori. Each of these women had a design for living; in it there was no place for a painful decline from stardom. While both sopranos, superb artists, have done some singing since their retirement from the Metropolitan, they are allowing their careers to taper off easily and naturally.

An amusing angle of Farrar's retirement is that both the management of the Metropolitan and the artist herself seemed to read each other's minds long before the event. A careful investigation reveals that the management, which was planning to offer Miss Farrar only half a season instead of the full season which had been her right for twenty years as one of the foremost artists of the company, predicted that she would not accept these terms. She, on the other hand, wrote a friend, a year before this offer, "I have a feeling they are going to ring the bell on me, and I intend to ring it first."

Geraldine Farrar, whom Gatti called the "beniamina" of

the American public, stands apart from many other artists in that she accepted wise counsels for the conservation of her earnings. The late Charles A. Ellis was her trustee, as he had been Melba's before her. Today, when she does no singing at all, she has ample means for a gracious way of life.

Lucrezia Bori meant to retire several years before she actually did. But the depression came along. It may even be that her personal finances were impaired. Her main objective for staying on, however, was her activity to keep the Metropolitan alive. She headed committees to collect funds. She became an executive as well as an artist. Those who know the quality of Lucrezia Bori's intelligence realize that, in her opinion, an artist best serves his art who gives it all his concentration. Since her standards were of the highest, she undoubtedly felt that her chairmanship of the Committee to Maintain Metropolitan Opera interfered with her self-imposed requirements as an artist. But she bore the double load cheerfully.

Bori was intelligent enough to face the fact that no singer can go on forever and that it is better for him to devise the time and means for retirement instead of waiting for others to do so. She looked ahead. She began to study sculpture for which she had had a taste all her life. She modeled in clay and planned to go on with marble. She agreed to act as a director of the Metropolitan and as a member of the board's managing committee. She planned to travel, to read, to see people; in short, retirement was not to be fatal as it had been to others.

Some artists go on singing when they have passed their prime because they refuse to admit that their voices and energies are going. Some know that their star is waning but, since they are without funds, they have no choice. There was Antonio Scotti, a grand seigneur as a human being and a fine, intelligent artist. He continued beyond his best years vocally, although some of his interpretations—Scarpia in "Tosca" and Chim-Fen in "L'Oracolo"—remained models of the actor's art even when the voice did not support the conception. Scotti had lost a large sum of money on a touring opera company in the early Twenties, and the remainder of his fortune was depleted by unfortunate investments. At the end of his life friends helped him with funds. His retirement, for all his brave showing before the public eye, was tragic.

In the line of newspaper duty, I happened to be with Scotti in the hours before his final performance. As he glanced at the mementoes in his room at the Vanderbilt Hotel, they brought back vivid memories to him and a tear came to his eye. A figurine of Caruso, his bosom companion, occupied a place of honor on the table. He caressed it. He glanced around at the photographs of dear friends of the opera world. Remember that Scotti was at the Metropolitan for thirty consecutive years, more than any other artist before or after. His career was bound up with New York.

As he waited for the time to leave for the opera house, he answered frequent telephone calls from well-wishers and friends. He spoke equably, but at the end of each call his eyes would become dewy. The measure of his friendships was those telephone calls. They came from friends in every walk of life. There were a banker, a painter, a broker. There was a call from an American actress who had been a dear friend. When he had finished speaking to her, Scotti showed his visitor a brooch with a photograph of a strikingly attractive girl. "That is Ina Claire," he said. "She was nineteen then. A beautiful woman."

Scotti had been a figure of distinction throughout his long career. He had the physique and the bearing to be the veritable Don Juan. And even in that final performance there was the air of the natural aristocrat about the man.

Other artists have not possessed the qualities of character to carry the burden of the final years with the same grace. They have become quibblers and trouble-makers. They have sought praise at every turn. There was a soprano who had been a person of geniality and kindness at the height of her career. She befriended young artists, gave them words of advice and encouragement. She was not above little acts of generosity to chorus and ballet. But when she realized that younger artists were moving up to vie for her place, she became irascible and unreasonable. She argued about distribution of roles, about length of rehearsals, about curtain calls, about the hundred-and-one things that a singer can find wrong if he puts his mind to it.

Aging singers develop amusing foibles. There was the basso who felt that his high notes had taken on a new breadth and refulgence. He would stop any one who would listen—his preferred victims were officials of the opera or the conductors—and would ask them: "Have you noticed my high notes? Did you hear the F-sharp? In the old days, I had no F-sharp at all. Now it is a magnificent note, is it not?"

Actually a good many singers face the hard fact that their range is not what it used to be when they were younger. They arrange for transposition of difficult passages. A dramatic soprano who must sing the "Siegfried" Brünnhilde will not attempt to hit the two high C's in the final act duet. Tenors transpose frequently.

A good many of them transpose even when they are at the height of their careers, especially in the French and Italian operas. In Wagner it is not necessary to transpose all the high notes, because a full orchestra can cover a multitude of shortcomings in a singer. Transpositions would also dislocate the effect, so meticulously do voices and orchestra jibe. But in the Italian and French repertory certain changes are used virtually all the time. The duet in the first act of "La Bohème" between Mimi and Rodolfo is almost always taken a half-tone lower, for the tenor's sake. The air, "Di quella pira," in "Trovatore" is customarily sung a half-tone lower.

The artist who worked out his transpositions with a thoroughness that was characteristic of his careful approach was the tenor, Tito Schipa. It was his habit to transpose some of his roles from a half-tone to a full tone and a half down. He had orchestrations prepared to match his transpositions, so that the instrumentalists would not be obliged to transpose on the spur of the moment. He had the parts ready and would distribute them to the men.

A tenor who transposed a great deal once made a speech and asked a colleague who knew him well whether he had heard the address. The colleague said he had.

"How did you like it?"

"Fine," said the colleague. "For the first time I heard every phrase of yours in the proper key."

II

A discussion of artists and their problems always evokes comparisons with the good old days. There is a great hue and cry that the seasons of yesteryear were the finest and that the artists of that period were supreme. Old-timers insist that the de Reszkes, Lilli Lehmann, Melba, and the rest were the true giants, and the younger element counters with claims for the current crop. Those of us who did not hear the singers of the golden Nineties nor even the crop that followed in the next decade or two may accept on faith the claims of their supporters.

Artists and Prima Donnas

But there is this to be said for contemporary artists: A new age has added to the things required of them. They must know more about costuming and acting. They must look reasonably like the figures they are portraying. The cinema has set up new standards of personal appearance, and younger audiences will not compromise the eye for the benefit of the ear. The radio has spread a little knowledge of the voice. People know languages. About ten years ago Chaliapin was the Mephistopheles in a performance of "Faust" at the Metropolitan. The Russian basso sang a big aria, but did not trouble himself to restudy the words. He fitted a gibberish of sounds to the air and did likewise through most of his lines during the rest of the performance. The audience laughed at him, some even hissed, and many complained to the management.

The conscientious artist, in the last analysis, remains conscientious in all times and all climates. Caruso made a habit of coming to the opera house at 6 P.M. on the evening of a performance. He would go through his entire part between 6 P.M. and curtain time, frequently singing in full voice. Lucrezia Bori always rehearsed the full role the day of the performance.

Rosa Ponselle does the same thing, but because of her nature she overdoes it and works herself up to a nervous state from time to time. Can it be that this is the reason why she no longer sings "Norma"? The Druid priestess in Bellini's masterpiece was easily her supreme interpretation, as it was also the finest Norma since Lilli Lehmann. But the hours preceding the performance were often trying for her. She would worry and doubt herself. Gatti-Casazza knew how to keep her calm and to restore her confidence. It should be emphasized that once she went out on the stage, Rosa Ponselle became mistress of herself and her role. The audience had no notice of her nervousness. She was an interpreter of sumptuous and controlled voice.

Kirsten Flagstad is another artist who carefully reviews every role in its entirety on the day of the performance. She prefers to go through her part at home in the early afternoon. Then she takes a nap. But she will not spare herself if she feels that a role needs attention. There was the time last season when she spent the morning and part of the afternoon singing in full voice at the dress rehearsal of "The Flying Dutchman." The season's first performance of "Lohengrin" happened to be in the offing as well, but there seemed to be no way of scheduling a rehearsal for this opera without conflicting with performances later in the week. It was Flagstad who suggested that "Lohengrin" be rehearsed that night. Since she had already rehearsed in full voice that day, the conductor and the officials suggested that an evening rehearsal would be too much. Flagstad demurred. She proceeded to sing in the evening in full voice. Her colleagues pleaded with her to use half-voice. "No," she said simply, "I want to be sure to get everything right."

Regarding Flagstad, her concerned admirers have inquired why the Metropolitan and her concert manager worked her so intensively. They have feared for her health and the pristine beauty of her voice. Both her manager and the Metropolitan reply that it is Flagstad's wish. She loves to sing. It is no chore for her, but a deep, abiding joy. She is grateful to America and Americans, moreover, that they have made her the current first lady of song in the operatic and concert world. For twenty years she was just another singer in her native land. America granted her unparalleled recognition.

Many stories have been told about the simplicity and unaffectedness of Kirsten Flagstad. I like this one best. She has saved crucial situations for the Metropolitan, and the truth is that the management would accede to any request she made, even before she stated it. She has but to ask and her wishes will be granted. One day Flagstad did ask for something. She hoped apologetically that the Metropolitan would let her sing Senta in a revival of "The Flying Dutchman." Her request was not made because she sought a new role, nor because she was responding to the clamors of her public for the revival. She asked to do "The Flying Dutchman" because her Norwegian husband had never heard her in it.

The measure of an artist's simplicity combined with disturbing premonitions was suggested in a letter that Caruso wrote from Sorrento to his manager, Gatti-Casazza. The letter was written on July 29, 1921. It was an answer to a telegram in which Gatti asked what Caruso's plans were for the coming season.

Here are the salient parts of the letter:

Mio caro Direttore:
I received your affectionate telegram in due time for which I thank you very much and today I received your dear letter of the 26th.

I am very sorry not to be able to tell you anything regarding my sailing for New York because new events are in prospect which are not quite clear to me.

[Here follows a detailed account of the tenor's illness, the latest treatments and a new plan for curing.]

Consequently I have decided to go to Rome next week and whatever there will be to do, operation or no operation, it will be there that I'll be skinned. I shall be at the Grand Hotel in Rome Wednesday next at 13.15 and immediately I shall get to work and whatever happens I shall let you know.

May I beg you now, Caro Direttore, inasmuch as the doctors have assured me that I shall be able to begin work not later than five months from now, to please wait for my word; otherwise I shall never get well due to the constant thinking which bothers my head. Steamers can always be found; if not, then we shall do without the next season. What is sure is that I don't want to die in order to please those who are waiting for me to judge me. First of all, I shall get well, then we'll talk.

If you can come to Rome I would be exceedingly glad to see you. At any rate as soon as I shall have heard from the doctors what will have to be done I shall telegraph to you. The side hurts me and my head is dizzy on account of fever, so I shall stop and throw myself on the bed.

It seems that the thing is very serious as my wife cries since yesterday without pause. She says it is because she sees me suffer but I believe that the doctors have told her something which they don't want to tell me. We'll see. Please accept my kindest regards and an affectionate hug from your

ENRICO CARUSO.

On August 1, 1921, Enrico Caruso died.

12

In the course of his career Caruso sang all manner of lyric and dramatic roles and his impersonations ranged from the gay young Duke of "Rigoletto" to the subtle, aged Eleazar of "La Juive." But his repertory, although it comprised fifty or more operas, was restricted largely to the Italian and French works. Whether he wished this to be so I do not know, but we have the evidence of James Huneker to show that Caruso knew some of the Wagner operas.

"It has often been a cause of critical wonderment," Huneker wrote, "why Caruso never sang the music of Richard Wagner. What a Lohengrin he would have been, what a Parsifal, yes, even a Tristan! He knew every note of these roles. Once for my delectation he hummed the plaintive measures of the dying Tristan. Tears came to my eyes, so penetratingly sweet was his tone, so pathetic his phrasing."

It will not profit us to speculate on the question of whether Caruso really would have been a great Lohengrin, Parsifal, or Tristan. Only a handful of exceedingly great artists have been able to range over the entire repertory with distinction to themselves and with justice to the composers. Lilli Lehmann and Jean de Reszke did it in days gone by. Florence Easton has contributed memorable performances in the French, Italian, and German operas, not to mention works by composers of other nationalities. There are a number of contemporaries who have touched on all the major styles and schools. For the most part, however, singers stick to their métier once they have found it. The wisdom of specialization has been amply substantiated in the careers of hundreds of artists.

Specialization is more common in this country where opera is sung in its original tongue. Since we import outstanding European artists, the theory is that we might as well bring over the best for each school of opera. It happens, therefore, that a singer who does every kind of role in his native land is confined to a limited repertory in this country. A Friedrich Schorr sticks to Wotan, Sachs, the Dutchman and Amfortas. An Emanuel List sings Hagen, Gurnemanz, Hunding and Baron Ochs. A Gina Cigna sings Gioconda, Aïda and Norma. A Giuseppe DeLuca kept on doing Figaro, Rigoletto, Amonasro and the like.

Some artists are satisfied to let their activities become grooved. Lauritz Melchior is eminently pleased to keep to his Wagner tenor roles of Siegmund, Siegfried, Tristan, Parsifal, Tannhäuser and Lohengrin. He knows them thoroughly, and since he is constantly singing them he does not have to worry about keeping his repertory fresh. He does not have to labor over new roles, and he has every assurance of

[133]

finding ample employment with his stock in hand. He is in
the fortunate position of being the outstanding tenor of his
day for his repertory, and he can work as much as he chooses.
When his New York season is finished, he can embark for
London at once, and appear on the stage of Covent Garden
the day after his arrival in England. No drawn-out rehearsals, no bother with new texts, no taxing practice periods.

There are artists who grumble at the limitations of a spe-
cialized repertory. The lyric singer thinks he has the talent
to be a dramatic artist, and the dramatic singer wishes to do
lyric roles. The Metropolitan once had a baritone who
played Beckmesser and Alberich successfully. His voice was
harsh and hard-bitten, but these deficiencies were not serious
in his roles. He aspired, however, to lyric parts, and when
he received them, croaked like a frog. There was the case
of Editha Fleischer, who was a valuable member of the Metropolitan for a number of years. She was required to sing,
with disheartening regularity, the roles of the Rhinemaiden,
the forest bird or the shepherd, minor roles in Wagner's
operas. Now and then she did a Zerlina in "Don Giovanni"
or a Marguerite in "Faust," but these opportunities did not
come often enough to compensate for her routined life at the
Metropolitan. She departed because, as she put it, she was
"tired of singing in a bucket, down a well or up a tree."

The singer of minor roles is not, of course, restricted to
any group of operas. He must know hundreds of works, frequently several parts in each. If he is a veteran and has more
than a bowing acquaintance with any opera that may turn
up, he may be more valuable to the company than a more
illustrious artist. The second-line artist may be comparatively
unknown, but he is not without honor. The manager, the
conductor, the stage director know how to value him, and
young singers have particular reason to be thankful that the

veterans are around. For an old hand on the stage may have a steadying influence on nervous youngsters. He may be able to whisper a word of help or encouragement to debutants. He may be a tower of strength in rehearsals.

How many casual operagoers know the name of Angelo Bada? He has been a member of the Metropolitan Opera Company for thirty years. He himself has probably lost count of all the roles he has done. His voice is not a glittering organ any longer, but that does not signify when contrasted with his importance in any performance. He knows not only his own roles but virtually all the others. When an emergency arises he can fill in almost anywhere—save, of course, in female roles—and often he has given a faltering young soprano her phrase or pitch.

Bada is not *sui generis* at the Metropolitan; nor is his kind indigenous to that theatre. An opera house of such pretension must have a handful of skilled, routined artists. They are the best insurance a company can have that the show will go on.

There are also the obvious blessings of the second-line artists. It is in the nature of their positions that they should not have airs, recriminations and bursts of temperament. They go about their work in business-like fashion.

13

One of the stock gags for poking fun at singers and opera is to open the mouth wide and to utter a series of Me-me-me-me's. There is no doubt that the sight and sound of a pompous tenor making these noises is comic, and as little doubt that some singers indulge in the Me-me-me-me's for effect rather than utility. Yet warming up the voice is part of the game, and as long as the artist does it in the privacy of his dressing-room he will be neither funny nor irritating.

Opera: Front and Back

A few artists are fortunate in that their roles or their peculiar equipment do not require extensive warming up of the voice. The Wagner music-dramas are so skilfully written that an artist may depend on most roles to give the voice a natural opportunity to warm to its work. The roles are, of course, so extensive that the singer cannot afford to use up energy for warming the voice, but occasionally he has no choice. The part of Isolde begins on a high tension, and the demands on the soprano are enormously exacting through most of the first and second acts. But the Isolde usually has to warm up the voice before going on.

The role of Siegmund in "Die Walküre" begins on a low plane and curves upward slowly and steadily, giving the tenor adequate opportunity to warm up his voice in the course of the performance. Wagnerian tenors do not have to spend much time preparing their voices before the show begins. And a tenor like Lauritz Melchior, because of personal gifts, does not have to spend any time at all. His voice is so well placed and focused, he is so completely in command of his repertory, that he can go on without uttering a sound in advance. He has been known to spend a week traveling overseas, during which time he has not sung a note, and then to walk on without any warm-up.

The artists who sing in the French and Italian operas have an entirely different problem. They must warm up their voices or they are lost. The composers have not provided natural curves of intensity. The tenor who sings Radames must tackle the aria "Celeste Aïda" in the first five minutes of the opera, and he must be ready to sing at the top of his powers. That is why the Italian tenor spends some time in advance of the performance warming up. Some singers actually devote as much time to warming up as they do to the entire role.

[136]

Singers will vocalize not only before the performance but during it. Some will warm up their voices before every entrance; others before each big scene. Most of them retire to the privacy of their dressing rooms for this function. A few, and they are the more pretentious citizens of the theatre, prefer to give the stage hands, the chorus and their colleagues the benefit of their vocalizing.

Each singer has his own whims. One tenor will drink hot water before every entrance. Another will take a slug of Scotch or rye. Some, like British tennis players, will imbibe hot tea between appearances on the stage. And one or two will have nothing less than champagne.

14

The measure of an artist's quality as a human being may often be estimated from observing his relations with the public and the press. Place at the head of the class those singers who do their work to the best of their abilities and serenely ignore what is said or written about them. On an equally high level are those who react to public and press with frank interest and with graciousness and intelligence. There are many who belong in either of these categories. There are some who fret and fume over every adverse comment and some who behave as if a personal insult were involved. There was the time when a leading baritone of the Metropolitan communicated with a writer of a New York paper, asking him for an early appointment. The baritone declared it was terribly important. A meeting was arranged. The baritone came right out with it.

"Tell me," he said earnestly to the writer, "is there something you have against me?"

"Nothing at all!"

Opera: Front and Back

"In your piece on 'Manon,'" the baritone said, aggrievedly, "you did not mention me. I sang Lescaut, the leading baritone role."

"Did I leave you out?" the critic was honestly surprised. "It was sheer accident."

Some of the finest artists are not above this concern with the slightest adverse criticism. Caruso once threatened not to sing in Boston because a young critic in that town roasted him. Gatti-Casazza had to reason with him and to point out that Caruso was the world's most famous tenor, while the young critic was virtually nobody.

Some artists boast that they never read criticisms, and it may be true of one or two. Most of them do. And some may be seriously affected by severe censure. I know of two prima donnas who literally took to their beds for several days after they had been burned to a critic's crisp for their portrayals of Carmen.

There is on record a historic personal encounter between a tenor and a critic. The latter, who happened to be in his cups that day, was no admirer of the tenor. They arrived in the office of the press representative at the same moment, and that well-meaning gentleman proceeded to introduce the tenor to the writer. The latter spoke his mind with the frankness of a man who had endured much.

"I don't want to know you," he assured the tenor, and how many of the critic's colleagues have not envied him this one glorious moment! "You sing like a dog!"

The critic turned and departed. The tenor let out a horrendous scream. He surged into Gatti-Casazza's office like a fullback plowing through tackle. He threatened to call the police, he offered his resignation, he said he was going to pack and leave at once. It is not recorded what form of mesmerism Gatti-Casazza employed, but he finally calmed the tenor, who had, to be fair to him, some cause for declaring himself insulted.

The public may impinge on a singer's preparation for a role. There was the time when a Cincinnati citizen filed a request in court in an effort to enjoin Leonora Corona, the American soprano, from wearing a scanty costume in "Thaïs" in an outdoor performance in that city.

"It's art," Miss Corona answered. "The opera is a great moral lesson. Furthermore, who could play Thaïs in a Mother Hubbard?"

The manager said: "Veiled in the moonlight, she will be amply protected by the shades of night."

The judge said, "No jurisdiction."

Nor was there any court or individual to gainsay Lina Cavalieri from granting an ordinary mortal what she considered to be a little moment of happiness. She was in her boudoir at the old Netherland Hotel, in the midst of her daily beauty treatments—she was noted more for her beauty than her vocalism—and a retinue of maids, hairdressers, masseuses, and manicurists were administering their beneficent services. La Cavalieri did not bother with clothes during these seances.

A knock on the door announced the approach of the waiter to take the singer's breakfast order. Some one reached to throw a sheet over the resplendent figure. But La Cavalieri waved the covering away.

"No," she said, "give the poor fellow's eyes a treat. His life must be so drab."

A comment about a pair of shoes once moved a distinguished artist, Marcella Sembrich, to action. A critic wrote that Sembrich's red shoes in one role looked "like a pair of lobsters." An emissary visited the writer post-haste. His re-marks were brief and to the point.

"Madame wants to know," he said truculently, "what kind of shoes *you* would wear?"

VIII

THEY WHO LEAD

THE men who give visual and aural unity to a performance of opera are the stage director and the conductor. A theatre such as the Metropolitan Opera has a staff of seven conductors, nine assistant conductors and three stage directors. The general public, however, knows little or nothing about these men who fuse the diverse elements into a cohesive production. The average person who runs and reads may be acquainted with histories of the stars, but he does not bother with the guiding spirits of a performance. No white light of publicity beats down on conductor and stage director, the one silhouetted in darkness, the other bound to blush unseen.

The glaring exception is Arturo Toscanini. Through a long storm-tossed career he has been news. For America he became a public figure when he arrived to conduct at the Metropolitan Opera in 1908, and he has remained in the public eye ever since. It is a curious thing about Toscanini. His concentration in his task is incomparably intense. No one has ever questioned his sincerity as a musician. He does not grant interviews. He does not make speeches. Yet he wins headlines with a Shavian regularity that must be the envy of people who spend fortunes to obtain publicity.

It must be borne in mind that such Toscanini yarns as do become current are only a fragment of the saga that has sprung up around the name of the little Italian maestro. If all the stories of him, well-founded and fictional, were to become public property, he would be in the news constantly. Around him events erupt, tempers clash and feelings mount high.

When Toscanini made his debut at the Metropolitan he had behind him a long record of service as an opera conductor. He had begun in Buenos Aires at the age of nineteen, where, as 'cellist in the orchestra, he had taken over the baton at the last minute and conducted "Aïda" from memory. He also had conducted literally all over Italy. No provincial theatre was too small for him. No opera was too low for him. He learned his job in the crucible of strenuous daily work. When he went to La Scala in Milan with Gatti-Casazza in 1898 he was just past thirty, but he had behind him a wealth of experience, and his fame was spreading beyond the confines of the Italian peninsula. In fact Heinrich Conried, general manager of the Metropolitan from 1903 to 1908, had made an offer to Toscanini to come to New York, but he had declined.

It was Toscanini who cast the die for Gatti and himself in the decision to come to the Metropolitan. The maestro's position in Milan had become—at least so he felt—untenable. One can guess what enemies Toscanini had made in Italy. For he had early developed the habit—it was, no doubt, an indivisible aspect of his character—of telling singers just what he thought of them, and composers and directors and instrumentalists as well. His abrupt departure from the Scala at the end of his fifth season there did not endear him to the Italian multitude. At the end of the second act of the final performance the audience clamored for an encore. Toscanini was infuriated. He flung down his baton and walked out of the opera house. An assistant conductor had to finish the performance. He took the boat for South America the next day. He did not return to the Scala until three seasons had passed, and then he remained for two years. But there were those who did not forget.

They Who Lead

Toscanini's years at the Metropolitan left an indelible mark on that institution. There are many persons still working in the Broadway opera house who recall the passions that swirled around the little Italian and the magnificent performances that he prepared and conducted. His debut on the opening night in "Aïda" was hailed with hosannas. Only one dissenting voice was heard, and the years have surrounded it with the ironic fragrance that belongs to the judgment of a forgotten contemporary of Beethoven who said that the "Eroica" was confused. The dissenting voice was Reginald de Koven, writing in *The World*. He thought that Toscanini's "Aïda" was lacking, of all things, in understanding.

Toscanini's presence at the Metropolitan made difficult the position of the other conductors. It is true that he replied, when asked whether he would be able to get along with Mahler, that it would be a pleasure to work with such a distinguished musician. Mahler did not remain long at the Metropolitan because his heart was in the symphonic field. And Toscanini's relations with other conductors were often strained. The first difficulties arose when he undertook to direct some of the Wagner music-dramas, "Götterdämmerung" and "Tristan und Isolde." Alfred Hertz believed he was the Wagner conductor. It can be imagined with what satisfaction he received the news that the Italian would deploy all over the repertory.

Save for those Toscanini years and the war period, the repertory has been evenly divided. One conductor has presided over the German works, another over the Italian, another over the French. After Toscanini had gone, Gatti-Casazza observed this division. When the war broke out and the German operas were placed on the index, Artur Bodanzky conducted a variety of works. More recently, Tullio Serafin did "Siegfried" once. But these have been rare exceptions. It may be that the Metropolitan learned a lesson from the days of conflict and resentment.

Toscanini was the hardest working conductor on the staff in his years at the Metropolitan, and by his own choice. There was no limit to the amount of time he would lavish on rehearsals, as the management learned to its sorrow when overtime had to be paid to the orchestra. Nor was there any limit to the performances he would undertake. In the first week of the first season at the Metropolitan, the second-line Italian conductor, one Spetrino, sprained an ankle during a rehearsal. A performance of "Tosca" was scheduled which Spetrino could not conduct, and Toscanini offered to direct. Gatti pointed out that there would be no time to rehearse. Toscanini said he would conduct anyhow. The cast was headed by Emma Eames and other artists who had never worked with Toscanini before. Yet he led a performance that was found to be as elegant, as precise and as well rounded as his "Tosca" at the Scala, where it had had hour upon hour of preparation.

Toscanini's rehearsals have become legendary. His eleven years as conductor of the Philharmonic Orchestra in New York have made that aspect of his preparation better known than his work at the opera. But the Metropolitan Opera rehearsals had all the storminess, intensity and abrupt contrasts that have marked later preparations. With the Philharmonic, Toscanini had only a hundred instrumentalists to contend with. At the Metropolitan he had singers, chorus and ballet as well as orchestra under his command.

There was the time when Toscanini came into conflict with a Bohemian soprano and an American contralto. Their treatment of one passage displeased him. They could not produce the effect he desired. He fell back on invective, unconsciously rhymed. Gossip said that he called the first artist "the Bohemian sow" and the other "the American cow."

More recently when a quartet of soloists were rehearsing with Toscanini for a choral work to be presented at a Philharmonic performance, one of the women in the foursome perpetrated a succession of errors, indicating that she was not adequately prepared. The maestro stopped the rehearsal imperiously. He called for an official of the orchestra, and in the presence of the other soloists, he demanded that the erring singer be replaced immediately by a more competent artist.

The maestro is aware of his reputation. Make no mistake of that. But once the fires of rehearsal conflicts begin to flame, he cannot stem them. There is a story of a rehearsal in Turin that illuminates this point. Toscanini was working with a quartet of singers. The mezzo-soprano had never sung under his direction before; she was, moreover, comparatively inexperienced and nervous. She did not make a certain attack properly.

Toscanini scowled and barked, "Da capo."

The mezzo-soprano made her attack in a wavering tone.

"Da capo," Toscanini snarled.

All that the mezzo emitted was a sniffle. There was a pause of deep silence, and the singer broke into tears. Toscanini sat at the piano, glaring. For many minutes he sat there without a word. With one hand he fingered his mustache, and with the other he fanned himself, gestures that have become familiar to people who have experienced the maestro's wrath. Finally the mezzo-soprano stopped sniffling. She dried her eyes and looked at her music. Toscanini waited until she was ready, keeping his anger under control.

Then he spoke with the air of a martyr. "And they say," he said, "that I am impatient! *Da capo!*"

Opera: Front and Back

Toscanini spared no one's feelings at the Metropolitan. When one of the first American operas was produced and proved to be a vacuous exercise in composition, Toscanini openly characterized it as "musica inutile."

There is another story told around the opera house that may or may not be true. According to the tale, an American opera was in rehearsal, with another conductor in command. Toscanini is said to have resented the expenditure of time on a score of no character or quality. He walked into the auditorium during a general rehearsal—so the story goes—and shouted his disapproval, upsetting every one on the stage and in the pit.

The story is characteristic of the legends that have mushroomed around the name of Toscanini. One thing may be said with certainty: Toscanini was not consistently the egotistic wild man that his detractors have made him out to be; nor was he always the self-effacing, consecrated votary of art that his admirers have insisted on calling him. He was a human being, with an incomparable gift for bringing to life the marks that composers had recorded on paper. He drove himself remorselessly to study and to learn and to recreate what his intelligence and instinct told him the composer had intended. He did not rewrite a man's music, he did not allow his singers to distort it. No tenor got away with long held high notes or with fake sobs when Toscanini was in command. The story is told of a famous tenor who sang under Toscanini at the Scala just after the war. Endowed with a beautiful lyric voice, the tenor sang like a musician and an artist as long as Toscanini wielded the baton. The tenor came to the Metropolitan and it became impossible to control him. He sang constantly to the gallery, giving values to passages in an aria that were fine for applause, but destructive of the essential curve of the music.

[146]

They Who Lead

A notation in the master score of Beethoven's Seventh Symphony in the archives of the Philharmonic-Symphony Orchestra is illustrative of Toscanini's insistence on observing the composer's instructions. It seemed that Mahler, when he was director of the Philharmonic, had made several minor changes in the score. Toscanini angrily crossed them out, and under Mahler's changes he wrote: "Unworthy of such a musician, Arturo Toscanini."

There have been occasions, however, when he did not hesitate to add to a score for justifiable musical purposes. When the Metropolitan gave Mussorgsky's "Boris Godunoff" for the first time in America, the opera was sung in Italian. It is almost impossible to fit one language exactly to the musical line devised for another tongue, especially when the languages are so divergent in rhythm, structure and sound values as are Italian and Russian. The Italian translation of "Boris" was a good one, but it was not perfect. Toscanini saw to it that text and music were as one. He added an occasional note to the vocal line so that a singer would not have to swallow his words.

And there was the occasion when Toscanini was leading a modern work which was an atonalist's holiday. In a spirit of fun or perhaps in retaliation for the assaulting of his ears, the maestro took the liberty of adding to the score a final C major chord, which sounded almost indecent after the turmoil of the clashing atonalities. The conductor took full responsibility for the emendation. Under the C major addition, he wrote, in a defiant hand, "My chord, Arturo Toscanini."

When Toscanini arrived at the Scala in 1898, his first opera was "Die Meistersinger." Antonio Scotti had been engaged to sing the role of Hans Sachs. He had been singing a season of opera in South America and he undertook to learn the difficult part in the twenty days of the trip. When Scotti

[147]

reached Milan he had a conference with Toscanini. Scotti's score had certain indicated cuts. Toscanini glanced at them and said, "I don't make these cuts." He demanded that Scotti learn the big chunks of the music-drama that he had omitted. It was only several days before the première, and Scotti protested. But Toscanini would hear of no other approach. Poor Scotti had to sit up nights mastering the remainder of the part. Toscanini would not compromise for a mere matter of a singer's convenience.

Will power and ruthlessness where art is concerned would not be enough, if there were not joined to these qualities an encyclopedic knowledge, a phenomenal memory and an unsurpassably keen ear. The stories that illustrate these Toscanini powers are legion. He can single out in an ensemble of a hundred a lesser voice that has not the right quality, even though it be on pitch. There was the time when a member of the Metropolitan orchestra used a clarinet in A instead of one in B-flat. Although the former instrument is pitched a half-tone lower than the latter, the clarinetist played the correct note. He was not off key; the tone of the clarinet in A had a slightly different quality from the same note played on the B-flat. Despite the fact that the entire orchestra was going full blast, Toscanini detected the difference in tone quality and accused the instrumentalist of using the wrong clarinet.

Toscanini's word has affected the fortunes and direction of New York's major musical institutions. When the Metropolitan was considering its next step, after Gatti-Casazza had resigned, it was proposed to the board of the Philharmonic-Symphony Orchestra that the two institutions merge. A plan was worked out, and its approval depended on Toscanini's acquiescence, since he was to be the guiding spirit of the new dispensation. He said, "No." The plan was dropped, fortunately for both the Philharmonic and the Metropolitan. Events have proved that the Metropolitan can go it alone, and the Philharmonic-Symphony is managing to do likewise.

Toscanini's disapproval was based on his feeling that the Metropolitan Opera House was not suited to symphony concerts, which, with performances of opera, were on the program of the merger. It did not mean that he had lost his interest in, or regard for, the Metropolitan. On the contrary! It is not known to more than a handful of persons that Toscanini offered to save a difficult situation at the Metropolitan several years ago. The season was to open with a performance of Verdi's "Simon Boccanegra," and Tullio Serafin was to conduct. Serafin became ill several days before the performance, and it seemed that there might have to be a change in operas, for "Simon Boccanegra" is not done frequently in the operas of the world and few conductors know it well enough to direct it at short notice. Toscanini knew "Simon Boccanegra," and when he heard of Serafin's illness he offered to take his place on the opening night.

Serafin recovered in time to conduct, and Toscanini was not asked to pinch-hit. The chances are that he would not have been asked in any event. The management of the Metropolitan was cognizant of the misunderstandings that follow in the wake of a Toscanini appearance; it knew of the jealousies and the displeasures of other conductors. It probably would not have taken a chance. And yet—what a story that would have been! Toscanini and Gatti-Casazza had just become reconciled after a feud of some ten years' duration. They had not met or spoken to each other. Toscanini's beau geste on the heels of the reconciliation would have been the perfect touch.

Opera: Front and Back

The conductors who were Toscanini's contemporaries at the Metropolitan labored under his shadow, as did his colleagues at other theatres and those with the symphony orchestras. At the Scala, when Toscanini had left and Cleofonte Campanini came to take his place, the latter seemed always to be seeing Banquo's ghost. For those who worked in the same theatre and at the same time with the Italian maestro the shadow was not of their own imaginings. It was real; it was omnipresent.

Campanini loomed large in New York's operatic picture in the days when Toscanini and Gatti-Casazza were new. He was the principal conductor at Oscar Hammerstein's Manhattan Opera, and when that company was transformed into the Chicago-Philadelphia Opera and left its New York center, he continued as the director and leading conductor.

Campanini was a conductor whose early musical training had not been thorough. He was frank about his limitations. For instance, he admitted that he had difficulty in reading the full score of an opera, with its bewildering array of parts for orchestral choirs, principals and chorus. He used a piano score, carefully annotated for orchestral entrances and nuances.

When he was preparing "Salome" with Mary Garden at the Manhattan Opera House, Campanini arranged to have one of the other conductors lead the orchestra through the entire score while he followed the rehearsal with his piano arrangement, making notes for reference in future rehearsals and in performance. At some points he stopped the conductor and asked him to repeat a passage. He wished to make sure that his annotations of the instrumentation were correct.

They Who Lead

Despite his limitations, Campanini was, on the evidence of contemporaries, a conductor of impressive gifts. He had power and magnetism, and his innate sensitivity was reflected in the refinement of his interpretations. Those who heard his performances of "Pelléas et Mélisande," "Louise," "Thaïs" and other works of the French repertory, where elegance of style is a major requisite, have testified to his accomplishments.

Mahler, a searching symphonic conductor, remained at the Metropolitan for a brief period, and only one year of his stay coincided with Toscanini's. He was a sick man at the time. He had come to America to make some money. Having earned enough he returned to Austria, built himself a house and died. While his leadership was distinguished, he left his mark on New York operagoers principally with his finely wrought interpretations of Mozart.

Mahler tried to overcome the obstacles of the large auditorium of the Metropolitan in his productions of Mozart. He devised a charming scheme to give an air of intimacy to the performance. He had the legs of a grand piano removed, and the instrument was laid on the apron of the stage, at about where the hood that covers the prompter's box may normally be seen. A high chair was placed before the keyboard, and Mahler sat perched on it, his back to the men in the orchestra pit. He himself played the recitatives, and since the piano was damped with newspapers, it sounded like the strumming of a harpsichord of Mozart's own time. The instrumentalists were able to follow the gestures of the tall, lean figure before the piano. His position in the no man's land between orchestra and performers gave a piquancy to the presentation that Mozart did not always have at the Metropolitan.

Mahler knew his job as a conductor, as did Toscanini. He knew many other things—history, philosophy and the like.

Opera: Front and Back

He inhabited the world of ideas. People who knew him well recall how this quiet, unworldly man always dominated an assembly of distinguished personages. His pleasures were not like those of a Nikisch, who delighted to sit up the whole night after a performance playing poker. Of Mahler's musicianship there was no doubt. Artur Bodanzky remembers a comment made by Richard Strauss during a discussion of instrumentation. "Mahler," said Strauss, "is the only man alive from whom I could learn anything about orchestration."

3

The Metropolitan has had, since the departure of Toscanini and Mahler, both expert batonists and mere routiniers. The qualities that go into the making of a first-rate opera conductor are many and varied. At the risk of resuming an old, old dispute, I must contend that the conductor of opera has a harder job than the conductor of a symphony orchestra. Granted that masterpieces require the same ingredients of musicianship, imagination and leadership from their interpreters, the opera conductor must marshal greater forces under his baton. He has not only the orchestra, but principals, chorus and ballet to command. His eyes must be sharper, his ears keener, his knowledge and control of human beings more comprehensive and subtle.

It will not hurt to review the job of the conductor at the opera house and to examine, as a natural corollary, the requirements of the man who will execute it most effectively. A conductor's task is to lead, and to lead well he must know thoroughly what he is leading. In other words, he must be the master of several dozen operas. He must have, as Hans von Bülow succinctly put it, the score in his head, not his head in the score. Study of the operas is a first step, but it is not enough. The conductor must have wide experience in directing in the theatre. Once theory has been enriched by practice, the conductor may understand precisely what is in the score and what he wishes to do with it to convey the gist of his understanding to the audience. Between him and his listeners are his performing forces, and to them he must communicate what he feels and knows, if his conception is to become a reality on the stage and in the pit.

The conductor, therefore, should be an expert orchestral leader. He must know what colors he wants from the various instrumental choirs and how to obtain them. If a horn player argues that a certain lurid color cannot possibly be drawn from his instrument, the conductor must prove that it can. He must know what bowings to demand of his string players. He must know what tone qualities his woodwinds can produce.

The opera conductor must be an expert on voice and the art of song. He has not the time to give his singers lessons in voice production, but he must know the capacities of the human throat. It is not his job to worry over a singer with a faulty method of emitting tones, so long as the desired quality and phrasing are achieved. There are singers who look as if they are strangling when they produce a high, full tone, and the chances are that their careers will not last long, but the conductor's only interest is that the tone be high and full when wanted. The tenor, Italo Campanini, who was an outstanding figure long before the turn of the century, used to turn a sunset-red when he sang, but the sounds were magnificent.

It takes more than knowledge to convince an experienced artist that his conception is wrong and the conductor's is correct. The conductor needs, above all else in the opera house, authority and the tact of angels. He must treat the nervous singer with kindness; he must be domineering when faced with an arrogant star. He must know when to smile and when to be severe. At all times he must behave with the utmost impartiality to all his forces, for there is nothing that creates greater ill feeling than the suspicion of favoritism.

Given all these qualities, the conductor must have fire and temperament and energy in abundance. For opera is a theatrical performance. It does not matter if the action on the stage is wooden and without imagination; the conductor can redeem deficiencies of this kind by a dramatic conception of the music. A seething orchestra, a subdued mass tone from the chorus, a skilfully phrased solo or duet will impart more meaning to the audience than the most artful acting.

There is no such thing, of course, as a conductor who has all the gifts. Toscanini triumphed by the sheer urgency of his own exhaustless energy. He knew what was in the score, and he did not care what feelings were injured so long as he got what he wanted from his people. A Mahler used gentleness to the same ends.

The methods of the conductor will vary according to the personality of each leader. A man who is irritable, explosive and verbose will have arguments and conflicts without end. A man who is precise, laconic and disciplined will have smoldering and unspoken resentments. One may implore; the next may order. One may deliver long explanatory discourses; the next will bark terse commands. One may observe the amenities with the courtliness of an old-world don; the next may be brusque, even uncivil. The approach of opera conductors may be as diverse as that of business executives who supervise large forces, and the results may be as varied.

4

Artur Bodanzky has said that if he feels a cold coming on, he will try to keep going during the rehearsal period, for that is where the performance is molded. Once it is shaped by his hand he feels that it will be safe for an assistant conductor to carry on. His method is the direct, laconic one. He is business-like in all his encounters. He leaves no doubt that he is the boss and expects orchestra and artists to follow instructions without ado. He will not countenance a singer taking liberties on the stage, and he will be sharp with his instrumentalists if they do not give him what he wants.

One of the things that upsets Bodanzky most is slovenly work on the stage. If the stage crew makes too much noise in moving the scenery, if the chorus chatters too loudly when it is not singing, if the acolytes in "Parsifal" march off the stage tardily, Bodanzky may be driven to a wrathful outburst. He may make acid comments that will freeze carelessness into strict attention.

Of the current crop of conductors at the Metropolitan, Artur Bodanzky is the most domineering and abrupt when irritated. He has occupied his post for more than two decades and he has developed absolute authority. Although he always believed in discipline, he could not achieve his aims in his first seasons at the Metropolitan. There was, in fact, a distinct let-down in tension in the years following the departure of Toscanini. Alfred Hertz, who went in 1915 when Toscanini did, was a conductor of the old German school, and he had a commanding manner of his own. There are instrumentalists who have not forgotten the bearded, bald-headed German in his place in the orchestra pit, shouting always, "Mehr! Mehr!" For Hertz could never obtain enough volume and sonority from singers or orchestra.

There has not been a recurrence of the sultry atmosphere that characterized the opera house in the days of Toscanini, Hertz, et al. But when Bodanzky is in command, he is the commander-in-chief. A young singer happened to be seated beside Bodanzky when the company was traveling to Philadelphia for a Tuesday night performance. She chatted with the conductor, discussing a number of things amicably. Then she said boldly: "Why is it you have the reputation of being such a Tartar? I find you quite human."

"Have I such a reputation?" Bodanzky was amused.

The young singer nodded.

"Have I ever been unkind to you?" he asked.

"Well," she said, "you told me to go to hell several times."

"But," Bodanzky replied, good-humoredly, "you didn't go."

"No," the singer dead-panned, "I was afraid I'd be late to rehearsal."

5

The wise conductor knows when to let an artist alone. An experienced tenor like Lauritz Melchior has arrived at his Tristan out of years of slogging effort in the opera houses of the world. A gifted musician and conscientious artist like Kirsten Flagstad studies her own roles assiduously and needs little or no advice from the conductor. The conductor will not hesitate to suggest changes, but he will not worry the capable artist with needless problems. He will attempt to unify the styles of the singers in the same cast, but he will not insist on coherence at the cost of other things such as loss of confidence or harmful change in vocal style.

There are conductors who are content to let well enough alone. They assume that virtually all the singers in a theatre like the Metropolitan know their business and that the men in the orchestra are perfectly dependable throughout the repertory. Such conductors attempt to familiarize the company with their beat and with a few general ideas. Once they feel that the performance will cohere, they do not attempt to impose further difficulties.

The truth is that there is a great deal to be said for the laissez-faire approach. One conductor who is too exigent can discombobulate the entire routine of an opera house. It is a routine that is carefully grooved, with no time for waste motion. If a conductor is insistent on having his way in every question, he may eat into the next man's time, he may demand more time for rehearsals—and extra rehearsals cost money. He may refuse to undertake more than one new show a year. The Metropolitan has no room for more than one such man at a time, and if it has one of his kind it must have several of the laissez-faire school to balance its schedule.

There can be too much of a good thing, and the laissez-faire approach can be overdone. There are singers who have little or no artistic sensibilities. Give them their head and they will run away with a performance. Tenors of this disposition will hold climactic notes to their heart's content and to the full extent of their breathing capacities, which are, unhappily, enormous. Sopranos will add flourishes to arias that the composer had not dreamed of. Orchestra players will handle their parts sloppily. Who has not heard at least one opera performance when the alleged artists all but trampled the prostrate body of a laissez-faire conductor?

There are also legitimate differences of artistic vision. But whatever his approach, a conductor is expected to remain consistent in his own views. In preparing a performance for the stage, one conductor gave his singers one tempo in the first rehearsals. At the dress rehearsal it was slower, and at the performance it was slowest. It was naturally a failure.

Divergences are often so far apart that an artist may despair at ever following the whims of each conductor. Friedrich Schorr, who has sung Wotan and Hans Sachs hundreds of times, once showed me his scores of "Walküre" and "Meistersinger." They bore a jigsaw of markings. One conductor made these cuts; another made a different set. Various maestros had radically disparate views of tempi. In one performance of "Walküre" most of Wotan's music in the second act had been elided. In another the glowing, tender, disillusioned and unforgettable "Wahn" monologue in "Meistersinger" was cut in half. Richard Strauss had conducted the fastest "Walküre" and Siegfried Wagner the slowest. There had been a difference of fifteen minutes between the two.

A shrewd conductor knows tricks of the trade wherewith he can make his work stand out. When Serafin was permitted to do a performance of "Siegfried," with Bodanzky acceding to this diversion of Wagner from his province, the former proceeded to restore to the music-drama cuts that had always been made and to eliminate passages that had always been included. The result was a presentation of the score that differed in many respects from the one that had become familiar to Metropolitan audiences over a period of ten years. It fell on the ears with a new freshness and vitality.

6

What is true of the conductor holds, in lesser part, for the stage director. He must know all the operas, their action and their music. He will not last long if he demands impossible things of the singers. He must realize that the music comes first and that the acting must be developed within the confines of the tonal pattern. A stage director must know the traditions, and it is not harmful if he has a little imagination. Unhappily, most opera régisseurs are gentlemen who do their jobs by rote. They have learned the routine, and they do not change a piece of stage business from decade to decade. They merely see to it that the rules are observed. Then, if instructions are carried out on the stage, their job is done.

At the other extreme is the stage director who must be, at all costs, original. He flouts all traditions, even if they are well-founded and wise. He will mass his forces in Russian style in an opera like "Lohengrin" and will ask them to hold the same positions for fifteen minutes until they look more like a tableau on the stage of Radio City Music Hall. Or he will decide that neither composer nor librettist knows his business, and he will introduce a character into the first act whom the composer and librettist have not seen fit to bring on until the second act.

The special bête noire of most opera managements is the mise-en-scène. They have learned that the staging of opera is always being taken for a sleigh ride; amateurs and critics indulge in the pastime with equal gusto. The manager hires traditionalists to direct and they receive a roasting. He engages bright young men, and they have the daylights kicked out of them.

The costuming is left to the individual artist, but the stage director must see to it that there is a unity of syle. He must also look after the lighting, and that is a problem that has made difficult the lives of many régisseurs. No two persons in an audience are satisfied with the same effect. What is darkness for one person is condemned as a glaring light by another.

A stage director may be blamed for the sins of a poorly equipped stage or an impoverished theatre which cannot afford new sets. The Metropolitan Opera, for example, has not been able to splurge on fresh décors, and when old operas have been revived ancient sets have been employed. Thus a stage director who approaches an old opera with a fresh conception of its action may find himself hogtied by the old entrances, exits, trapdoors and either excessive or limited spaces. Take the case of Herbert Graf and a recent revival of "The Tales of Hoffmann" at the Metropolitan. The sets were old and limiting. He wished to treat the fantastic opera in a new way. He tried to; his attempt was unsuccessful. Perhaps he would have been better advised to follow the traditional staging which was in keeping with the old set. His work would not have been condemned. But the true artist wishes to express ideas of his own and is willing to take chances.

The whims of a prima donna may distort a stage picture, and the régisseur will be held accountable. Some singers refuse to let any one stand as far forward as they. I have heard of one soprano who had to sing a duet with a tenor while both sat on a bench. But the prima donna was not interested in the requirements of the libretto. She refused to let the tenor sit beside her. She insisted that he stand several paces behind her. And because her influence and determination were greater than those of the tenor and the régisseur, she had her way.

The stage director, like the conductor, should be a cosmopolite. For the world of the opera is the most cosmopolitan that there is. Every language is spoken, and the stage director and conductor must be able to communicate with their forces. There was the occasion when Alexander Sanine was preparing the mise-en-scène for the American opera "The Emperor Jones" and he was confronted with a group of Negro singers and dancers. He did not speak English, but he had had no trouble with the principals and chorus, most of whom understood Italian or French. The Negroes, however, could speak nothing but English, or so he thought. As Sanine hesitated over the few English words that he knew, a Negro woman stepped forward.

"Speak Russian," she said, "I will translate."

They Who Lead

It developed that she had worked with Sanine in European theatres and that she was a linguist of parts herself.

It was Sanine who contributed one of the most surprising performances at a Metropolitan rehearsal of "Simon Boccanegra." In the midst of a mass scene, he held up his hand for quiet. The full complement of stage hands, orchestra, chorus paused. Sanine invoked, at a terrific cost to the company in rehearsal time, a prayer to Verdi, and took minutes to do it.

Conductors and stage directors often come into conflict. The amount of time allowed to each may become a bone of contention. And the conductor may differ violently with the stage director's ideas. One season at the Scala the conductor, Leopoldo Mugnone, was preparing a performance of Tchaikovsky's "Pique Dame." A régisseur had been imported from Russia to give the mise-en-scène verisimilitude and to follow the Russian traditions in the presentation. But Mugnone fancied himself an expert on stage matters as well as the music. He would not let the Russian régisseur, a young and nervous person, get a word in edgewise. Mugnone simply took over the stage direction; the production was entirely his. And when the première was over—it had been well received—Mugnone gave the Russian stage director a parting word of advice.

"Now you can go home," he said, "and teach those other Russians how 'Pique Dame' should really be done."

The production of "Falstaff" that Toscanini directed at Salzburg in recent festivals was said to be in good part his in staging as well as musical conception. Herbert Graf was the young régisseur assigned to the job, and he willingly accepted the maestro's ideas. They were evidently good. At any rate, the music and action had the humor and lightness of spirit that suffuse this incredible ultimate score of Verdi's.

[161]

7

We return to Toscanini and to Salzburg, where the maestro is closing his operatic career. He would have preferred to round out his work as a conductor at Bayreuth, as he has confided to his friends. The Bavarian Festspielhaus is finely designed, its acoustics are good, the conductor and his musicians are hidden from the sight of the audience and it is the theatre which Wagner himself wrought. But it was not to be. The accession of Hitler and the Nazification of Germany built a high wall between Bayreuth and Toscanini's democratic principles. The maestro's hatred of fascism exceeds even his loathing for sham and triviality in his art; he is incapable of compromise with either.

His work at Salzburg is a protest—and a second choice. And recently there was the danger that Toscanini would also abandon Salzburg. It was he who demanded that Wilhelm Furtwängler, Germany's leading conductor, be barred from the Austrian festival. Although Furtwängler protested that for him art was above politics, Toscanini replied that whatever the German's secret ideals might be, he was put forth as Nazism's shining light of the podium. Vicious gossips attempted to distort Toscanini's motives by whispering that he was against Furtwängler because the latter was too fine a conductor. The truth was, however, that Toscanini continued to admire the German's musicianship; Toscanini, in fact, had recommended him as his successor with the Philharmonic-Symphony Orchestra.

Yes, Toscanini is a superb artist, a genius, if you will, in the field of interpretation. But for men of good will his glory is the greater in that he has dared to fling the gauntlet of his independence into the teeth of both Hitler and Mussolini. He has acted with high courage. The little maestro with the rim of gray hair, the sharp face and the soft voice has not feared to remain true to himself in his native land. Mussolini, who has been brave enough to shower bombs on hapless Ethiopians and Spaniards, has not dared to join issue with a musician of flaming spirit who has continued to make his home in his beloved Italy.

IX

IN THE PIT

PITY the poor orchestra player! He and his fellows are probably the most maligned group at the opera. In recent years the tattoo of condemnation beat down so heavily on the backs of the instrumentalists at the Metropolitan that a new management was driven into activity. A turnover in orchestra personnel, affecting about 30 per cent of the men, occurred. Is the end in sight, either of criticism or change? Probably not, so long as the Metropolitan adheres to its current repertory and critics retain the freedom of the press.

Under a dispensation such as is in effect at a theatre like the Metropolitan, the orchestra player is the hardest-worked individual in the company. From the day that rehearsals begin until the end of the season he has no rest. He must scrape his fiddle until his arms become leaden; he must blow until his breath comes in gasps and his lips begin to dry; he must pound until his wrists ache and his ears split. Whatever the opera, the orchestra player has to perform. The chorus has a night off when "Walküre" or "Siegfried" is done, and the ballet is excused from time to time. The principals, even those who are called upon oftenest, can pass several days each week without plying their trade. The conductors have to wave their baton at three or four performances a week at the most. Even the general manager takes an occasional night off. But the orchestra? During the season it may well plead, with Thomas Hood's downtrodden shirtmaker, for "a respite however brief, no blessed leisure for love or hope, but only time for grief."

In the Pit

The orchestra player does not complain about the amount of work. To him it is a job, and a seasonal occupation at that. Under present conditions he receives about twenty weeks of work. In the old days when the season ran for twenty-four weeks and was followed by a tour, the instrumentalist had a reasonable length of employment. Added to his weekly wage, he had about three weeks of pre-season rehearsals, for which he received payment. The total was a respectable sum for a year's income. Today the orchestra player still has the pre-season rehearsal period, and the spring season has been introduced for good measure. He gets by financially. But, leaving out of consideration for the moment the problems of the opera house, does it make sense for the orchestral player that he should toil strenuously for less than six months and have nothing to do the rest of the year?

This is not an apologia for the misfeasances and malfeasances of the slovenly musician. I am as indignant as the next man when the golden-voiced horn of Siegfried develops asthma at the climax of the call; I would cheerfully blow out the brains of the trombonist whose tone cracks in the apocalyptic finale of "Parsifal"; and I would condone mayhem committed on the miscreant who distorts the brief trumpet passage allotted to the stage band in "Aïda." But only under the stress of the moment when the unfortunate musician has cast a pall of disillusion over my absorption in the music.

When the rational processes begin to function once more, it is time to inquire why the instrumentalist perpetrated his foul misdeed. For some players there is no excuse. They are congenitally careless or nervous and they can be counted on for breaks at the most stirring points in an opera. Others are simply incompetent and they should be dispatched to greener fields. There is a wind instrument player, an able musician with a good technique, who seems to be scared by Bodanzky.

[165]

Opera: Front and Back

Whenever Bodanzky is in charge, the player, who is otherwise dependable, is apt to bog down just when he is most anxious to be at his best. But the most reliable of musicians have their off days. There is no utter infallibility in orchestral playing any more than in any other human endeavor. Even the vaunted instrumentalists of the major symphony orchestras crack momentarily. There was the time when the trombones broke on a phrase in Siegfried's Funeral Music from "Götterdämmerung" with Toscanini conducting the Philharmonic-Symphony Orchestra. The maestro, in one of his mountainous furies, stormed out of Carnegie Hall on a wintry, snowy night, forgetting to take his hat or coat, and his friends chased after him along the streets of New York. Toscanini refused to direct that composition with the orchestra thereafter.

If the opera orchestra cracks oftener than the symphony players, it may be because the Metropolitan cannot afford to pay as high a rate to the solo musicians as does the Philharmonic-Symphony. The opera personnel does not begin and end with the instrumentalists and conductors, as does the symphony set-up. The opera has singers, chorus, ballet and stage crew—a huge staff—on the payroll. What is more, the opera musician works harder than the symphony player. The Philharmonic-Symphony musician contracts for nine services a week—five rehearsals of two and a half hours each and four performances of two hours each. If he chooses to do outside work that is his affair; if his outside work interferes with his accuracy and competence, that is the Philharmonic-Symphony Society's affair.

Let us consider, in contrast, the work of the opera orchestral player in any week. He plays every night: full opera performances at the Metropolitan every evening but Tues-

In the Pit

day and Sunday; a concert at the Broadway theatre on Sunday and an out-of-town opera performance on Tuesday. Then there is a matinee every Saturday, and either a benefit matinee or a Wagner cycle matinee in the middle of each week. Sometimes there is a total of three matinees a week. A performance of opera is not a two-hour concert. The shortest full-length operas run over two hours, and when they are too short, two works and possibly a ballet are added to the program. Several times a week the productions run close to four hours. Thus the orchestra at the Metropolitan has a minimum of eight operas in public a week.

In the words of John Donne, "when thou hast done, thou hast not done, for I have more." Each week there are rehearsals. The management attempts to distribute these humanely. If the orchestra has two performances during the day, a rehearsal is not called unless there is no alternative. Rehearsals are scheduled generally in the mornings when there are only evening performances. It adds up to an average of two full sessions each day, with the exception of Sunday, when rehearsals are not scheduled.

During this period the orchestra may work with seven different conductors. Each man has his own approach, and the musicians must master the divergences if they are to get on amicably with their leaders. One may have a sharp, incisive beat that is easy to follow. The next conductor may swing like a pitcher with a roundhouse curve, and following him requires another adjustment. Tears are shed for the poor member of the symphony orchestra who has three or four conductors during a season, each one for a stated length of time. What about the opera instrumentalist who has four or five conductors operating on him in the course of a week?

The opera routine does not let up for at least sixteen weeks.

[167]

Opera: Front and Back

It is not to be wondered at that the men become weary in mid-season or toward the end. It would call for superhuman stamina to play with keenness and freshness at every performance of the season. A string player's left hand tends to become calloused under the constant pressure. The embouchure of the wind players becomes less dependable, for the toughest lips wilt under the constant application to the mouthpiece of an instrument. In any one day the orchestra may have to play through a four-hour Wagner opera in the afternoon and return for duty for a three-hour French or Italian work in the evening. It is not surprising if the night performance lacks in glow and spontaneity, even if the players manage to carry through with accuracy.

What is the solution? In some of the opera houses of Europe, two sets of solo players are engaged. They alternate at public performances and they retain a measure of vigor. The problem in such a scheme is to find solo players of equal competence and to train them so that they will function smoothly with the rest of the orchestra. This procedure works with reasonable effectiveness, and Edward Johnson once told me that he hoped to establish it at the Metropolitan as soon as he had the necessary funds.

A double orchestra was tried back in the days when the Metropolitan operated not only its Broadway house but the New Theatre on Central Park West, later known as the Century Theatre and still later demolished to make way for a modern apartment house. But the double orchestra was an expensive proposition, and it lasted for one season. It helped to incur a tremendous deficit that year.

In other American cities where opera seasons are short, the orchestra is usually the same as the one used for the symphony season. The repertory is not as extensive as is that of the Metropolitan, and the opera orchestra does not suffer the invidious comparison of having its standards set beside those of the symphony orchestra, as it does in New York.

The opera orchestra has not always been condemned, nor is it even today universally censured. In the days when Toscanini conducted, he drew from the instrumentalists performances that were said to be finer than those of the contemporary symphony orchestra. Toscanini, of course, was able to extract from his men the last ounce of energy. If the conductor the next night had a tired body of players on his hands, that was his bad luck. He had the misfortune of being a contemporary of the most exigent conductor of our time.

When Artur Bodanzky arrived in New York and conducted the Metropolitan Opera orchestra for some seasons, he gave it as his opinion that it was an excellent ensemble. He had seen and heard the kind of orchestras that filled the pits of European opera houses—he had even directed some of the best—and he declared that the Metropolitan orchestra ranked high. There have been other defenders of the orchestra.

The censure became most intense after a period of years when there had been no changes in the instrumental personnel. It may be that some of the players had become antiquated. In any event, the management confirmed the attacks of the critics by proceeding to overhaul its entire ensemble and by weeding out those men who were not up to snuff. Many heads fell. Among those who lost their jobs were some who have never ceased to execrate the critics whom they blamed for all their troubles.

How does an opera house overhaul its orchestra? Each man at the Metropolitan was given what amounted to a blindfold test. The conductors and the general manager and his assistants sat out front, while each instrumentalist played behind a screen. Newcomers were selected in the same way.

Opera: Front and Back

If you would like to know what the ingredients of an orchestral test for opera are, here are some of the passages that the musicians were asked to play:

Violin: The finale of the duet of Ortrud and Elsa in "Lohengrin"; the introduction to the second-act duet of Elisabeth and Tannhäuser; the finale of Beethoven's "Leonore" Overture No. 3.

Viola: The judgment scene in "Aïda"; a passage from the third act of "Tristan."

'Cello: A passage from the "William Tell" Overture; the introduction to the third act of "Tosca" and the same "Tristan" passage as the violas.

Double bass: The Sparafucile scene in the second act of "Rigoletto"; the introduction to "Walküre" and the unison in the last act of "Otello."

Flute: A passage from the "William Tell" Overture.

Oboe: Ballet music from "Lakmé"; the Nile scene in "Aïda."

Clarinet: The fourth act solo in "Gioconda."

Bassoon: Pages in "William Tell" Overture and in the "Leonore" Overture No. 3.

Trumpet: Prelude to "Parsifal."

Horn: Siegfried's call; entr'acte in "Fidelio."

Trombone: Finale of "Parsifal"; intermezzo in Thomas's "Hamlet"; pages from "Otello" and "Falstaff."

All the test passages have not been listed here, nor have all the instruments. The trial sections were selected to test the various qualities of the musician: the facility of his technique, the color and luster of his tone, the sensitivity of his interpretation. Each candidate was also allowed to play one solo of his own choice with piano accompaniment. He chose music that would give all his capacities a chance to shine.

The test was not all. A newcomer to the opera orchestra

In the Pit

had to show that he knew the full repertory of the theatre, plus operas that might crop up at any time. It is a taxing repertory and no mere neophyte among musicians can get by in it.

And there were some instrumentalists who had to be taken because no one could be found with a knowledge of the repertory. Recently the Metropolitan engaged a new first desk man for one of the woodwind sections who had never played in opera before. He was a good musician, and an assistant conductor was assigned to work with him all summer.

The size of an opera house orchestra depends on the space in the pit. The Metropolitan has a pit that can accommodate a capacity of 92 players, more than any other pit in the country and as many as the largest theatres in Europe. There are 1000 square feet in this pit. Years ago, the first two rows of seats were taken up for "Parsifal," providing an enclosure of 1240 square feet. But that is not done any longer. The regular Metropolitan orchestra, at full strength, is 90 men; for "Parsifal" it used to be 106 men. There is a nucleus of 70 players who are guaranteed eight performances a week. Certain instruments are hired for the full season on a guaranteed basis, although not for the full eight performances. The Wagner or tenor tuba, used only in the Wagner operas, is such an instrument. The men who play in the stage bands play less than the full eight performances a week, and they help to bring the orchestra to full strength by playing with it in the pit several times a week. The Wagner operas use the full ensemble, and in "Parsifal" the men sit together as closely as subway riders in the rush hour.

When the Metropolitan gives two performances out of town on Tuesday nights, as it sometimes does, it must have two orchestras. In that case, it has available what amounts to an auxiliary ensemble. The first-desk men are divided up between the regular group and the auxiliary unit. The remainder of the latter unit is recruited from experienced symphony and operatic instrumentalists. They are drawn from the radio, theatre bands and occasionally from the Philharmonic-Symphony Orchestra. The men are as dependable as the regular orchestra; sometimes, because they have not played as often during the week, they are fresher. Nevertheless, the management takes no chances. There is always a complete rehearsal for the auxiliary orchestra before it leaves town. The conductor runs the orchestra through the score, but not with singers or chorus.

The rate of pay is fixed by contracts with the musicians' union, which has a closed shop at the Metropolitan as well as with the Philharmonic and Philadelphia Orchestras. The union appoints a contractor who is the personnel manager of the orchestra and the clearing house for most differences between management and players. At the Metropolitan the contractor is Simone Mantia, who was a trombonist at the opera for two decades. The one non-union orchestra among major ensembles is the Boston Symphony, which quelled a strike several decades ago and never permitted the union to intrude. The Philharmonic-Symphony minimum is $90 for a week's nine services, while the Metropolitan pays its nucleus $16 a performance for the guaranteed minimum of eight performances a week; in other words, $128 a week. Several of the solo players may receive more than the minimum. Whatever the sum is, it is less than most major symphonies pay to first-desk men. The Metropolitan has tried to get some of these men into its orchestra but could not pay enough. There was one instrumentalist on the Pacific coast who turned down a Metropolitan offer because, with his orchestra and moving-picture engagements, he was earning about $100 a day—or more than most opera conductors.

In the Pit

In the days when Grau and Conried were the general managers of the Metropolitan no payment was made for rehearsals. That has changed. Nowadays all rehearsals are paid on a fixed scale. A three-hour rehearsal in the morning or afternoon costs $5 a session for each man. For every fifteen minutes of overtime, there is a charge of 50 cents. Evening rehearsals are paid for at the regular performance rate. As a result, virtually all orchestra rehearsals take place during the day; only a major crisis would cause a session to be set for the evening. Overtime for performances and for evening rehearsals is 75 cents for every fifteen minutes.

Some one who did not admire the manner in which the musicians and their union drove a hard bargain once declared that the members of the orchestra played only for the money in it, not for any love of art. Assuming that the charge were true, why not? That seems to be the way of the civilized world, or the greater part of it. I dare say that the singers, the conductors—even Toscanini—insist on the best remuneration the traffic will bear.

Actually the men of the orchestra, whether it be the Metropolitan, the Philharmonic, or a WPA orchestra, have a large measure of affection for their work. Despite calumniators, they are not like the fiddler of the story who played through a season with a lugubrious expression and who, when asked whether he bore any grudge against his colleagues, conductors, audience, replied, "Not at all. I just don't like music!"

The musicians in the Metropolitan Opera orchestra know how to admire fine music and great interpreters. When a debutant shows signs of talent in a rehearsal, they do not hesitate to indicate their approval. And if a singer perpetrates bulls during a performance, the instrumentalists have a language of their own for evincing their discontent. When an

[173]

American or German artist sings in Italian and mangles the enunciation of the lines, the Italians in the pit will scrape their chairs, make little noises with their bows and some will mutter under their breaths, "Cane!" The audience, of course, cannot hear these things, nor can the singer. Only the musicians' colleagues are aware of it, and possibly the conductor.

When an Italian sings in German and murders that language, the German players wince. But they are better disciplined. They restrain their impulses. They indicate their resentment by glaring at the culprit and by tearing him to shreds in their conversation in the musicians' rest room during intermissions.

The orchestra at the Metropolitan today is a better disciplined group than its predecessor of two decades ago. The shakeup in personnel has caused the men to fear for their jobs. There was a time when they assumed that they had lifetime posts, and some took advantage of it. The players do not bait conductors, as some have been known to do in the past. It is a practice that characterizes some symphony orchestras. I have heard of a number of tricks played on the conductor, especially a newcomer; apparently the idea is to test his ability. A 'cellist will deliberately play out of tune to see whether the conductor can detect him in the midst of a hundred other instruments. An oboist will hold an eighth note in a phrase just a little longer, in the hope that he can put one over on the conductor. Unhappily, there are conductors whose ears are not keen enough to hear these slight distortions. Then the conscienceless instrumentalist may have a Roman holiday. But when the maestro has the ear, the training and the will power to deal remorselessly with these playful scoundrels, he will have no trouble with them whatever.

[174]

In the Pit

The Metropolitan Opera orchestra does the best it can. Of this I am certain. And the men have a keen interest in the people of the opera. Caruso was a buddy of many; and there are artists today who are the friends of the men in the pit. Martinelli is one of them. Some years ago, when the men were tuning up before a performance, they played little snatches of lullabies. The early arrivals in the audience did not understand why. It seemed that the instrumentalists, in a sentimental mood, were paying their respects to Martinelli, who had become that day a proud father.

X

A COMMUNITY OF VOICES

IF THE opera orchestra is denounced with regularity, the chorus seems to be taken in good-natured stride. It is, in fact, a source of innocent merriment. Not deliberately. Not musically. The singing of the Metropolitan Opera chorus is disciplined, unified, sonorous. It is the "acting" of that heterogeneous body that adds a comic touch not intended in most productions. The choristers mean well. They plunge into their assignments with the best will in the world. They add original bits to the picture. They are not chary of their talents or their energy. They are—bless them!—irreplaceable.

To the chronic operagoer the faces and figures of the chorus are dear, familiar things. Principal singers come and go; several hang on for twenty or twenty-five years. But the choristers average a quarter of a century of service; some have been around much longer. Their smiles, their gaits, their gestures, their marvellously diverse builds are engraved on the consciousness of the regular customers. There is the bouncing girl, the one with the gold tooth, the lady with the haughty, aristocratic bearing, the short swarthy gent, the pot-bellied bandy-legged hombre who looks as if he were going to burst out into "Santa Lucia" at any moment.

Among one's souvenirs of opera performances, the most fragrant are scenes in which the chorus does its stuff. Be it a playful or a stately scene, depend on the chorus to do its share with gusto. Remember the sportive apprentices in "Die Meistersinger"? Those apprentices! They are supposed to be young lads, brimming over with healthy spirits and joie de vivre. How they brim over! Wagner had the temerity to demand of his apprentices that they sing soprano, alto, tenor and bass parts, and the Metropolitan choristers meet him more than half way. You see ladies of a certain age squeezing their ample curves into tight-fitting shirts and breeches. You see tall, stolid louts and paunchy youngsters. They pound, chase, kick each other with the vigor of lively bear cubs. They prance and they preen. They jump and they run. Do they have fun!

Then there is the grand parade in "Tannhäuser" when the noble ladies and gentlemen march into the grand hall for the song contest in the second act. It is the chorus that bears the burden of this scene. The costumes are purple and gold, and if they do not fit perfectly, it must be borne in mind that the couturiers in Tannhäuser's time were not what they are to-day, and that these ladies and gentlemen would not qualify as models in any period. They stride in with regal bearing, provided they have no minor defects such as round shoulders or pigeon toes. They bow to their lord, the Landgrave Hermann, and his daughter, the beauteous Elisabeth, with delicate courtesies; only some are not as spry as they used to be and get a crick in the back or a pain in the side if they bend over too ceremoniously.

Another quick change and we are at a performance of "Carmen." Our chorus women are now hell-raising cigarette girls of Seville. Those that fight with Carmen have been known to outdo that hoyden in a fair and square fight. In fact, on one occasion Carmen became so indignant at the scrappiness of her opponent that she hauled off and started to swat in earnest. The gentlemen of the chorus are rough-and-tumble Spanish customers. Later on in the opera they become smugglers, and a more villainous lot of ruffians you have never seen, not even in a Hollywood quickie. Hissing would be too good for them.

In "Aïda" the men are priests in the temple of Phtha. They wear long, flowing robes, and short black beards. These roles are probably their métier. Nothing covers a multitude of physical shortcomings better than robes that flow down to the ankles. And a priest does not have to move around much. The ladies are waiting maids for Amneris, the Princess. If they do not appear comely in Egyptian costumes, the audience can afford to be indulgent. Who does? The tenor, singing the role of Radames, looks like a tired business man at a fancy-dress ball, and the usual portly Amneris could well be his middle-aged spouse.

Turn to "La Bohème" and our choristers are a crowd of carousing, careless Bohemians celebrating before the Café Momus. In "Rigoletto" they are ladies and courtiers of the court, and in another scene the men are bravos and kidnappers. In "Faust" they are unpretentious villagers, and that perhaps suits them best. In "Parsifal" the men are Knights of the Grail, and the women are a celestial choir that is heard from offstage. Glance down the calendar of opera and you will find the chorister almost everywhere. Only Wagner, in "Rheingold," "Walküre" and "Siegfried," and Debussy in "Pelléas et Mélisande," dared to omit him.

Individuals of the chorus are entrusted with bits. A woman will act as a page and will hand a tenor his sword. Several ladies will be the servitors of the contestants in the song competition in "Tannhäuser" and will hold the lutes for their liege lords. Two women of the chorus lead Beckmesser and Walther von Stolzing to the grassy mound in the final scene of "Meistersinger," where those gentlemen compete for the hand of Eva. Men of the chorus are constantly appearing as servants or valets or fellow-conspirators. They are often in the thick of action.

Many people will recall the accident one year when, at a rehearsal of "Caponsacchi," Lawrence Tibbett, playing the role of a villain, lashed out with a knife and gave one of the choristers a glancing blow on the arm. The chorister sustained a severe gash, and some hours later he died. The coroner held that death was due to a heart attack, and that Mr. Tibbett was not responsible. The chorister received the initial shock in the line of duty. There was nothing amusing about this piece of acting.

Make no mistake about the chorister. His is a taxing profession. He may look funny, but his principal business is to sound fine. The mastery of his job requires study, concentration and hard work. It takes a lifetime to develop a first-rate, versatile chorister, and when the opera company has one it will cling to him through the thick of the audience's laughter and the thin of his acting. What good is a youthful, streamlined chorus if it cannot remember its music or sings off key!

Even so, they make mistakes. The audience may not be aware of them, but the conductor, stage director or chorus master knows of them only too well. There was the time when a male chorister marched in the wrong direction and found himself the only male in a group of women choristers. He happened to be a powerful-voiced gent, and he sounded as if he were singing a solo.

The chorus in a theatre such as the Metropolitan must sing in more than thirty operas each season nowadays; it used to be in excess of forty. While the fundamental repertory remains the same through the years, each season sees as many as a half dozen novelties and revivals. The chorus must learn new parts each year as well as refresh the old. The veteran chorister who has been at the Metropolitan for about twenty-five years may have a repertory of as many as 200 operas. Two hundred operas! Consider how few the principal artists are who cover that many operas in a career! The chorister must learn his music and text by heart. He must be able to sing in four languages—Italian, French, German and English. He must make an effort to fit into the stage picture. He is bothered with stage movement, with costumes, wigs and make-up. If he has no aptitude for these arts, what would you for a modest salary?

First and foremost, the chorister must be able to sing. If he is a good musician, life is easier for him and the opera management. At any rate, he must know how to read music easily at sight. The voice of the average chorister is reasonably good. The chances are that it is not unusual enough to warrant a career as a solo singer. It is, in most cases, a dependable voice; sometimes it is big, strong, and somewhat uncultivated; in other cases, it is smooth but not large enough for individual show. Some young men and women with voices join the chorus in the hope that it will lead to promotion as a principal. And there have been several instances where a chorister has moved up to a place where he can sing secondary roles. For the most part, however, the chorister remains in the chorus throughout his service.

At the Metropolitan the full chorus encompasses ninety-six men and women. They are members of a union, the Grand Opera Choral Alliance—which is represented in the Chicago Opera as well. The union has a contract with the Metropolitan Opera Association, and no person may become a member of the regular chorus without joining the union. The weekly minimum wage of the chorister is $65. In the days of Grau and Conried, before the union came into being, choristers were paid as low as $25 a week. Now their pay checks constitute a sizable sum in the opera's budget.

The chorus begins rehearsals four weeks before the beginning of the season. Virtually all preparations are under the direction of the two chorus masters—one of whom is responsible for the Italian and French operas and the other for the German. During the pre-season rehearsals, the chorus studies the new operas and the revivals. Occasionally the stage directors take them over for long sessions, and the stage business is worked out.

Building a good chorus is no easy task. It requires excellent musicians as chorus masters. Giulio Setti, who was at the Metropolitan for twenty-seven years, was an expert chorus master. His forces were a superbly trained ensemble. The balance of the various choirs, the quality of the tone, the flexibility of control, the responsiveness to requests for the most delicate tints as well as the most massive effects were not unlike those of a well-trained orchestra. Setti's successors have attempted to carry on in his footsteps.

The full chorus is used in the majority of the operas. In a music-drama such as "Tristan und Isolde" only a chorus of sailors is needed in the first act, and the women receive a night off. Most of the week the choristers are in action. In the operas that call for tremendous mass effects, the chorus of ninety-six is not enough, and the Metropolitan will recruit perhaps another forty or fifty singers from its chorus school.

The chorus school, which is under the direction of Edoardo Petri, was instituted by Gatti-Casazza, who had found it useful in his theatres in Italy. The chorus school will take on about one hundred men, women and boys. There they are trained in vocal method and in the operas of the repertory. Instruction is free and the opera asks in return occasional appearances. The singers who are drawn from the opera school are placed in group scenes. They are not given important parts, and they are not entrusted with the front positions in any group. In the triumphal scene in "Aïda," for example, they help fill the auditorium with the vast blocks of tone that Verdi demanded from his chorus. One of the thrills of opera is the massed choral effects.

The chorus has large dressing rooms in the upper reaches of the house. The men are on the Thirty-ninth Street side of the Metropolitan, and the women on the Fortieth; that is the way the Metropolitan divides the sexes for the principals and ballet as well. In their dressing rooms the choristers, most of them mature men and women, relax for long periods when they are not needed on the stage. The women will sit around and knit; some will gossip. The men play pinochle and poker and bridge.

The old-time chorister is experienced in the ways of the opera. He has seen many singers come and go. He has been on friendly terms with some of the great stars. He will reminisce of momentous events and famous names with the éclat of any operaphile.

There is the dean of all choristers, Mme. Maria Savage, who calls herself "the oldest chorus girl in the world." She has been in the chorus of the Metropolitan for thirty years, and before that she had sung leading mezzo-soprano roles such as Donizetti's "La Favorita." Her family shut her out when she took to opera, but it didn't help. She made her debut in Namur in her native Belgium in 1897. Now, at the age of seventy, she is still on the stage, one of the most dependable choristers at the Metropolitan. If the stage director requires tall, stately dignity, Maman Savage, as the youngsters of forty and fifty call her, is the choice. She came to this country in 1908, traveling on the same boat with the new general manager. By her own account, she flirted with Gatti-

A Community of Voices

Casazza, thinking he was a fellow-artist. In the off-season she teaches voice, and she numbered the late Jeanne Eagels among her pupils. But once the opera season begins, her heart is in the theatre. And her family is, too. Her daughter is also a member of the chorus.

Like Maman Savage, the other choristers take pride in their work. They look after their voices with the solicitude of prima donnas. After all, it is their living. The women will not smoke or drink; all of them are careful of draughts.

Where does a chorister come from and how does he get that way? A few are graduated from the ranks of the chorus school. Others are trained in the opera houses of Europe as well as in other American cities. Thirty years ago, choristers were as difficult to find in this country as leading singers. They had to be hired in Europe, and shipped back and forth, just as if they were $2,000 a performance stars. Now they are all residents of this country, and most of them either native or naturalized citizens.

The majority of choristers are men and women who have begun preparations for careers as singers and have realized, before it was too late, that they would never amount to anything as soloists. They had the intelligence to compromise with their ambitions. If the theatre is in your blood and you love music, the chorus is the next best thing to being a leading artist. At least you live in the world of the opera and it is thrilling beyond explanation to join with your fellows in pealing crescendos of tone.

New choristers receive auditions, just as principals do. They are required to sing in four languages. The trials may include choral excerpts from "Gioconda" and "Aïda," "Lohengrin" and "Tannhäuser," "Faust" and "Carmen" and "Peter Ibbetson." The candidate must know all the standard operas by heart.

[183]

Opera: Front and Back

It may surprise you to learn that the average chorister regards the music of some of the Italian operas more difficult than the Wagner works. One of the toughest operas for chorus is "Gioconda." It requires the chorus to be on the stage longer than any other opera. Ponchielli, moreover, has written concerted passages for chorus with intricate, contrasting tempi and rhythms. The chorus was confronted with perhaps a more difficult score only when it sang Rimsky-Korsakoff's "Sadko."

If you admire the quality of the chorus singing at the opera, give some of the credit to the men who drill it. The job of chorus master is a difficult one, and the musician who holds it does not have many moments in the limelight as does the conductor. Fausto Cleva and Konrad Neuger, the Metropolitan incumbents, are not known to the average operagoer. Neuger said wryly recently that he was thinking of joining the chorus himself. His work gave him many more responsibilities and not much more compensation.

The choristers are loyal to their leaders. When Giulio Setti substituted at one performance on the podium in place of Serafin, who was ill, the chorus sang its head off for him.

During rehearsals the chorus enjoys a certain camaraderie with some of the artists. In "Parsifal" Melchior wears a short tunic. In truth he looks "the poor fool" he is playing; his huge figure resembles an infant Gargantua. The flower maidens have to play up to him in the second act, and the bold choristers among them have been known to tickle the big tenor. He cannot stand it. He pleads with them, "Please, ladies, do not! I am so ticklish."

XI

SWING IT, GIRLS!

ONE of the major attractions of opera to many of its devotees is that it combines within one form many of the arts. Music, drama, poetry, painting, sculpture and the dance are held to be the ingredients of the well-rounded opera. The theoreticians and analysts may discuss these matters to their hearts' content, but the average man will justify the inclusion of the dance on a simple basis. Granting the charms of music and the passions of the drama, the spectator may weary of watching the cavortings of a group of hefty principals or the meanderings of the awkward chorus. A dance or two by a sprightly ballet offers a refreshing interlude. Even if the dance is not artfully designed, there are always the ballet girls.

They have youth, verve, grace and shapeliness. Ask any tired business man. Ask any member of the stage crew who works behind the scenes at the Metropolitan. Normally these hard-boiled citizens ignore the proceedings on the stage. But when the girls are dancing, they crowd the wings and follow the movements most attentively. They may not care about the design of the dance, but they know what they like.

Samuel (The Great) Goldwyn—even he gets into this book —is quoted as not being impressed with the ladies of the American Ballet ensemble, which is the Metropolitan Opera ballet these days. Mr. Goldwyn engaged twenty-six members of the ballet for "The Goldwyn Follies." The contracts were signed without Mr. Goldwyn's personal observation of the ballet in action, and he requested that some of the dancers be screen-tested. This was done in New York, and the tests

Opera: Front and Back

were shipped West. After the showing, Mr. Goldwyn is said
to have made one of those cryptic comments for which he has
become illustrious. "Those girls must be good dancers," he
said, "they look awful funny."

Nevertheless opera audiences respond to the ballet. A good
many patrons look upon the dancers as manna from heaven
in the arid waste of singing. There are people who perk up
noticeably the moment the ballet appears on the stage. They
watch intently and they applaud with fervor. When the ballet is over they slide down into their chairs with an air of
resignation. The ballet, of course, is taken much more seriously in some of Europe's opera houses. Paris, Moscow, Len-
ingrad, Rome, Milan, Stockholm all have large corps of
dancers. Who has not heard the tale of the first performance
of "Tannhäuser" at the Opéra in Paris, when the members
of the Jockey Club precipitated a furor because the ballet
came at the beginning of the opera instead of in the middle,
where they insisted it belonged?

The opera houses of America have always had a ballet
corps of one kind or another. The major reason has been that
the operas called for them. There has been no indication that
the opera managements valued the ballet for itself. They
have not attempted to develop ensembles that would have
character and distinction in their own right. If they have attempted it, they have failed. The Metropolitan Opera, in
fact, has recently gone out and engaged an independent ensemble for its productions, in the hope that a separate direc-
torate would bring individuality to the dances of the opera.
The Chicago City Opera also has a separate ballet—Ruth
Page's ensemble.

In the days when Rosina Galli was the ballet mistress the
corps of full-time dancers was larger than the present one
at the Metropolitan. There were about fifty-three girls and

twenty young men. The ensemble of dancers could be augmented beyond a hundred by using the youngsters of the ballet school which the Metropolitan conducted as an adjunct of its ballet. The school is still in operation at the Metropolitan, but it furnishes fewer extras for the large ballet. Its principal product is the children who appear in several of the ballets and in such operas as "Parsifal," where they are young acolytes, and "Rheingold," where they play the roles of Mime's host of dwarfs.

Considering that the members of the ballet have a short opera season, they are paid modest salaries. As the American Ballet, added earnings may be available to them in outside work, such as the movies and tours throughout the country. The modus operandi today is a contract between the Metropolitan Opera Association and the American Ballet calling for the payment of a flat sum to the latter. In the old days the dancers were paid directly by the opera company. Salaries ranged from highs of $45 for the favorites of the ballet mistress to $20 a week for those who were liked least. Dancers who had solos of whatever length received $10 extra for each appearance of this kind. Thus a girl or a boy who had two or three solos each week—and it was not rare for the leaders to have such opportunities—was able to earn about $75 a week. Nowadays ballet salaries are better equalized so far as the rank and file of the ensemble is concerned. The rates are from $45 to $30 a week. The American Ballet began the apprentice system last year, engaging three girls at $10 a week.

The chief divergences in salaries between the Galli days and today are in the pre-season rehearsals. When Miss Galli was in charge and the ballet was the Metropolitan's, the dancers were paid their regular salaries during the four weeks of rehearsals that preceded the season. Now they are not paid at all. I do not know who is to blame: whether the

Opera: Front and Back

Metropolitan is paying too small a sum for the season to the American Ballet or whether the American Ballet chooses to do business this way, on the theory that it is providing compensating opportunities for off-season employment to its dancers.

There seems to be slight doubt that the ballet today costs the Metropolitan a good deal less than in the old days. The principal difference may be that Galli was paid a large weekly fee. Some said that it was as high at $1,000 a week in the boom days of opera prosperity.

Another change, and perhaps a more important one, is the transfer of ballet headquarters to the studios of the American Ballet. In Galli's time rehearsals were held on the roof stage of the opera house. Now all preparations take place in the American Ballet's studios. The latter are more spacious and better equipped for dancing. The dances are designed and worked out in the American Ballet studio with the proportions of the opera stage in mind. The ballet master confers with the stage director, the conductor and the scene designer and he knows exactly how much space and time he has for his figures. The dancers are not brought to the Metropolitan stage until the ensemble rehearsals of an opera are called. Then they go through their parts with the rest of the company. There may be one ensemble rehearsal with piano and two with orchestra. In its studios the ballet works with piano. The dancers have a scant number of rehearsals on the stage itself.

The questions have been raised: Was not the ballet a more integral part of the Metropolitan Opera House in the old days and is it not more concerned with other things outside that theatre today? The answers to these problems require a study of artistic results. Students and critics of the dance contend that there is little to choose between the old ballet and the present. In Gatti's regime the ballet, they say, tended to cheap and tawdry conceptions; now the emphasis is on flashiness, flamboyance and artificial designs. If the critics are correct in their judgments, the kernel of the trouble is in the artistic vision of those who have conceived the ballets. Assuming, however, that a choreographer came along who not only understood the needs of the dance as a part of opera but was actually absorbed in solving that problem, would it not be better if the ballet corps lived in the atmosphere of the opera house and were saturated with the spirit of the operas? So ask the critics, and they argue that the obvious answer is in the affirmative.

Leaving artistic considerations aside, there is the practical problem of causing the forces of the ballet to live happily with the other elements of the lyric theatre. With the present corps rehearsing away from the opera house, there is less conflict in the distribution of the Metropolitan's limited rehearsal space. However, other headaches crop up.

There is constant warfare between the chorus and ballet over the amount of stage space required by each during a performance. The dancers need all they can get, and they cry out that the chorus is loath to give it up. The chorus takes its place for an elaborate mass scene, and it does not budge. The stage director begs the choristers to make way for the dancers. Sometimes they do; more often they do not. The dancers are careful to tread on the feet of their natural enemies, and the chorus retaliates with sly kicks and pokes. But the dancers never expect a final, satisfactory conclusion to this perpetual quarrel. They expect it to go on and on, like the war between men and women.

Mention the word "ballet girl" and there is always a snicker from the prurient. The two words seem to have the same effect on certain types of males as that other combination, "show girl." Whence comes this repute? It is said that in some of the sophisticated European centers the directors of the opera regard it as a perquisite of the job that the ballet girls shall be nice to them. Similar innuendoes have been leveled at some sopranos and mezzo-sopranos who were endowed by nature with more looks than voice. I have no doubt that such things happen in the world. I have even heard the yarn—but I choose to label it apocryphal—of the antiquated basso who heard some years ago that a ballet girl at the Metropolitan was injured and came dashing backstage, breathing hard with anxiety, to discover which one it was. It is possible that his interest was purely humanitarian.

I have heard of another Metropolitan leading singer who was constantly on the make for ballet girls. It was said of him that he examined each newcomer in the corps with a practiced eye. If she was attractive and pleasing to him, he would say to her, "Nice—I like," with a broad, sensuous enunciation of the vowel sounds. Several times the singer's wife became suspicious of her mate's attentions to ballet girls and had detectives set on their trails.

These stories are not indigenous to the opera house; you hear them wherever there is a theatre. Not being an Anthony Comstock or a purveyor of erotica, I have not checked the facts. I only know that I have seen the mothers of the ballet girls wait for their daughters after each performance. I have observed that the young men and women of the ballet go about their business as conscientiously as the next person.

They work, in fact, harder than most people in the opera house, for theirs is the strenuous life. A dancer, like an athlete, must always keep in form. Sometimes he must be prepared for emergencies that tax all his energies, like the occasion of a recent performance of "Carmen." The soprano who sang the title role was assuming it for the first time at the

Metropolitan. In the second act, Carmen has an aria in which she dances several steps as she sings and continues dancing at the end of the song. This passage is preceded by a brief dance by a group from the ballet. The new Carmen told a young male dancer that, just before she began her dance, she wished him to do several steps. She informed him, at the rehearsal, that she would clap her hands as a signal for him to dance. The boy agreed, but made no special preparations, thinking that he would be expected to dance to a couple of measures.

The Carmen gave the signal at the performance when the music had six pages to go. The boy thought that she had done so accidentally, and did not begin dancing. But she clapped her hands imperiously, and he started to dance. She kept centering attention on him, making him dance. The poor fellow was obliged to improvise. He began to breathe hard, as he waited vainly for Carmen to take up the dance. She never did. Finally three of the ballet girls, who were standing on the fringes of the stage crowd, joined the dance and all four improvised the remainder of the scene.

It might be said, in passing, that this was not merely a heroic feat on the part of the dancers, and a mean trick on Carmen's part. It was a stupid thing for her to do, because the scene is designed to focus attention on the Carmen, and this Carmen insisted on turning interest to members of the ballet corps.

There have been other improvisations for the ballet corps. Once, some years ago, a group of girls became confused in the Bacchanale of "Tannhäuser" and turned it into a veritable hash. Some girls followed the beat of the music; others drifted around like sailboats in a fog. Talk about messes! The ballet mistress was rabid for days afterwards. To add to the hilarity, the music critics termed the ballet an improved version of what had been done in the previous season. To which the innocent bystander may add: Maybe it was at that.

The ballet master has one of the toughest jobs in the opera house. The run-of-the-mine opera director, when he has faced the problem of gathering into one happy family singers and conductors, chorus and orchestra, backstage crew and administrative staff, is not inclined to give much thought to the dancers. He leaves problems of discipline, design and rehearsal to the ballet master. Only when the ballet clashes with a member of the staff does the executive worry. Once, in a dress rehearsal of an important novelty, a ballet girl accidentally jabbed a prima donna in the rear with a spear. The prima donna let loose an unholy yell and stalked off the stage, refusing to go on with the rehearsal. That was one problem the opera executive had to deal with.

Others occur when the ballet master differs with the other heads of departments, such as the stage director, the conductor and the scene and costume designers. Recently a dance was prepared, then the conductor decided to cut several passages out of the ballet music. It took the wisdom of a Solomon to persuade the conductor and ballet master to compromise.

Usually the conductor wins. If the ballet master is a determined person, he may triumph. Rosina Galli used to win her way more often than not. There was the time that a Rimsky-Korsakoff opera was being revived. Serge Soudeikin designed the sets and worked out colorful costumes for the ballet. The dancers wore their costumes for the first time on the day of the first general rehearsal. Galli did not like the costumes. She had a pair of scissors brought to her and proceeded to cut up the costumes. The dancers wore the renovated outfits at the dress rehearsal, and when Soudeikin saw them he was furious. But there was no time to restore the costumes, even if Galli could have been overridden.

In the recent revival of "Coq d'Or" an amusing example of internal jealousies developed. The leading roles were taken by Ezio Pinza as the decrepit, sotted old King Dodon, and Lily Pons as the beauteous Queen of Shemakhan. Each character has a brief dance in the second act. Pinza prepared his with George Balanchine, Metropolitan Opera ballet master, and Miss Pons went outside the opera house to seek the services of Michel Fokine. Miss Pons's action was interpreted as a slight by Balanchine, but the première brought solace to him. Lily Pons's dance was received with polite applause. Pinza's finely exaggerated steps, designed with Balanchine's flair for the grotesquely comic, brought down the house. Balanchine was said to have informed the backstage people that virtue had had its own reward.

Rosina Galli, whatever else may be said of her work with the ballet, took a personal interest in her corps. She watched over her girls with a maternal care. She was, in fact, jealous of their activities at the Metropolitan and would refuse to let her dancers appear elsewhere. Her ballet once had an opportunity to dance at the Lewisohn Stadium, but Galli turned down the offer. Her prima ballerina, Rita de Leporte, had offers to dance at Roxy's and at the Radio City Music Hall in the opera's off-season, but she was prevailed upon to forego these opportunities.

Despite Galli's vigilance, her charges managed to get into trouble on occasion. Once, while the company was on tour, a ballet girl accepted an invitation to join a party that the stage-hands were giving in their car. The company was en route from Baltimore to Rochester. The girl joined the party, costumed in her lounging pajamas, thinking she would stay a little while and return to her own car to go to bed. But the party was lively, and the girl remained until 3 A.M. When she set out for her car, she found that her section of the train had disappeared.

The train had been broken up into two sections, with the car in which the stage hands rode routed in the first division because they had to be in Rochester much earlier to set the stage. It was a difficult situation for the girl. She had no money and no clothes but her lounging pajamas. She had to wait alone in the train on a siding until the second section arrived several hours later and her roommate hunted her up, bearing a change of clothes.

In a performance of "Mefistofele," a ballet girl, dressed as a demon, emerged through a trap door, and as she leaped forward she felt a distressing bareness. The tail of her costume had caught in the door and ripped away the seat of her tights.

One of the principal complaints of the ballet used to be the raggedness of the stage floor. The dancers tripped over cracks and collected splinters. A new floor has been provided. That difficulty should be no more.

The ballet begins formal rehearsals four weeks before the opening of the season. At the American Ballet classes start in August, and work on the dances for new operas or for revivals as well as for separate dance compositions begins long before the pre-season rehearsals. The ballet rehearses the standard repertory thoroughly, and if there is a rehearsal before the first performance of the season, the ballet joins in it. The dancers appear in all ensemble workouts when new works are concerned. If the ballet is difficult or if it is one of the central elements of a production, as it was in Gluck's "Orpheus," extra rehearsals may be arranged with orchestra.

Swing It, Girls

The Metropolitan ballet is generously roasted, year in and year out. Sometimes the criticisms are justified. But the ballet does have excuses for being ragged. The Metropolitan does not allow it frequent rehearsals with orchestra because the cost of such preparation is prohibitive. A number of the dances, the friends of the ballet claim, would look better if more time were spent in unifying them with the music and with the sets and lighting.

We are now back where we started. What does the customer want at the opera anyhow? Singing or dancing? Maybe there ought to be a referendum.

XII

THEY ALSO SERVE WHO
ONLY STAND

MOST opera houses believe that the grandest effects are achieved by filling the stage with a
huge mass of people. The more human beings
crowded behind the footlights, the more lavish the spectacle.
Hollywood has the same general idea, and so have the more
spectacular stage shows of the film cathedrals. The chorus,
the ballet, and the principals give an opera house a stage
contingent of more than 200. But that is not sufficient. Several hundred supernumeraries are hired, togged out and
paraded onto the stage. They are distinguishable from the
choristers in that they do not sing and are kept usually in the
background.

If there is any one in the entire world of the opera without the slightest vestige of temperament, it is the super. The
chorister may harbor delusions of grandeur, once he gets a
small bit, and the ballet girl may have visions of becoming
a leading lady in the dance. The super knows that he helps
to form crowds. He receives a modicum of attention from
the company, if not from the public. He is the forgotten man
of the opera. More likely than not, he may also be the forgotten man of our social scheme—a down-and-outer earning
a small piece of change.

At the Metropolitan and the other great lyric theatres of
the world supers are employed in most of the operas. They
perform a variety of functions. They are soldiers, priests and
hostages of war in "Aïda," picadors and matadors in "Car-

[196]

men," peasants and villagers in "Cavalleria Rusticana" and "Pagliacci," a crowd in a Hindu market-place in "Lakmé," priests and altar boys in "Tosca," members of the medieval guilds in "Die Meistersinger" and servants in "La Traviata."

Most frequently supers are cast as soldiers and priests. They are minions in the armies of manifold realms and centuries; they are communicants of every order that has been set upon the stage, from Montsalvat to St. Francis of Assisi.

The super has a brief moment on the stage. He may be in a procession that is just passing by. He may walk on with a tray and depart instantly. Or he may stand by as part of the populace at a public fête and listen to a moment's singing by famous artists. Of the present contingent of supers at the Metropolitan 60 per cent, it is estimated, are not impressed by the fact that they may hear the most expensive voices in the world. Being a super is a job that pays a dollar a night, and in hard times or good a dollar is a dollar. The other 40 per cent do care. They would cheerfully contribute their services to stand on the same stage with a Bori, a Flagstad or a Tibbett. They are enamored of opera and its people. They are the devotees.

For the management—in New York, Chicago, San Francisco or wherever opera is sung—the super is a problem as well as a necessity. Two hundred men and women must be outfitted in "Aïda," about one hundred in "Carmen," "Lakmé" and "Coq d'Or." To Borodin's "Prince Igor" goes the palm of requiring the largest number of supers—more than 300. Having been costumed, the supers must be rehearsed in their stage business. They must be kept out of the way of the performance and the backstage crew. Finally, they must be watched everlastingly for the unexpected.

More than two decades ago the Metropolitan Opera Company responded favorably to a request from a group of local colleges that students be used as supers. In theory it was a fine arrangement. The students would have the educational benefits of contacts with opera, and the management would have their services without cost. For a time the youthful brigade was a blessing. The young men and women were intelligent, attentive, well-behaved.

One night, however, they carried undergraduate habits into the opera house. It was the end of the second act of "Aïda." Lillian Nordica had sung the title role magnificently, and in the smashing ensemble that concludes the act her high tones had soared over the voices of her colleagues and the chorus. When the curtain rose in response to applause and Nordica came forward for a bow, the phalanx of supers contributed its meed of tribute to a great artist with a yell: "Rah, rah, rah! Nordica! Nordica! Rah, rah, rah!"

This incident did not bring the end of student participation. The next did. Since this was an educational experience for the young folk, the management permitted them to remain within earshot of the singers during the entire performance. When their work was done, the supers were allowed to clamber to the topmost bridge above the stage where they could hear the opera, if not see all the action. One evening a student dropped a lighted cigarette from on high. Remember, smoking is strictly forbidden backstage. The Metropolitan decided that the cost of education might become too expensive.

The management went back to the use of mature supers, men and women who were interested in the pay. At that time the Metropolitan gave each super 75 cents for an evening's work. One night there was rebellion in the ranks. The supers were in their dressing room, wearing the clerical tunics, the military uniforms of Egypt and the manacles of the vanquished Ethiopians, ready for the triumphal scene in

the second act of "Aïda." The call came to march upstairs
to prepare for the entrance. The supers refused.

They argued that they were underpaid. They demanded
a dollar for their services. The stage functionary was frantic.
He pleaded, threatened, but the supers were obdurate. Word
was hurried back to Giulio Gatti-Casazza, the general manager, who gave a peremptory order: "Throw them out!"
The supers were dismissed, and the chorus and ballet did
the best they could with the grand march. The triumphal
scene of "Aïda" had a skimpy look that night; it seemed
that the Egyptian populace had unaccountably remained at
home, and the handful of prisoners belied the fact that the
celebration was for a famous victory.

The boss of the supers at the Metropolitan is Jules Judels, who has accumulated, in forty-seven consecutive years
with the company, an assortment of tasks. The hardest is
looking after supers. His father, Maurice Judels, was responsible for the extras in the Eighteen Eighties, when Ed-
mund C. Stanton was the general secretary of the company.

Mr. Judels recalls that in those days supers were paid
twenty-five cents a performance. After the show they would
congregate across the street at Schultz's Café, which had
sawdust on the floor and a generous free lunch. There they
would be paid off. The procedure, designed to keep the
supers from clogging the stage entrance, was all right with
Mr. Schultz. The twenty-five cents was usually spent on
beer. And Mr. Schultz was happy when the opera was
"Aïda."

In those days about 120 supers were used in "Aïda." Ap-
plicants turned up at the stage door and were taken on just
before the performance. Today the management does not
rely on such a hit-or-miss system.

The opera has a list of more than 300 names in its files

Opera: Front and Back

and each year it receives several thousand applications. The supers who are required are notified by postcard. They are told to be at the Metropolitan Opera House at 7 P.M., but arrive well ahead of time. No one is admitted without a card. The guardian of the stage entrance must see to it that the men are clean-shaven, unless the opera calls for beards, and sober.

The contemporary supers are, for the most part, men and women who have no other regular employment, and in the winter the dressing room is a warm, comfortable place to sit and read, to discuss the state of the nation or to play a friendly game of pinochle or penny-ante poker.

The dressing rooms at the Metropolitan are fairly commodious. The men have a spacious chamber on the north side of the basement of the opera house. The women have theirs on the other side. Rows of lockers are ranged along the walls, with long low benches in front of them. In the center of each room there is a huge table for the costumes.

The wardrobe man, a graduate from the ranks of the supers, has the job of distributing clothes and accessories. Shoes, helmets, tights, tunics must fit. Generally they do. The wardrobe man knows his supers. He remembers the size of their feet, the sag of their shoulders, the shape of their heads.

Occasionally, of course, a soldier looks as if he were rattling around in his uniform, or a page wears stockings that crinkle around the ankles. But with an orchestra going full blast, with principals and a chorus singing and several hundred persons behind the footlights, the observer out front must have a keen or wandering eye to detect a super who is badly fitted.

If the stage crowds are not always sartorially right, the circumstances may be judged extenuating. When the supers form a military detachment, men of the same average height are selected. Giants and lilliputians are ruled out. But having recruited a group of reasonably uniform height, how can you possibly guarantee that one man will not have spindly legs, that another will not bulge in the wrong place, and that a third will not have round shoulders?

Accidents will happen in the best of regulated opera houses. Supers who have arrived for their evening's work without a trace of liquor on their breath have managed to imbibe enough, during a long wait in the dressing room, to be wholly unreliable by the time the crowd is required on stage. And you cannot frisk every man for a bottle.

Somehow drunks are kept off the stage. There are many eyes backstage to detect a serious inebriate before he goes on. Minor crises, such as a super's toppling off a platform or marching in the wrong direction, occur at intervals.

Perhaps the most disturbing of these happened during the war in a performance of Liszt's "St. Elizabeth," when a super stationed in front lost his trousers. He was wearing a size too large and had omitted to fasten the trousers securely. He was as amazed as the conductor and the stage forces. He let go his spear with a thud, and clutched at the offending garment. The rest of the act never did recover its gravity.

How are supers trained? For intricate maneuvers in operas that require hundreds of them, many rehearsals are held. A work like "Coq d'Or" needed at least six. The supers do not object; they receive regular rates for rehearsals.

The Metropolitan retains six leaders all season on a weekly salary. They are supers who have proved themselves under all conditions. They know all the operas. They are asked to perform the important tasks, to execute the difficult gestures, to stand in prominent positions. When many leaders are wanted, male members of the ballet, provided they are not dancing, are drafted.

Opera: Front and Back

The easiest operas to man are those with the most elaborate scenes—"Aïda," "Carmen" and "Meistersinger." The average super is told to follow the leader; yet some supers have had attacks of stage-fright under the burden of the simplest of assignments. Heavy work is done by veteran supers. A husky squad of extras lifts the slain Siegfried, usually a tenor of generous proportions, and carries him off slowly as the orchestra chants the incomparable funeral music of "Götterdämmerung."

The length of certain operas has caused trouble in the past. There is on record the action of one super of independent mind who decided that he had remained on the stage long enough and stalked off angrily in the middle of a scene. When "Aïda" is being done, protests are to be heard frequently from supers who are cast as priests and not as soldiers. The priests must work in the Nile scene of the third act, whereas the soldiers are through at the end of the second.

There is and always has been an element that chooses to "super" for the fun of it. A subscriber who had seats in the orchestra would frequently work as an extra. She and her daughter would come and make up with the other supers and go through the same maneuvers on and off stage. They preferred acting as supers to occupying their $7 seats.

Several painters found that being supers was not only amusing but provided them with ideas. Well-known lawyers, judges, physicians and teachers have served time on the Metropolitan stage as supers. Alfred Piccaver, the tenor, who has sung leading roles extensively abroad, began as a super at the Metropolitan.

Some years ago, during a performance of "La Bohème," Enrico Caruso, who was not singing that night, decided suddenly to join in the proceedings. The super who was to be the waiter at the Café Momus in the second act was standing in

the wings. Caruso took his apron and the tray, with its de-
canter and glasses, and walked on. The audience did not recognize the rotund waiter. The singers did, and one of them
was so surprised that, tradition has it, he skipped a phrase.

An opera such as "Parsifal" requires a procession of young
children. Usually youngsters from the ballet school are
brought in. Years ago Mr. Judels used to bring the children
of his neighbors into the opera house for this work. The children of these children, now mature citizens, come to the Metropolitan to ask to be allowed to emulate their parents as
youthful supers.

The $30,000 a year which the Metropolitan spends on its
supers pays for impressive crowds and a measurable amount
of trouble. Mr. Judels has been in charge of the supers at
the Metropolitan for twenty-six years. "The job," he sums
up, with a reasonable show of being dispassionate, "is no
joke. Sometimes it's a toothache. Supers get old and we have
to let them go, and they call me inhuman. They hang around
the opera house to complain and to curse me."

But depression years have tamed the supers. They are
easier to handle. In other days one of the difficult problems
was the petty larceny practiced by some. Most of them merely
wanted souvenirs.

The things that were taken were of no great value: a helmet, a torch, a pennant. Once, however, the lingerie of a
prima donna disappeared from her dressing room, and the
supers were the first to come under suspicion.

When the opera is on tour, supers are engaged in each city.
Many years ago, before the word "racket" became known as a
method of extortion and easy living, out-of-town supers were
induced to pay for the right to serve on the stage. In the days
when Lilli Lehmann, Jean de Reszke and the rest packed
them in, people who could not obtain low-priced tickets would

cheerfully pay $2 a head to be allowed on the stage. The boss of the supers in those days made a pretty penny in this way.

Many supers develop the autograph craze. It is irritating enough to most artists to be badgered off stage, but between the acts—a pestilence thrice compounded! Some supers are fond of chatting; they will stop a singer on his way to his dressing room to compliment him on his singing, to comment on the audience or to discuss Art. The best of supers have spells of this amiable habit. Then there are the violent congratulators. What is an artist to do when he finds, as the curtain drops on a great aria, that a super is wringing his hand, slapping him on the back or shouting "Bravo!" in his ear? Some tenors, the gossips say, like it; other singers do not.

XIII

ARTISANS OF ILLUSION

THE artisans of illusion at the opera are the stage crew. They are not seen and should not be heard, at least by the audience. They, not Loge, surround Brünnhilde with magic fire; they convert the boards of the stage into the majestic waters of the Rhine; they are the makers of wind and rain and lightning; they are the movers and shakers of a hundred operatic worlds.

The stage workers have come by their skill through an arduous apprenticeship in the lyric theatre. For the problems of opera exceed those of any other stage. Not only are the words set to music, but every stage effect. If working out a repertory is no pushover, consider the task of managing the sets, the lights and the props for a theatre which averages eight different shows a week and more than thirty in a short season. The stage workers know as much about the operas as a good many of the artists; there are some who know more.

They must. The opera that has three acts is rare. Most works require four or five, with a couple of scenes for some acts thrown in for good measure. "Pelléas et Mélisande" has thirteen scenes. "Don Giovanni," an even ten. There are wheels within wheels: transformations and visions as in "Faust" and "Tannhäuser" and "Thaïs." In one week the Metropolitan may mount a street in Verona, a garden in Japan, a vista of Valhalla, the ramparts of a castle in Cornwall, the banks of the Nile, a great hall in Lammermoor. You may think the sets are old-fashioned or unimaginative.

Opera: Front and Back

You may marvel at their splendor. To the boys backstage they are one thing—hard work.

Opera's pretentious settings require the adjustment of numerous hangings, back drops, sky and leaf borders, side tabs, built up sets and stage platforms. If elaborate productions are scheduled for afternoon and evening, almost every available batten—there are 100 of them—is in service, and the side and rear areas used for stacking are jammed with the canvas and carpentry that spell dreams.

These things are in the province of the scenery gang. The light and prop men have equipment of their own to dispose and to set. Although the stage area at a theatre like the Metropolitan is enormous compared to most Broadway playhouses, it is a glutted cosmos at performance time. Because space is limited, the operations backstage require a larger crew than would a fully equipped and more spacious stage.

The Metropolitan has a staff of about eighty men who work in and around the stage, in addition to a contingent of nine who take charge of sets at three storehouses. The crew has five divisions: electricians, carpenters, property men, stage hands and night staff. For the most elaborate operas such as "Aïda" and "Meistersinger," additional men are engaged on a per diem basis. The regular crew is paid weekly salaries at standard rates during the weeks that they work, as well as for pre-season rehearsals. The rates for stage workers at the opera are higher than for the spoken drama because of the greater difficulty of the work. Electricians receive $12 a day and $9 a show, making a total of $21 for about 12 hours' work. When there are matinees the preliminary work is scaled down to half a day. The night crew is paid $12 for a tour of duty. Stage hands, carpenters, prop men get $10 a day, plus $8.50 a show. In other words, electricians earn about $125 a week, and the others about $110. Do you wonder why opera tickets come high? A closed shop contract between the Metropolitan and the union, the International Alliance of Theatrical Stage Employees—IATSE to the trade—covers working arrangements.

The general lines along which the labor is divided is not unlike any other theatre, but the night crew is a wrinkle peculiar to the opera. The eleven men of this contingent come in at midnight when the opera is over. They take away the show and cart it off to the storehouses, where every item is placed by the warehouse men in its assigned location. The Metropolitan has complete sets for about eighty operas, with thousands of items in all, and each bit of canvas and woodwork —each piece has a number and a record is kept of the numbering—must be placed in its appointed spot where it can be found instantly. The regular crew has time only to set each show and to handle it during the performance. Since the New York City Fire Department does not sanction keeping more than one production on the stage at any time, a squad of nocturnal toilers must be employed.

The Fire Department ruling that allows no more than one show on the stage at any time explains why sets are stored temporarily on the street. People who have strolled along Seventh Avenue between Thirty-ninth and Fortieth Streets, which is the backstage side of the yellow brick building that resembles a well-appointed stable rather than America's ranking opera house, have seen piles of scenery neatly rolled against the wall. Tarpaulins cover it, but never thoroughly. You can descry the abbreviations of the operas to which the sets belong. And the rain, snow and sleet of New York's winters occasionally inundate drops and tabs, causing a painted ship upon a painted ocean to fade and become even more unreal.

Let us put a shoulder under one of the rolled-up drops

which, because of the height of the stage, are sixty to seventy feet in span and let us stagger in under the burden of the "damnably heavy" load—an old stage hand who used to tote these burdens named himself and his fellows "bugger luggers." Let us stand by as the boys perform the miracles that are indigenous to opera.

Let us begin with a few figures to obtain an idea of the size of the stage. The proscenium opening is 52 feet wide and 50 feet high, although the draperies cut down the height to 40 feet. The height to the gridiron behind the proscenium is 90 feet. The complete backstage area is 70 feet deep and 100 feet wide. There remains a space of 24 feet on each side and whatever is not used for the set in the rear is employed for the stacking of scenery for the next acts, for the assembling of chorus, ballet and supers for their entrances and for the moving of principals, assistant conductors and stage officials behind the scenes.

On the sides of the proscenium, level with the top of it, are two "fly" floors from which side tabs are handled and on which spotlighting and special equipment is operated. At the rear at the same level is a paint bridge. At points high on the sides are the sound machines for thunder, wind and rain, which are operated electrically from the call board below. Underneath the stage there is a labyrinth of traps and elevators. Virtually the entire area on which the performance takes place can be raised or depressed. Deepest underground is located the intricate mechanism, known as the thyratron-reactor units, which is the foundation of the new and most advanced lighting system obtainable, recently installed. The switchboard is directly under the front center of the stage in a fireproof compartment. Beside the hood which is the prompter's box there is a smaller opening in the footlight trough, through which the master of the switchboard can view the stage.

This, in sum, is the theatre of the stage force's action. The scenery gang hang canvas and place the solid elements of the set in place. The prop men bring out the implements of opera: the spears and shields for "Carmen," more spears for "Aïda" and still more spears and shields for "Götterdämmerung," bulrushes for "Siegfried," the swan and the swan boat for "Lohengrin," baskets of fireproof snow for "Bohème," the drinking horns for "Walküre," the drum for "Pagliacci" and the pen and parchment and heavy tomes for "Meistersinger." The catalogue is long, through many operas ranging. The electricians see to it that their eight light borders, the footlights, the special spotlights are focused. The electrical storeroom is scoured for the proper special equipment: the Holy Grail for "Parsifal," Isolde's torch for "Tristan," the fireflies for "Madama Butterfly," the tiny head lamps for the Norns in "Götterdämmerung," the lanterns for the fête scene in "Lakmé," the torches for "Elektra" and still more torches for "Götterdämmerung." In racks are gelatin color screens for clouds, running water, ripples, smoke, fog, flames and rainbows.

The stage crew operates everything. It works on the principle that the artist is to be allowed to do his singing and not to be bothered with gadgets. If a candle is to be blown out or a torch extinguished, the stage force prefers to do the job itself. Years of experience have proved that most artists are not to be depended upon. They are nervous, indifferent, impatient, forgetful. For every singer like Jeritza, who was clever at managing stage effects, there are dozens of artists who are inept.

In "Bohème," for example, Mimi blows out the light of a

candle in the first act. The light is a tiny electric lamp. It would be simple enough for the Mimi to snap a button in the candle as she blows out the flame. Too many times, however, Mimi has puffed and puffed, but the light has kept on burning. Now the candle is connected to a circuit on the side of the stage, where an electrician snaps the button as Mimi puffs. It is a wise precaution.

Then there is the torch in the second act of "Tristan und Isolde." The torch, if you know what is happening on the stage, is central to the action. Isolde extinguishes the light as a signal to Tristan that it is safe for him to appear. There have been occasions, however, when Isolde forgot to snap a button, and the light burned on through the night. Even if Melot had not been about to fill King Mark's mind with suspicions, the torch light would have informed the monarch's loyal retainers that something was afoot in the garden. The torch, therefore, is operated from offstage.

Not every Isolde would forget to press the button that turns off the torch. But there is another reason for working it behind the scenes—a practical reason. The torch has a strong flickering flame. A small motor inside the torch turns a fan that causes a ribbon to flicker like a flame when illuminated by a lamp inside. The ordinary storage battery would last for three minutes, if it had to keep a motor and light going at the same time. The torch must be on for about thirteen minutes, and it would have to be filled, therefore, with four or five batteries. The weight of the torch would then become burdensome for the Isolde, and the opera officials do not wish to fatigue their dramatic soprano before the love duet. The torch is connected to one of the light pockets on the extreme side of the stage, where an electrician sees to it that the juice is cut off when it has to be.

Precautions are taken against every conceivable mischance.

Artisans of Illusion

In "The Tales of Hoffmann" a circular chandelier of gas lights has to be lit in the prologue. The lights—electrically operated, of course—are adjusted so that they will go on clockwise, one at a time. If the lamplighter were to move in counterclockwise direction, the effect would be ludicrous. The result is that an electrician attires himself in a costume and acts the role of the lamplighter. For this extra bit of service he receives the regular super's fee of $1.

Some things must be left to the artist. At the end of the first act of "Siegfried," when the young hero has completed the forging of his sword, he smites an anvil down front and cleaves it in two. The splitting is accomplished when the sword is brought down on a spring on top of the anvil. Melchior is dependable; he always hits the spring. There have been occasions when a tenor did not, and all he had for his efforts was a rebound of the sword. The curtain comes down quickly on this scene, and it may be questioned whether the audience would know that the young hero and his sword had been found wanting.

The truth is, every one in the audience may not be aware of the deficiency. Possibly only a handful would be expert enough in the ways of "The Ring" to know its requirements. But some one always sees the failings. The stage workers are sometimes goggle-eyed at the infinitesimal things that some spectators will discern and at the fact that they will take the trouble to inform the management of these deviations. A customer complained once because one brass-headed nail in a long row of nails was missing from a throne-like chair in "Rigoletto." Another operagoer pointed out that the wrong saddle was used in "The King's Henchman"; a modern saddle was provided instead of one of mediæval style because Edward Johnson who sang an aria while seated on horseback had to be comfortable while singing; the medieval equipment may have been all right for horsemanship in the Middle Ages, but it was not exactly the thing for an opera singer.

For the pyre at the end of "Götterdämmerung," the opera's chief electrician, Jacob Buchter, who is a resourceful veteran, has invented an effective gadget—a large log, which can be raised and collapsed. The flames are obtained in the usual way, colored lights playing on ribbons that are fluttered by a blower underneath. But this fire is being fed constantly by new logs, and it must become an impressive pyre. As the choristers throw new logs in the general direction of the blaze, the log is raised and the fire looks as if it is mounting ever higher. When Brünnhilde plunges in and the scene has to undergo a quick change, the log collapses like the innards of an accordion.

A rapid-fire scene change at this point in the music-drama produces an effective illusion. Gunther's house must collapse, and the Rhine must overflow the stage, with a sunburst in the background. Gunther's house seems to be collapsing. Actually the scene gang is pulling out the set at lightning speed and lowering another drop that gives the effect of the inundating Rhine. The crumbling of Gunther's walls is what the audience sees instead of the rapid dismantling and moving by the stage hands that is taking place.

One of the most startling and stirring moments in the whole calendar of opera occurs in "Parsifal" when Amfortas picks up the chalice that is the Holy Grail and holds it aloft to his disciples of Montsalvat. The Grail lights slowly and becomes blood red. The stage is darkened, and the crimson of the Grail dominates the scene with awe-inspiring impressiveness. Here again the Amfortas is not relied upon to turn the light on and off. Hidden under the altar-like structure upon which the Grail is set is a stage hand. There is an opening in the structure, and as the moment comes for the revelation of the Grail, the stage hand turns a little knob at the bottom of the chalice. The Grail is connected to a dimming device, and it irradiates slowly. It is possible to operate the Grail in this way because it begins to light up just as Amfortas touches it and it need not be dimmed and extinguished until he sets it down again.

In the old days, the Grail illumination was not a simple matter. In the first place, there was no modern equipment such as the Metropolitan has today and the transfiguring light of the Grail had to come from above. In the second place, there were no permanent bridges on the light borders and it was sometimes necessary to hoist a man up to that level in a portable bridge called a basket. The man who went aloft in the basket had to start up more than an hour before the illumination of the Grail occurred, and remain dangling in mid-air until the signal from below. Once when the assistant conductor waved a white handkerchief to give the electrician above the cue to illuminate the Grail, nothing happened. The stage remained shrouded in gloom, and the bewildered Amfortas held up a chalice that was visible only to himself and his immediate neighbors. What had happened? The electrician aloft had fallen asleep.

The stage officials try to insure their effects by various precautionary measures. Lightning, for example, is obtained by the use of a thin gauze drop on which is sewed a jagged line of canvas. An explosion of a photographer's flashlight bulb brings the jagged canvas line into momentary and brilliant relief. One bulb would be enough, but it might not go off. Five or six are usually set off. Before flashlight bulbs were developed, the stage lightning was produced by an explosion of a calcium compound.

The opera stage heads do not hesitate to use the latest ideas in props and illumination. They are not, of course, responsible for an old-fashioned scenic design. They would be happy to co-operate on the newest devices. The flowers in the garden scene of "Faust" used to be illuminated by little lights in the leaves. The effect was all right, but improvement was possible. With the new lighting equipment an ultra-violet ray is thrown on the flowers from above, giving them an eerier and more magical appearance.

Some things are worked in the same old way because the tried method has proved effective. The black bird of ill omen in "Götterdämmerung" is swung out on wires, presumably invisible, as is the flying spear in "Parsifal." Actually the wires are seen by persons down front. A striking effect, simply contrived, is the shooting of the apple in "William Tell." The boy is always placed near a tree trunk behind which a stage hand is hidden. As Tell shoots his arrow, somewhere into the wings, the apple is swiftly removed from the boy's head. Another apple falls to the floor in halves, while another arrow suddenly drops like a lever, the tip lodged in the tree, so that it looks as if it has come from Tell's bow.

The manner in which steam is used to make a vaporous curtain for the end of "Walküre" or a change of scenes in the last act of "Siegfried" has not changed much. Years ago the Metropolitan manufactured the steam in its own boilers. Now it is bought from the New York Steam Corporation and piped in from its lines underground, at a pressure of eighty pounds. There are little slots in the front of the stage, and these are opened before the beginning of the act in which the steam is required. A steam made from a chemical was used to provide a murky atmosphere for one scene in "The Man Without a Country." But singers object to this chemical compound. They complain that the odor and taste bother their voices, and its use is discouraged.

What of the stage workers themselves? They average

more than twenty years each at the Metropolitan. They have been exposed to enough of the feel and color of opera to have developed a deep affection for, or a violent antipathy to it. If they like the opera and its people, they have not become softies about it. They still wear the crusty shell of the typical stage worker.

They have witnessed the great events of operatic history as well as the minutiæ of temperament, trouble and dispute that never seep through the walls of the old theatre. Scratch a stage hand and you will discover a man with a collection of reminiscences. Most of them cheerfully share their information and experience. One or two tell you that they have a book in their systems but hardly ever get around to writing it.

There is the stage worker who has never lost his veneration for Caruso and Farrar, and another who recalls Jean de Reszke with emotion. They listen disdainfully to the new crop of leading singers, although they may have a kind word for an artist like Flagstad. It may be that they treasure a memento from Caruso. The tenor was an adroit caricaturist and he would make sketches of his friends among the stage staff while waiting for a cue. Philip Crispano, the chief property man, has never forgotten or forgiven the skunk who pilfered one of his most treasured memorabilia. Some weeks before he died Caruso drew, between acts, a large caricature of himself as Canio in "Pagliacci" on the drum which he used in that opera. Crispano clung to that drum as if it were a princely heirloom. Some time after Caruso died the thief cut the drumhead out of the instrument and carried away Crispano's priceless caricature.

Hero worship of the stars does not go down easily backstage. Old hands have less patience with airs than the manager himself, and they can better afford to show their distaste openly. On the other hand, a regular fellow is speedily recognized and treated not merely with respect but with hearty comradeship. Lawrence Tibbett is considered one of the boys by the backstage crew. He has a jest or a kind word for them, and he does not hesitate to play a practical joke on them.

In fact, the boys once decided to play one on him. It was a performance of Manuel de Falla's charming one-acter, "La Vida Breve," in which Tibbett played the role of a swashbuckling Spanish muleteer. In the course of the opera Tibbett had to smoke a long black cigar. He does not smoke at all off the stage, and it was arranged to have for him the mildest cigars obtainable. One night when the company was in Philadelphia for "La Vida Breve" Tibbett found that his cigar, which looked the same as those he had smoked at previous performances, had more of a tang. He did not like the taste of it but had to continue smoking it. He realized that it was becoming stronger and stronger, at least so it seemed to him. He felt a queasiness inside. He managed to stagger through the opera, and then he was ill. The boys had supplied him with a villainous stogie that looked innocent enough to a non-smoker.

Difficulties on the stage with props, sets and lights that embarrass an artist are generally accidental, although some have been diverting. There was the time that Richard Crooks seated himself on a sofa in a scene of "Traviata" to find that the thing did not support him. He sagged to the ground, his feet up. It was more like a scene from comic opera. And in a performance of "Manon Lescaut" in Montreal, where opera is not performed regularly, the prop men dug up what furniture they needed in various antique shops. They found an old chair, a beauty, and placed it down front for the prima donna, Frances Alda, to sit on while she sang an aria. Alda began her song, then seated herself. She discovered she had a competitor. From underneath the seat of the chair there emanated a tinkling tune. No one had discovered until this moment that the chair had a hidden music box which worked when sat upon.

The heads of the various departments of the stage crew are men who have been around as much as thirty years at the Metropolitan. They have helped to mount more than two hundred operas by as varied a group of composers as the world has produced. It would not be an exaggeration to call them among the most knowing in the theatre, but they would hate you if you did.

The technical director used to be the late Edward Siedle. Until he died about ten years ago he was the czar of the stage force. Now the executive authority for each department is given to its head. And each leader has shown an aptitude for triumphing over the physical limitations of the Metropolitan. Jacob Buchter, the chief electrician, has invented a variety of gadgets, and he worked out the major part of the design of the new electrical system. Inventiveness backstage seems to be a tradition at the opera house. Years ago when Conried was the manager he suggested the development of a movable floor for the orchestra pit. It was done, the first in the land perhaps. It is dropped as low as it will go in the Wagner operas, so that the singers will not be swamped by the mass of orchestral tone. It is raised all the way for the works of lighter texture such as Mozart and Puccini. The only trouble with this floor is that it vibrates, and the instrumentalists complain that the lights on the music stand shake, causing them to see blurred images of the music. A cynical stage hand observed that the musicians are always looking for excuses.

The electricians also developed an early public address system, still in operation, which makes it possible to communicate throughout the backstage area, from the basement to the loftiest flies, and during rehearsals, from the rear of the auditorium to any part of the stage.

The carpenters who construct the solid sets have built some massive outfits in their time. For the Metropolitan follows the tradition of most opera houses, save the rare progressive experimenter such as the Cologne Opera before Germany underwent Hitler's "gleichschaltung"; it prefers heavy, solid décors. The carpenters, under their boss William Warren, have even been asked to rebuild the floor of the stage. Last summer they did this job after the end of the spring season, receiving welcome off-season salaries. In 1911 when the stage was last rebuilt the carpenters were the artisans.

The boss of the scene gang is Fred Hosli, another back-stage veteran. Hosli is a man whose life in the opera house has left him with a glowing appreciation of its tradition. I have seen him—he is a bulky, solidly set citizen—shedding a tear on the day that he came to the pier to say good-by to Giulio Gatti-Casazza at the close of the latter's career at the Metropolitan. I have heard of Hosli knocking out an ob-streperous bird backstage with one punch.

Out of his work at the Metropolitan Hosli has developed an ingenious side line. He buys up the sets of Broadway shows and carts them off to a warehouse he has rented. Broadway flops can be had for the taking, and Hosli has an eye for a useful drop or for a solid set. He resells his equip-ment to other Broadway hopefuls, and the Metropolitan management has learned that it can buy sets from him, that are usable, with slight changes, for less than it costs to build them. In the spring season the mansion set in "The Man Without a Country" came from Hosli's warehouse, and so did one of the scenes in "Marouf."

Naturally you will rarely find a manager who has a kind word for his stage hands. Their union is powerful and not to be hoodwinked. Working conditions are strictly observed, and the management is kept to its word, be it in the payment of overtime or in the hiring of extra help. One thing the stage hand in the opera house or in any other theatre cannot be accused of: he does not prattle about Art.

XIV

AND OTHERS

AN OPERA house like the Metropolitan employs more than 750 persons during the season, from the general manager down through scrubwomen. This chapter is dedicated to the miscellaneous workers in the opera vineyard behind the scenes and in the theatre auditorium.

There are all sorts of odd jobs in an opera house and there are some you would expect. There are the house superintendent and his staff of ninety-seven porters, cleaners, watchmen, doormen and ushers; the wigmaker, with his four assistants; the costumer and his twenty-one workers. There is the staff of five for the Thirty-ninth Street office whose duties include operating the telephone call board, acting as reception clerks, handling mail and supplying information to callers regarding the length of operas, the curtain hour, the time of intermissions. There are the scholarly librarian and his assistant. There is an engineer department of six men who look after such things as the heating and ventilating systems. There are a scenic department, a call department, a paymaster, a transportation man, a baggage crew of seven, a publicity man. There is even one man whose job is to post bills; he puts up the three-sheets around the opera house and distributes the snakes—the long sheets with the week's operas and casts—to the hotels and ticket agencies.

2

Consider the job of the call department, operated by Jules Judels. He used to be the entire department; lately he has acquired an assistant, for he has to look after the supers as well. Judels has been with the Metropolitan for forty-seven years and he may be described with a variety of titles—master of rehearsal calls, master of supers, master of tours. He started life at the Metropolitan as a call boy backstage, then he became Maurice Grau's office boy. His career at the Metropolitan highlights the manner in which the opera house maintains a tradition of keeping people employed for a lifetime.

As master of rehearsal calls Judels's job is to notify every artist of his scheduled rehearsals and performances When the repertory has been fixed by the manager and his assistants, the musical secretary charts the rehearsal assignments in a large, specially designed notebook. As soon as the assignments are filled in—usually they are worked out at least two weeks in advance—the call department goes to work. Judels and his assistant leave nothing to chance. They send the artists a printed notice, they call them by phone, they remind them personally. Even the announcement of the week's bills that goes to the newspapers is sent to the home of the artists. And when the snakes come off the press, copies are dispatched to the singers.

Nevertheless, there are some who come late. In the Grau and Conried days, when the star was virtually the court of last resort, he could get away with anything. Gatti-Casazza began to make changes. He insisted that artists must arrive at rehearsals on time, and he gave to Judels the right to fine those who came late. Judels confesses that he never used it. He looked upon himself as a minor factotum, and he reasoned that it would only raise the devil if he slapped a fine on a major artist.

The call department learned to be tactful and subtle. He discovered that no artist came late for a rehearsal with Toscanini when that dynamic maestro was at the Metropolitan. Even the most careless singers managed to arrive in good season. If they arrived late once, they were treated to a sampling of Toscanini's indignation and they never came late a second time. Judels always omitted the name of the conductor on the rehearsal notice in those days. The artists figured that the electric maestro might be in command, and they took no chances. The trick is still employed. The conductor's name is not revealed in the notice, just to keep the singer guessing.

The call department has learned that you have to tell a singer not only when he rehearses but when he sings. There was a matinee performance of "Meistersinger" in Boston once when the Pogner, Robert Blass, did not turn up at curtain time. Frantic telephone calls were made, but Blass could not be found. Finally an assistant conductor undertook to sing a minor part, and the singer of the latter role assumed that of Pogner. At about 4 P.M., when "Meistersinger" was more than half finished, Blass sauntered up to the box-office window. Conscious of no wrongdoing, he greeted the box-office director gaily and asked for a favor.

"Can you spare a pair of tickets for me," he said, "for tonight's 'Meistersinger'?"

3

The librarian of the opera is a personage who seldom basks in the public limelight. At the Metropolitan he used to be a man who, even if he could have personal publicity, preferred the obscurity of his little office on the third floor of the opera house on the Thirty-ninth Street side. He was Lionel Mapleson, and he held the record for seniority of service. He was with the Metropolitan from 1889 until his death in December, 1937, and he taught his son to be a musician and to

And Others

follow in his footsteps. The younger Mapleson has a record of eighteen years of service.

The librarians have three rooms as their domain. Two of them are used, for the most part, for the storing of music. The third is both storeroom and office. This room used to be fragrant with the personality of its venerable occupant. The elder Mapleson was a sentimental man who retained, during the years of his American work, a love for his native England. He had hung on the walls of his office photos and letters of Britain's heroes of land and sea, Wellington and Nelson. The room overflowed with opera mementoes. Autographed photographs of the great singers of the Metropolitan's history stood in frames and were hung on the walls. He had assembled letters, autographs, writings that related to opera. Here was an operaphile in the completest sense of the word. A casual visitor to Mr. Mapleson's office could find material for hours of observation and study.

Before coming to the Metropolitan, Mapleson had been a violist under Hans Richter in London. His father and grandfather worked in the opera house, and his uncle was the famous Col. James Mapleson who ran the Academy of Music in New York as well as opera houses in England. In Lionel Mapleson's arsenal of musical memorabilia were some of his uncle's records. One was a copy of a contract with Adelina Patti with its requirement of $4000 a performance to be paid before the curtain went up, and a copy of a receipt signed by Patti. The pictures on the wall included Richter, Mahler, Verdi, Puccini, Gounod and dozens of others, all with a characteristic comment or a suitable inscription.

When he was younger, Lionel Mapleson toured with the opera company and made the earliest photographs of the stars—Melba, Lilli Lehmann, Plançon, de Reszke. He was perhaps the first man to record the voices of these artists. He set up his own apparatus on the paint bridge, long before recording became an industry. Once he placed his instrument in the prompter's box and made a recording of a scene by Melba. He played it back to her. It was the first time she heard her own voice when she was not making the sounds herself. Mr. Mapleson was asked by various companies to allow them to transmit his old records onto modern disks, but he declined, for fear that the original soft impressions would be spoiled. The old records sound as if the voices were being heard from the family circle.

The librarian's job is to keep the Metropolitan scores in order. If a conductor wishes to make new cuts in an opera, the librarian must see to it that all the orchestral parts are edited. If a conductor decides to restore a former cut, the librarian does the work of restoration. When a cut is made, the music is not blotted out. The librarian merely pastes a sheet of brown paper over the measures that are to be eliminated, and he removes this sheet if the passage is returned to the performance. The Wagner opera scores have gone through a multitude of changes of this kind, because cuts are made to suit the taste of each conductor. Fortunately, Artur Bodanzky has been in charge of this repertory for more than twenty years and there has been less tinkering in this period. Nevertheless, the Metropolitan presents the Wagner operas with cuts during the regular subscription performances and does the "Ring" without any excision in the matinee cycle. The librarian must have the parts in order for these performances.

The Metropolitan does not own an enormous library, as some might expect. It buys only those scores that are staples of the repertory. Novelties and revivals that remain in the active lists for a season or two are borrowed. It costs about $1000 to purchase a master score and the various orchestral parts, and the librarian must see to it that they remain in service as long as possible. The master score, known as the partitur, is the most expensive single item. It costs $100 to $150 alone. Some partiturs last longer than others because the opera is not performed as often; also some conductors are especially hard on the score. Bodanzky, for example, fairly fights the score, and in the depression days he was asked to relent. Even his partiturs now have a longer life, for he has toned down his violent page-turning. Recently a new master score of "Parsifal" was purchased; it was the first time it had to be replaced since Conried obtained it for the initial performance of "Parsifal" outside of Bayreuth. The "Parsifal" partitur had a long life comparatively because it is not given more than once or twice a season.

The librarian learns a great deal about the musicianship and idiosyncrasies of conductors. Mapleson remembered how Toscanini prepared for the world première of "The Girl of the Golden West." The maestro took the partitur home, and each morning, lying in bed, he studied it, holding it, as was his habit and necessity, several inches from the eyes. This procedure was followed for several mornings, and he was through. During rehearsals and performances Toscanini did not look at the score at all. And the scores themselves sometimes tell a story of their own. The partiturs that Toscanini used had notations in the maestro's hand, but they are now gone. The librarian has to keep all scores clean; he erases all signs and notations left by previous maestros. Which is a pity.

The librarian is privy to the secrets of conductors and composers. There was the time when a new opera was being prepared. The composer gave the conductor careful instructions on the interpretation, making notations throughout the partitur. After the composer had gone, the conductor ordered the librarian to erase all the instructions.

[225]

Opera: Front and Back

"Don't tell the composer about it," he said. "He knows little enough about composing, he knows less about interpreting his own score."

And Mapleson recalled how a real composer, Puccini, did not hesitate to change his score. When the Metropolitan gave his "Manon Lescaut" in Paris in 1910, Puccini realized that his second opera could be improved. He proceeded to rewrite the instrumentation.

4

Then there is the costume department, in the custody of Nicholas Lanzilotti, who bosses a crew of cutters, fitters and seamstresses on an upper floor of the Metropolitan Opera House. Lanzilotti came to the Metropolitan thirty-nine years ago when Maurice Grau was the manager. He left to work for Hammerstein and the Chicago Opera, returning some years later. He has made costumes for musical comedies as well as opera. He knows the styles of many epochs. He is in charge at the opera house of a stock of costumes that encompass every period from the era before Christ to modern times.

The Metropolitan has a store of about 7000 costumes, a complete set for all the standard operas. Although many of the principal artists own their own wardrobes, the company must have costumes for those who do not. Among the singers of the past, those who did not have their own costumes were the exception. Among contemporaries Flagstad, Melchior, Maison, Crooks, Martinelli, Ponselle, Grace Moore, Tibbett have their own. Lily Pons, Rethberg and Wettergren have some of their own and use the company's for other roles.

Here is a notion of how many costumes are needed for the standard operas. The Metropolitan has complete outfits for these works:

And Others

Opera	No. of Costumes
Aïda	420
Bohème	114
Carmen	300
Faust	181
Götterdämmerung	67
Juive	160
Lakmé	231
Lohengrin	241
Lucia di Lammermoor	187
Manon (Massenet)	228
Meistersinger	256
Pagliacci	122
Parsifal	110
Rigoletto	132
Siegfried	7
Tannhäuser	166
Tosca	130
Traviata	92
Tristan und Isolde	79
Trovatore	243
Walküre	15

In pre-depression days the costumes for one opera cost the Metropolitan a pretty penny. The most ever spent for one show was the $28,000 on "Turandot," and Jeritza, who sang the leading role, had her own costumes made at a cost of more than $1000. It was not unusual to devote more than $10,000 for a new opera or a revival in those days. About $12,000 was spent on Stravinsky's "Rossignol."

Nowadays several thousand dollars is a large appropriation for the costumes of an opera. And the costumer must resort to a great deal of doubling and faking. The costumes of "Turandot," which ran briefly, can be employed in "Traviata" and works of a similar period. Other costumes are transformed for operas of a comparable period. And there is but one costume for each leading role. At the Metropolitan one role may be taken by three or four singers in a season. If the artist has not her own outfit, the company's costume must be refitted and resewn, because no two singers have exactly the same build, and the variations in physique are sometimes extreme. No wonder some costumes have short lives, or do not look perfect.

The price of individual costumes has come down, but not as much as might be expected. It may still cost a soprano about $1000 to outfit herself for a role such as Manon, and a tenor about $800 for Des Grieux in the same opera. Rosa Ponselle spent about $1000 on her "Carmen" costumes. A reasonably elaborate costume for one scene may cost about $200 and may take two weeks to make.

Virtually all the costumes, whether for the singer or the company, are made at the opera house, under Mr. Lanzilotti's direction. He has found the process of preparing them fraught with many of the problems that confront the conductor, the stage director or the manager. Temperamental singers can give the costumer as much trouble as any other worker in the theatre. There are artists who know what they want in the way of costume and make their wishes clear. There are others who do not know what is right but are willing to rely on the costumer. There are the third and troublesome group who do not know what they want and do not think that any one else does. Mr. Lanzilotti has met them all.

The women can be more troublesome than the men. There are some who worry about their figures and demand that the costumer perform miracles of streamlining on a subject for which nature had other designs. One prima donna demands that her costumes be drawn in and tightened so that she will appear to be svelte. Another in Chicago insisted that the natural curves should not be disturbed by the cut of her clothes.

And Others

"They are," she told the costumer, "the best things I have."

The fine artist is easy to manage, by and large. Singers like Caruso, Bori, Tibbett, Flagstad are easy-going and understanding.

Preparing costumes for the opera poses special problems. The singer must have a certain amount of freedom at the throat, the diaphragm and chest, so that the production of the voice and breathing will not be disturbed. The necks of some artists swell when they sing, and their collars must be loose. Pinza's neck muscles bulge when he sings, and his costumes must be designed with this in mind.

Years ago the women and some men wore corsets. They were specially designed to give the artist the maximum amount of muscular freedom as well as shapeliness. Modern devices—readers of the advertisements in the newspapers and magazines need not be told what they are—have simplified this problem, or so the advertisements say.

It is important, of course, that the costumes of the principals in one cast should be of the same period and style. And the costumer and stage director must be watchful, where some artists have their costumes made outside the opera house, that there will be no deviations. Yet they occur. A disturbing incident took place once in a performance of "Mignon" some years ago. Bori had her costumes made outside the theatre, and Marion Talley's were made in the opera house. In a scene where both singers wore lavish gowns, Bori and Talley walked on in costumes that were—horror of horrors!—almost the same shade of pink.

Costumes have undergone many changes in the past decades. There may be a greater awareness of the difference between what constitutes a beautiful gown *per se* and what will be beautiful to an audience. Sembrich as Violetta wore a costume that had delicate handiwork. It was the kind of costume that Violetta might have worn in such an environment and that might have caused her friends to study it admiringly and enviously. But the craftsmanship of the intricate design was visible to perhaps the first few rows in the audience. Bori in the same scene of "Traviata" wore a gown that had brilliant, contrasting slashes of color. In a drawing room it might have seemed garish. On the stage it was better than Sembrich's, for its effect was inescapable in the rear rows of the family circle.

5

Wigs and make-up come under the supervision of Adolph Senz, known to the denizens of the opera house as Papa Senz. He has been connected with various operas for more than four decades and has been in and out of the Metropolitan for more than thirty years. His sons have followed him in his craft; one of them works with him at the Metropolitan and another with a moving-picture company.

Senz, like Lanzilotti, has his own shop, where he makes his wigs, and he has his workroom at the Metropolitan. He has a contract with the opera company under which he supplies his services and the use of his stock of some 12,000 wigs. Many of the principals have a complete set of wigs of their own for all their roles, but Senz and his staff look after them, keep them clean, brushed and dressed. The wigs for each role are kept in separate boxes for each artist, and once in a while, though rarely, wigs are placed in the wrong boxes; never, however, on the wrong head. The wigs for the rank and file of the company come from Senz's stock.

There is more to wigmaking than meets the eye. The problem of obtaining the hair is a difficult one. Human hair is generally employed, save for white wigs such as are used in

And Others

"Manon," and the hair for these is from the angora and the yak. Human hair comes from China, Bavaria and some of the Scandinavian countries. American hair is not to be had. Women wear it too short. But the peasant folk of some foreign countries do not cut their hair often, and when they do, they have fine, long strands to sell. Chinese hair is the cheapest, about $2 a pound, while Bavarian hair at its finest is worth about $2 an ounce. The hair of the angora and yak sells for about $8 a pound. The most expensive wig may cost about $200, although $250 was spent for Flagstad's Brünnhilde wig by Paramount for a filming of the Valkyr's cry in "The Big Broadcast of 1938."

The fitting of a wig poses the usual problems. The good points of a singer's face must be emphasized and the bad camouflaged. And sometimes the singer thinks wrongly that she knows what suits her best. Wigs must be fixed so that they will not interfere with the singing. When a beard is put on a male singer, he must stretch his mouth as wide as he can, so that the beard will not snap off when he opens his lips to sustain a high note. A few artists, if they are generously endowed by nature, use their own hair. Some do, in part. Bori, for example, had curls attached to her hair in "Traviata."

The wigmaker and make-up departments have reason to see the artist at the moment when he is under the greatest tension—before the rise of the first curtain. Some singers insist that a make-up man work swiftly and get out. Others like him to be leisurely. Some like him to chat. Others demand that he remain silent. The make-up man must know the preferences of each.

Through some quirk of nature the veteran singers are sometimes the most nervous before an initial curtain. They fidget and fret and fume. There are artists, of course, who are perfectly relaxed and at ease. They are pleasant for the make-up

[231]

man to work with. Some artists arrive at the opera house an hour and a half before curtain time and get done in good time. And some, not many, rush in at the last possible moment.

The average principal, of course, should and does put on his own make-up. But there are some who, after twenty years in the theatre, still require the services of the make-up staff, which makes a tour of every dressing room before the performance. The wigs go on first. Then the costumes, and attendants from the wardrobe department are available everywhere. The last person to look at an artist before he goes on is the make-up man. And sometimes, through no fault of his, a slip occurs. In a recent performance Martinelli, wearing metal armlets, swung his arm past Castagna's head and her wig, which she had attached herself, came off on the tenor's mailed fist.

6

The scenic department now consists of Joseph Novak and one assistant during the season. In prosperous times he had five helpers and he contends that he still needs them. He labors in his small studio on the fourth floor of the Metropolitan or on the paint bridge. He has been at the Metropolitan for many years. He does a variety of tasks on the mise-en-scène, but seldom receives public recognition. He repaints faded sets, working in season and out. He has a notebook with a complete record of every drop and border and when they were made or last retouched. He can tell you in an instant the condition of every décor that the company owns. Before the curtain goes up he will work on a set up to the last minute, perched on a ladder and equipped with a brush and palette.

With finances in a poor state, Novak has worked arduously to convert old sets into new. He will paint fresh backgrounds on old canvases. A sky can be turned into another scene, but it is difficult to do anything with an ornate, thickly painted drop. There have been occasions when Novak has painted sets that well-known artists have designed, sometimes he has made them, thanks to his experience, fit the stage where the artist did not.

Novak can work rapidly and persistently. He painted a huge drop for one opera in about forty-eight hours, working alone. He works even during performances, provided the lights on his paint bridge do not interfere with the illumination of the scene. If the stage is dark for a section of a matinee opera, the paint bridge lights must also be turned off. Then Novak stands by and listens. And he has heard them all, and has opinions on the capacities of several generations of artists.

Novak has also built models of sets and has designed important stage objects. He constructed the Holy Grail and the columns for "Parsifal." He made the well for "Juive," the panels for the ship and the Celtic ornaments in "Tristan." He painted the portrait of the Flying Dutchman who transfixes Senta in Wagner's early opera, and he was the artist of the painting that you see on Marcello's easel in "Bohème" and of the one on Mario Cavaradossi's in "Tosca."

7

The house staff is under the supervision of Hugh R. Brown, who is responsible for almost everything that happens in the opera house except the activity behind the footlights. He has been at the Metropolitan for twenty-seven years and he officiates at the center door of the Broadway entrance as the chief ticket taker. His staff is comprised of old-timers. The doormen, the ushers, the watchmen, the porters, even the cleaners and the scrubwomen, have been around from ten to thirty years. When Brown first came to the opera house he put everything on a schedule, but he found it was impracticable. You can't even clean the theatre on a regular schedule. It is a cardinal sin to dust during a rehearsal, and there is no regularity about the time that rehearsals take place.

The entire staff is not kept on during the off-season. Only a few porters and cleaners are retained, for the opera house must be kept shipshape. The expensive rugs are covered with camphor flakes, giving the auditorium the smell of a New England parlor in winter.

During the season Brown must remain vigilant at all hours of the day. For his staff, next to the box-office workers, have the greatest direct contact with the audience. The Metropolitan prides itself on making its patrons feel as if they were at home. The doormen get to know the regular customers by name, as do the ushers. The ushers and doormen are not paid large salaries. In fact, they are paid so little that the job would not be worth much if the men could not count on occasional tips. The ushers receive seventy-five cents a performance. They are, for the most part, men with outside jobs. One is a court functionary, another works in a brokerage office, a third in an accounting firm. They usher at the Metropolitan for a little extra money. They have also come to enjoy the passing show. They know the foibles of the regular customers, and even though they are not likely to admit it, they know a good deal about the opera and its traditions. I have heard ushers comment on singing, on the quality of the reeds in the orchestra, on the cost of a production.

The doormen have outside employment or are on the regular Metropolitan house staff. One old chap, who takes tickets on one side of the house, is a former semi-pro pitcher from a small Southern town. He found his arm going and he asked Hugh Brown one day whether he had a job for

brilliance and shrewdness. He had wit and gusto and urbanity. He loved the lyric theatre and knew its shortcomings. He understood also the implications of some of the things he had done in his time. There was the night when he sat with several old friends. He was feeling disgruntled and perhaps seeing things clearly. Suddenly he began to wring his hands violently, as if washing and purging them.

"When I think," he said, " of all the things I have done in the name of Art, like Pontius Pilate, I wash my hands of it, I wash my hands of it!"

XV

BIG BOSS

THE general manager's lot is not a happy one. Philosophers may sing of the troubles of a king, but they ought to look into those of the man who runs an opera company. The qualities required of the head of an opera house are business acumen, artistic sensibilities, discriminating taste, the tongues of angels and of scorpions, the hardihood of a lion tamer, personal charm and courtliness of manner, a command of languages, a knowledge of music and the instinct of a showman. Nor are these all. You could enumerate the calendar of human accomplishments and there would be only a few that the opera manager could not use to advantage. You could make out a case for the patience of the flagpole sitter, the trickery of the sword swallower, the ruthlessness of a dictator and the lung power of a hog caller. I do not know how the talent of the chap who can eat a barrel of oysters at one sitting would help, but careful research might unearth a moral even there.

Why men should willingly seek the job of running an opera house is, like trying to become President of the United States, one of those mysteries. At least a President is elected for a set term; even if he has to wear a hairshirt or be a tough guy, his tenure is for four years. Opera managers depend for their jobs on the whims of the board, the response of the public, the appeal of the singers and dozens of unpredictables. The reign of Giulio Gatti-Casazza, who held his post at the Metropolitan for twenty-seven years, is probably unparalleled in operatic annals. Although his gifts for the job were remarkable, the auspices had to be felicitous. The local hierarchy on his arrival read no such rosy prospect in the stars.

Where do opera managers come from? Usually from the ranks of the lyric theatre, from among the conductors, singers, régisseurs. On rare occasions a man is bred to the job, as was Gatti-Casazza, who attended the hard school of the provincial theatre, where he did his first overseeing as a lad of twenty-three. Sometimes a business man has been selected for the post; on occasion, a concert manager. Edward Ziegler, who has been assistant manager at the Metropolitan for twenty-one years and who chose not to become manager when Gatti left, was a music critic. There are men who have in their blood the desire to run opera companies, and they become impresarios, although they may not have done operatic work themselves. Oscar Hammerstein was perhaps the most audacious of American impresarios of this caliber. Europe, especially Italy, has always had impresarios, and save for one or two exceptions, they have always ended up broke.

Look at the current crop of opera managers. Edward Johnson was a tenor. Sir Thomas Beecham at Covent Garden in London is still a conductor. Jacques Rouché in Paris is a manufacturer. Paul Longone in Chicago was a personal representative of artists. Gaetano Merola in San Francisco is a conductor. John Forsell in Stockholm was a basso who sang for several seasons at the Metropolitan. Winifred Wagner at Bayreuth happens to be the daughter-in-law of the incomparable Richard.

Ordinary mortals may wonder why an accomplished conductor like Sir Thomas Beecham should seek the heartaches of directing a company, or why a good tenor like Edward Johnson should turn to management. One may say to Johnson as Clemenceau is supposed to have said to Paderewski when the latter deserted his career as a pianist to become Premier of Poland: "What a come-down!"

Nevertheless, men accept the task of administering opera companies. Some seek it, and some give the appearance of having a good time at it. There must be satisfactions to balance the sorrows. Otto Kahn once said of Giulio Gatti-Casazza that he could have been a successful executive of a large business and have earned five times his Metropolitan salary. The thought of working in another sphere never entered Gatti's head, save in his most despondent moments, and then not for long. Edward Johnson gives the impression of a man who savors his work, and you cannot dismiss him with the phrase, "Once a tenor, always a tenor." He is that rara avis, a person of profound sensibility and intelligence who happened to sing in the tenor range.

Working out the program for a long opera season must give a manager the same satisfaction as does, on a smaller scale, the solving of a jigsaw puzzle. Keeping a company of about a hundred singers, conductors and régisseurs contented is probably akin to running a successful menagerie. Obtaining an adequate budget from a board of directors may have its hidden attractions. And explaining casts and choice of operas to subscribers may have charms of its own. There must be something to the job. It couldn't be the salary alone. Or could it?

There are many ways of running an opera company. The best method is probably that involving careful preparation with an eye for every contingency. There are those who use the way of improvisation which may be more tumultuous but also more brilliant. There are some who combine both methods. The chances are that compromise is necessary at both extremes. The best-laid plans may come to grief because a set of germs have invaded an expensive throat; quick thinking may be needed to save the day. The finest improvisers may have to employ a little planning. An opera cannot be put together with the smoothness of a new automobile on the assembly line, nor can it come into being full grown like Minerva out of the head of Jupiter.

Oscar Hammerstein was a brilliant improviser. He played hunches at tremendous costs. He went to see Nellie Melba in London once to induce her to return to New York and to sing in his company. She asked a guarantee of ten performances at $3000 each—an enormous price in those days. Hammerstein did not consult a board of directors and he did not ponder the idea for months. He walked around the block, made up his mind, and signed Melba at once.

It was a bold move, and a successful one. For Melba's performances packed them in. But Hammerstein's hunches did not always pay dividends.

2

Giulio Gatti-Casazza brought more system to his job than any man who preceded him at the Metropolitan. He also brought rare personal qualities not given to many executives. His ways are worth examination, for his mark is still on America's ranking theatre. Edward Johnson has followed many of his ideas, as have managers of other lyric theatres.

Gatti held it as a cardinal principle that the manager of an opera company had to be both a business man and an artist. He felt that the manager must be both Don Quixote and Sancho Panza, cognizant of both the ideal and the practical at all times. He realized that opera was an art, but he insisted that it was also a business undertaking susceptible to the rules of such enterprises. From Giuseppe Verdi, greatest of Italian opera composers, he learned early in his career the meaning of box-office results. When Gatti was serving his initiate in the Teatro Communale of Ferrara, he produced one of Verdi's operas and wired the maestro, after the première, that the performance was successful. Verdi replied that it was more important to know what the opera would take in at the second and following performances. And it was Verdi, then in his eighty-fifth year, who gave Gatti his best-remembered advice when he assumed the post of manager of the Scala in Milan.

"Remember," Verdi counseled, "the theatre is meant to be full, not empty. Study most attentively the box-office."

Verdi also advised that the manager should not read the critics, for they seldom agreed and were almost never consistent. The only dependable reading matter, he affirmed, was the figures of ticket sales. Gatti followed the advice of the composer who knew how to be popular and artistic in the truest sense. But Gatti also learned that even this rule required compromises. He discovered that the howling of the critical pack could not be ignored. A bone had to be tossed to the wolves, sometimes an expensive bone. Once in a while the critics were right and the gesture of appeasement turned out to be profitable.

Gatti-Casazza collected a horde of detractors during his years at the Metropolitan. The most piercing note of the anvil chorus of dissent was the accusation that here was an Italian who saturated an American opera with a pungent Italian flavor. The accusers maintained, moreover, that Gatti was a man of tawdry taste, and that his productions represented his artistic credo.

But let us look at the record. When he was at the Scala in Milan this same Gatti-Casazza was excoriated by the inevitable chauvinists for his alien tastes. He had the temerity to begin his career there with Wagner's "Die Meistersinger." He introduced into Italy Strauss's "Salome" and Debussy's "Pelléas et Mélisande" when both these operas were young and cordially hated. He gave Wagner in profusion.

Big Boss

Upon his arrival in America he was the first Metropolitan manager, repeatedly and liberally, to produce native operas and to encourage American composers to write them. He ranged the seven seas for lyric works. He introduced to the Metropolitan such varied fare as Mussorgsky's "Boris Godunoff," Dukas's "Ariane et Barbe-Bleu," Gluck's "Armide," Humperdinck's "Königskinder," Smetana's "Bartered Bride." It is true that he did not put on Alban Berg's "Wozzek." But it was an instance where Sancho Panza prevailed.

The point is that Gatti himself is a man of culture. His selection of repertory did not represent his own tastes, but his conception of his duty to a cosmopolitan audience. I know that he himself had no use for the coloratura soprano nor for the vapid music that had generally been written for her. If he had run the Metropolitan to suit himself, he would not have bothered with this species of singer. But he knew that the public flocked to the theatre to hear a woman who could rove beyond high C easily and who could hit an E flat or an F above high C and hold it indefinitely. He always sought a capable coloratura for his company.

Gatti also clung to the belief that the "star system" was an abomination of the theatre. He contended that the stress should be on the ensemble and on the score, rather than on the individual. He often recounted how Toscanini and he, in the ardor of their youth, first came to the Scala in Milan determined to root out the vicious star system, and how they tried to wipe it out at the Metropolitan. They effected an improvement. In the days of Grau and Conried the star was omnipotent. The secondary singers were, in the term of the day, "cats and dogs." The chorus and ballet were small and the sets were rudimentary. The star had a voice even in the choice of repertory. Gatti never wearied of telling how he made up the week's repertory in the first days of his tenure. In his office were ranged before him the husband of one singer, the mother of a second and the manager of a third. All three had vigorous ideas. They sought to protect the rights of their charges. They tried to tell the manager how to manage. Gatti eliminated this practice. He established himself as the Boss, with a capital B. His authority was not to be questioned and he insisted on discipline. It took hard fighting to score this victory, for a clique of the biggest stars intrigued against him and went so far as to petition the board against him.

Gatti was a hard fighter who asked and gave no quarter once the war was declared. Having won the war, he established in the Metropolitan a smoothly functioning machine. He attempted to buck up the elements that had been neglected in the past. He hoped that the emphasis on the star would die out. What thanks did he get? The stars never waned. In his very last year it was a new star, Kirsten Flagstad, who packed them in. He admitted ruefully that there seemed to be no cure.

Another grievance was that Gatti had no business making and saving money at the Metropolitan. It was contended that a theatre of the pretensions of the Metropolitan should have lost money every year, lavishing more funds on productions and saving less for the future. This charge was not exactly fair. It was not Gatti who decided the financial policy of the organization. There was a board and there was no subsidy. If the opera was to continue, it had to do so on its own. Gatti's husbanding of resources justified itself in the end. When the dark days of the depression came he had a large reserve fund, reported to be more than a million, to tide the company over for several years.

This is not an apology for Gatti. He made mistakes.

Big Boss

There were operas that should have been produced that he did not undertake. There were singers who belonged at the Metropolitan whom he did not engage. There were other singers whom he brought to New York when they had passed their peak. He retained conductors who were, at best, second-rate. He produced novelties that should have died still-born.

Whatever was done in Gatti's regime had the stamp of professionalism. His belittlers condemned him. But since his departure, some of these have had a voice in the affairs of the Metropolitan, and their counsel has brought little of the amelioration they shouted for. There are some observers, in fact, who say that singers and productions are tolerated nowadays that never would have seen the light of day in the past, and that the taint of amateurism has left its mark on some portions of the repertory.

Gatti's failings were the concomitants of his virtues. He was a deliberate man. He never made a major decision without sleeping on it for a night. He liked to give himself time to reflect. If he took his time in bringing in new operas and new artists, he made fewer mistakes than most managers.

When action was necessary he could move rapidly. He discovered upon his arrival in America that Oscar Hammerstein had stolen a march on the Metropolitan. He had obtained the rights to a new repertory, including "Pelléas et Mélisande" and Charpentier's "Louise," and the services of a group of interesting artists like Mary Garden and Maurice Renaud. The Metropolitan could have had them first, but up to this time was not interested. Gatti learned of this mistake and proceeded to prevent another like it. He went to see Debussy and obtained the rights to any new opera he might write. He did as much with Charpentier.

Debussy was weighing three themes for operas: two were

[247]

Poe stories, "The Fall of the House of Usher" and "The Devil in the Belfry," and the third was "The Legend of Tristan." Gatti paid Debussy $2000 for the rights, but the composer never got around to writing the operas. Years later Gatti went to see Debussy in Paris when he heard that the French composer was considering writing a ballet. Gatti offered to buy the rights for this, but Debussy laughed.

"You have already made a poor bargain," he said. "I don't know if I shall ever write those operas. You shall have the ballet first, and you need pay nothing more."

Debussy never finished even the ballet. Charpentier did produce an opera, "Julien," and the Metropolitan presented its world première. But it was not another "Louise."

Gatti had the bearing of the natural aristocrat. What was an innate reserve was construed as pretentious aloofness such as is affected by certain movie stars. Gatti never mastered the English language, although he tried. He did learn enough to read easily—he could make out the tenor of a criticism as readily as any of his hypersensitive charges. If he did not talk English fluently, it was because he would not trust himself to speak in a tongue which he did not know accurately in all its nuances. He loathed inexactness and slovenliness. He did not move about in society, calling on the boxholders during a performance or allowing himself to be lionized in their homes. He had a deep aversion to these superficialities. He preferred an intimate circle of intelligent friends. In their company he was not tongue-tied or diffident. He conversed freely and wittily on a wide range of subjects.

"A manager," he was fond of saying, "should be judged by his productions, by what the audiences see and hear in the theatre. How would it help my productions if I were the best linguist in the world or if I became a social lion?"

When he spoke for publication, Gatti insisted on absolute accuracy, even if it took three languages to do it. I recall conversing with him in French and setting down his comments in English. When I submitted them to him for a final check, he had them translated for himself into Italian, and the changes were turned into English.

Gatti did not stretch the truth for the benefit of the newspapermen. If they came to him for verification of a story, he would tell them the truth, if he was able to. He was not, however, the man to spoil a good story. Occasionally he would respond laconically, "Ben trovato," meaning that the tale was well founded, or, perhaps, well invented to carry conviction. The interrogator could not tell by studying the large, impassive face whether Gatti was holding something back or was merely laughing inside.

In his dealings with the company Gatti used as few words as in his contacts with public and press. Yet, when his wrath was aroused, he could pour forth a torrent of abuse, always in Italian. I understand that his vocabulary was exceeded in luridness only by Toscanini's. There was a time when his outbursts caused his physician to warn him of the damage he might do his heart. His assistants were admonished that he must not be allowed to become wrought up. Because his Italian was most dependable as a vitriolic force, it was his compatriots who bore the brunt of his fine rages. How he could tear into them! Occasionally an assistant would enter his office during one of these grandiose bawlings-out to admonish Gatti about his health. Gatti would stop his harangue. He would shrug his shoulders, smile, say, "Va bene," and dismiss the miscreant.

Gatti could drive a hard bargain. A long line of singers will bear testimony to his shrewdness in making a deal. He could ring all the changes of dispute—from amicable persuasiveness to outraged abruptness. Artists knew his word was as good as his contract. Agreements were frequently made that were not put into writing until months later.

Managers in other theatres have resorted to guile to win the good will of their leading artists. Cleofonte Campanini in Chicago had a delightful trick at contract time. He kept a picture frame on his desk. Just before a prima donna entered his office to talk terms, he would insert her photograph in the frame. She was flattered by the place of honor the manager gave her. As soon as she left, her picture was removed and the photograph of the next victim was substituted.

Gatti did not need to rely on a trick of this kind. He could marshal impressive silences or a single word that would turn away displeasure. His absolute control of his forces was not an accident. He knew how to squelch temperament and skittishness.

He did not have to resort to force majeure to avenge himself for his previous indignities as did another opera manager who preceded him at La Scala. This manager, a little man named Corti, had suffered the trouble-making of Victor Maurel for a full season, biding his time and his temper because he needed the great French star's services. At the end of the season, however, Corti obtained revenge. He invited Maurel into his office, asked him to seat himself, then pounced on him like a ferocious beast on its prey. He clutched Maurel's throat with one hand—he was a strong little man— and with the other pummeled the baritone's head. Maurel was so surprised and battered that he offered little resistance. And when Corti let up and the bewildered Maurel made for the door, the little manager shouted at him, "Now, my dear Maurel, we are even!"

Gatti knew how to handle them all—fire-eaters and sulkers, extroverts and introverts, chatterers and silent ones. On one occasion a catty prima donna commented audibly on the plain features of a mezzo-soprano. "What an ugly face!" she said. The mezzo stormed out of the rehearsal and would not take the stage with the insulting prima donna and you could scarcely blame her. But the mezzo was the only one available for the role—the opera was Henry Hadley's "Cleopatra's Night"—because the other singer who knew it was ill. While the conductor tried to work out a scheme whereby the duet for the prima donna and mezzo could be eliminated, Gatti persuaded the offended singer to come to his office. He said he was sorry for the incident, especially regretful that the mezzo would not sing, because he had planned to let her do Azucena in "Trovatore" as her next role. The mezzo had always wanted to sing Azucena, considered it her best role. She calmed down.

"All we want you to do," Gatti continued, "is to sing the opening and closing phrases of the duet in 'Cleopatra's Night.' "

The soprano was indignant. "If I sing anything, I sing it all!"

Gatti developed a smooth machine, backstage and in the administrative offices. He commanded the loyalty of his staff, and repaid it by taking the responsibility when something went wrong and giving the credit to others when things went well. If some one perpetrated a bull, Gatti knew how to reprimand him, but so far as the public was concerned the management was to blame. Incidents that illustrated Gatti's capacity for handling his charges hardly ever came to light. They are worth telling.

There was the time when Chaliapin was a guest artist at the Metropolitan, preparing for a revival of "The Barber of Seville." Chaliapin, who was to do Don Basilio, was behaving with characteristic aplomb. He had no hesitation in telling his colleagues how to sing, act and conduct. During the general rehearsal the stage crew was setting up one of the new décors designed by Joseph Urban. Chaliapin took one of the stage hands by the arm and led him around the stage.

"This door," said the Russian basso with his air of undisputed authority, "should be where this window is. That window where that door is. That door where this window is. This, here. That, there."

The stage hand followed the masterful Chaliapin in bewilderment. The impact of Chaliapin's commanding gesture and speech had robbed him of his own power of invective. The rest of the company looked on in amusement.

Gatti rose from his seat in the auditorium where he had been watching the rehearsal. He walked slowly down the aisle and up the temporary stairway which connects the auditorium and the stage during rehearsals. His thumbs were under the armholes of his vest and his gait had a massive dignity. He approached Chaliapin and spoke quietly.

"Ecoutez, Feodor."

"Yes, dirretore."

"Is there anything," Gatti said, as he looked him in the eye, "in your contract about the scenery?"

On another occasion there was a dress rehearsal of "Dinorah." A dispute arose between Galli-Curci and Gigli, and presently they were shouting at each other. DeLuca was also in the cast and he tried to intervene, and in a moment he was one of the parties to the squabble. Serafin, in the orchestra pit, attempted to pacify them and he was drawn into the fight, which had now reached proportions that alarmed some of the stage people. While the rest of the company listened to the shrill disputants, and the goat that appears in "Dinorah" stood by munching a blade of grass, some one hurried off to summon the general manager.

Big Boss

Gatti entered on the stage with characteristic gait, the thumbs under the vest holes. He uttered no word. Galli-Curci reached him first and poured out her complaint. Gatti said nothing. Gigli took his turn and chattered away, telling his side of the story. Gatti listened, but said nothing. De-Luca told his version. Gatti said nothing. Serafin ended the post-mortems with an account of the quarrel as he regarded it. Gatti still said nothing.

He turned and walked toward the wings. He stopped beside the goat, patted the animal gently and spoke for the first and last time during that dispute.

"You are," he said to the goat, as he headed back to his office, "the only intelligent one on the stage."

3

Edward Johnson's methods vary, because his personality is different and because he was brought up in a different environment. He likes to speak. He is an excellent mixer. He has the enviable capacity of making every person whom he meets feel like a bosom friend. He prefers a full and open discussion to inscrutable silences.

He realized in his first season that he had a great deal to learn about his job and he was big enough to admit it freely and to lean heavily on the counsel of those who were experienced. That does not mean that he has no ideas of his own. The contrary is true. Johnson overflows with plans for the opera. He has ideas for the refurbishing of the repertory, the improvement of the company, the expansion of the season. But he is obliged to move slowly. He was lucky enough to come in when the curve of the economic cycle had turned up. Business was improving at the opera. But the budget was limited and changes could be made only in easy stages.

Johnson wanted, in his first season, an inventory of everything the company had in the way of costumes, sets, properties. He would have preferred to undertake it in advance of the season. But that would have cost extra money, which he could not afford to spend. He devised the scheme of asking each department head to survey comprehensively the equipment for each opera before it was put on. By the end of the season the inventory was complete.

The problems of the opera house are onerous. Johnson confesses as much. But he likes to struggle with them, and whatever happens, he does not let them get him down. His cheerfulness and enthusiasm are his shock absorbers. And he has one consolation: he no longer has the worries of a singer.

"I don't get up in the morning," he says, "wondering whether I'm all right. I can eat anything. I can drink anything. And if my throat acts up, let it act up. My livelihood is not involved."

His colleagues and his singers call him Eddie, and Johnson prefers it. Many of the people in the company were his comrades on the stage and he has an affectionate regard for them. He finds it difficult to be the employer with them. But new faces are coming in, persons whom Johnson himself employed, and with these artists he could more easily act the part of the boss if he chose to, but he doesn't.

Edward Johnson has an immense enthusiasm for his job, and he does not keep it a secret. He discusses a season's plans with animation, and when he talks about an impending revival he illustrates his point by singing snatches of the music in a remarkably well-preserved voice.

A capacity for making quick decisions would seem to be one of the requisites in the modern world of business, and Johnson has this quality. When Rosa Pauly made a sensational success in a concert version of Strauss's "Elektra" with the Philharmonic-Symphony Orchestra, Johnson engaged her and decided to put on "Elektra" for her. When the first opera of Gian-Carlo Menotti, the fresh, inventive, spirited "Amelia Goes to the Ball," was performed by the Curtis Institute and received with excitement, Johnson earmarked it for the Metropolitan.

Johnson will need his tact, curiosity and awareness of the contemporary scene as time goes on. A characteristic development of the past few years is the organization of a union for artists to which the singers belong. Johnson will have to deal with the Associated Actors and Artistes of America as well as with the unions of the instrumentalists, choristers and stage crew.

Even the limitations of the Metropolitan Opera stage do not depress Johnson. He has adjusted his plans to a long stay at the Broadway house. He knows that Otto Kahn told Gatti-Casazza in 1908 not to worry about the old house and to expect a new theatre in several years. He knows that Kahn said the same thing to Bodanzky on his arrival in 1915 when the latter criticized the shape of the orchestra pit. He remembers how Kahn's plan for a new theatre—Kahn had even obtained an option on a site in Fifty-seventh Street—was frustrated. The present manager is making the best of what he has. He has a scheme for the realization of the most urgently required improvement. He would like to have a huge tower built on the Seventh Avenue side of the opera house, and in the additional space he would have ample storage room. Thus the Metropolitan would not have to rent four storehouses in various parts of the town, and there would be a saving in the cost of moving the sets as well as an increase in their longevity.

Edward Johnson has brought a modern note into the business of running an opera house. But he can never forget that he was once a singer, on the other side of the fence. He hopes that as manager he is continuing his career as an artist.

[255]

XVI

BIGGER BOSS

TWO kinds of directors populate most opera boards: those who direct and those who lend their names to the enterprise and do nothing else about it. The majority fall into the latter category. A few into the former, but how important these few have been in the history of American opera!

The Abou ben Adhem was Otto H. Kahn. For more than a quarter of a century he lavished his time, his energy and his money on the Metropolitan Opera, not to mention his patronage of a hundred other undertakings in the arts. He was enamored of music, especially opera. He made the Metropolitan his principal avocation. His contribution to what might be termed the era of good feeling and prosperity in New York's opera was of tremendous significance, although it was not always widely recognized.

The relationship between Kahn and Gatti-Casazza during this period was perhaps the ideal working arrangement for management and the board. There were not too many cooks to spoil the broth. Kahn, by virtue of his ownership of a large majority of the stock of the Metropolitan Opera Company, was, in effect, the board. Meetings were called from time to time, but they were only for the record, mere formalities. Kahn had the power to make decisions, and he did not hesitate to assume it.

The modus operandi was simple. Gatti and his assistants worked out a program. Kahn approved it, and the management had authority to go ahead. If a problem arose it could be solved by a telephone call.

[256]

Bigger Boss

Kahn rarely made demands of the management, but he did make many suggestions. He was musical and intensely interested in the opera. He traveled a great deal and met a wide variety of people. He kept his eyes and ears open for new ideas and talent for his opera company. What could be more natural?

There was one occasion when Kahn forced Gatti to agree to do an opera which the latter considered unsuitable for the Metropolitan Opera stage, and, in the end, he did not have his way. The opera was Richard Strauss's "Ariadne." Kahn was fond of this score. When he was abroad he never missed an opportunity of hearing it. He suggested that the Metropolitan produce it, but Gatti contended that the New York stage and house were too large for the intimate opera. Finally Gatti submitted to Kahn's wishes.

The contract was signed, and several weeks later Strauss arrived for a visit in America. The composer sat in Kahn's box during a performance of "Rosenkavalier," and presently he began shaking his head. Before the evening was over, he informed Kahn that "Ariadne" was too small for the Metropolitan and that he would not consent to its performance.

On another occasion, after the American première of Berg's "Wozzek" in Philadelphia, Kahn returned to New York and paid Gatti a visit.

"We have made a mistake," he said. "We should have accepted the chance to do this opera. It is an exciting work."

Several weeks later the production was put on in New York for one performance. Kahn saw it and observed to Gatti at the end that he had been wrong.

"I agree with you," he said, "it does not hold the interest. I was bored this time."

When he was in New York, Kahn, despite his vast business and banking interests, was always on tap for the Metropolitan. He could be reached at his office if the problem was urgent. Sometimes he would ask Edward Ziegler, the assistant manager, to come down and see him at the day's end, and they would discuss the question in hand as they drove up to the Metropolitan. By the time they reached Gatti's office, Kahn would have a grasp of the problem and they would arrive at a solution in a few moments. Occasionally he would take Sunday lunch with Gatti. Or Ziegler would go for a walk with Kahn on Sunday mornings. When he was in Europe, Kahn would pay Gatti a visit, or Gatti would travel to see him. Conferences were easily arranged.

Kahn took a hand in the Metropolitan's affairs in Conried's time. Before Conried the Metropolitan season was a direct undertaking of the Metropolitan Opera and Real Estate Company. With Conried's arrival it was decided to form the Metropolitan Opera Company, the operating unit, and Kahn became a stockholder, associated with William K. Vanderbilt, at that time the majority stockholder. These two men supplied the sinews of war in the fight with Hammerstein; they brought Gatti to America, and they bought out Hammerstein and established the best part of his troupe as the Chicago-Philadelphia Opera. Kahn became so interested in the opera that whenever a block of stock in the Metropolitan Opera Company was placed on sale, he was usually the purchaser. At the time of his death he owned most of that company's stock. Today its value is small. It owns some costumes, properties and sets; nothing more.

The operating unit is now the Metropolitan Opera Association, a membership corporation. The board must vote on all major policies. Because it is difficult to convene a quorum —most of the directors have far-flung business interests and no time or inclination for the opera—a management committee has been formed to handle immediate problems.

Bigger Boss

The manager has a contract with the board, and all other contracts are made with him. The management now works out plans for a season, and the full board meets to approve or to suggest alterations, which are not infrequent these days. When the plan is finally approved, a budget is drawn up, which must have approval of the full board. The board makes changes in the budget, if it chooses. The management committee comes into operation when the program begins to be administered. Problems in the larger framework may be dispatched by the committee, and there are many such problems.

Conceding to the members of the management committee the best will in the world, not all its members know the opera and its problems as well as Kahn did. Nor do they possess his taste and experience. It takes a lifetime to learn about the ramifications of the lyric theatre.

If there are differences of opinion today, there were disputes even in the halcyon Kahn-Gatti days. The bitterest was over the Diaghileff ballet. Kahn invited the internationally famous Russian troupe to visit the United States and to appear under Metropolitan auspices. Gatti was against it. He went, in fact, to see Diaghileff in Paris, and spread a map of the United States before the Russian impresario. He pointed out the immense distances in this country and the hardships of touring here. Diaghileff was impressed. But the war was raging in Europe and he was pleased to find a large new sphere of activity for his ballet in America.

The first season went well. When Kahn renewed the invitation for another year, Gatti protested vigorously. One of the most violent disputes in twenty-five years of contact between the two men took place. And the ballet came back. This time the tour went badly and the deficit was about $300,000, which came out of the Metropolitan Opera reserve fund.

Opera: Front and Back

In the depression, when $300,000 would have been a god-send to the foundering Metropolitan, Gatti recalled the tour with bitterness and regret.

Otto H. Kahn never made public the extent of his expenditures on opera. But when he died several years ago it was estimated that he had spent somewhere between $1,000,000 and $2,000,000, most of it between 1906 and 1910, in the years when the Hammerstein-Metropolitan competition was under way and when the New Theatre gave the Metropolitan—in 1909–10—two theatres to manage instead of one. He also contributed to the support of other companies with various operatic purposes. New York probably never had a more open-handed patron of the lyric theatre.

It is possible that Samuel Insull lavished more funds on the Chicago Opera in the years before the crash. It was said that he spent as much as $500,000 each year, and Harold McCormick, before him, had been equally open-handed. In the season when Mary Garden was the general manager the deficit ran up to $900,000, with McCormick as the principal contributor.

Samuel Insull was a dominating figure in Chicago's opera. Singers who were associated with the company during his ascendancy assert that Insull really loved opera. He would recall at intimate dinner parties the time when, a poor struggling lad in London, he had sat often in the topmost gallery at Covent Garden to hear Adelina Patti. Nevertheless, it must have pleased him for other reasons to be in command of the opera which was Chicago's most exclusive undertaking, socially and culturally.

The artists who knew Insull say that he was a kindly, generous man in his contacts with them, whereas in his office he had the appearance of a man of granite. He developed the habit of coming to the theatre at about 3 P.M. each day. He would stay through rehearsals and he attended virtually all performances.

Whoever the general manager was, Insull was influential in working out a policy. He was responsible in large part for the assembling of one of the finest companies of singers in this or any land. It has been claimed that the Chicago company, just before the debacle in 1929, outshone the Metropolitan in many respects. Insull paid singers the highest prices in America and he made sure that his prize catches would not desert him for New York's theatre. The Metropolitan, then at the crest of its own prosperity, was not interested in engaging in a price war for artists. It had an enormous subscription, and although there were some who crabbed about the superiority of certain Chicago singers, the Metropolitan went about its business, serenely indifferent to complaints.

The dangers inherent in one-man support of an opera house were never better exemplified than when the Insull empire of utilities, holding companies and the experts alone know what other financial houses of cards came tumbling to earth. The Chicago Opera collapsed and closed. It was not until several years later that it was reopened, under much more modest financing, with Paul Longone as the director. Longone succeeded in bringing opera back to Chicago because he persuaded the bank which had come into ownership of the theatre that the tax of $125,000 could be eliminated by establishing an opera company as an educational institution.

When I say one-man support, I do not mean that Insull paid every last nickel of the deficit. There were others who contributed. But he was the ruling force. And he induced others, by moral and perhaps business suasion, to join him in his artistic enterprise.

In the early years that Harold McCormick and his wife,

Opera: Front and Back

Edith Rockefeller McCormick, dominated Chicago's opera, the general manager was Cleofonte Campanini, and his relation with the leading figure in the board was not unlike that of Gatti-Casazza and Kahn. The arrangement made for a minimum of friction and headaches. Old hands at opera management speak of those days in Chicago with dreamy looks in their eyes. The late Louis Eckstein was another generous supporter of opera—at Ravinia Park in Chicago—until the depression.

Members of a board of directors can be helpful and bothersome, if they begin to show an interest in opera. In a provincial Italian theatre there was once a physician who was elected to the board. He promptly devoted all his spare time to the opera. His hobby became the rehearsals. He did not miss any of them. One day he came to the manager with a bitter grievance.

"There has been a rehearsal," he complained, "and I have not been invited to it."

The manager was astonished. He had given orders that the good physician was to be invited to every rehearsal. He ordered that the stage manager be sent for.

"Was there a rehearsal to which you did not invite Signor the director?" he asked the stage manager.

"It was merely a rehearsal for sets. It was nothing."

The physician broke in. "Never mind what kind of rehearsal it was! Please notify me of every one. I shall decide whether it is nothing."

At the Scala in Milan, before the turn of the century, there was a genial, simple-minded soul on the board who knew what he liked and what was fashionable. He heard one day that the management was considering a performance of "Tristan und Isolde." He rushed to the manager to protest. His daughter, a pianist, had asserted that "Tristan" was impossible, and he wished to warn the manager that a serious mistake was about to be made. The manager promised to consider his advice. In the end it was decided to give "Siegfried," and when the director heard of this decision he was relieved.

"Bravo," he said, "that is much better. 'Siegfried' sounds like something fine."

"Siegfried" was produced in due time and the director came to visit the manager. He wore a sorrowful expression. He held forth on the impossibility of understanding "Siegfried" with its long-winded dialogues. It was hopeless.

"I never want to see that villainous 'Siegfried' again," the director said, as he turned to go. "I have made a grave mistake. Give your 'Tristan und Isolde.' It cannot be worse."

The Metropolitan has had, from time to time, directors who were actively concerned about the administration of the opera. Often the public knew little or nothing of their participation. For example, some persons have always believed that J. P. Morgan the elder, who was on the board of the Opera and Real Estate Company, was instrumental in giving the Metropolitan a dual management for two years. When Gatti-Casazza was engaged and the board was apprised of this engagement, it was Morgan who insisted that Andreas Dippel be given a place of authority, inasmuch as he was his candidate for the managership. In those days Morgan's word was law. Dippel became administrative manager, with powers almost equal to Gatti's, and he held his position for two years.

There are men today who devote a great deal of attention to the problems of the Metropolitan. Whatever one thinks of their ideas and the value of their influence, they give of their time and energy with the utmost sincerity. They like the opera and attend its performances regularly. The incumbent president and chairman of the board, Paul D. Cravath, has observed that his favorite opera is "Tristan und Isolde" because it sends chills up and down his spine. No matter. He is a constant attendant at the Metropolitan, occupying his accustomed seats down front on the aisle. He always brings a large party. He may be a conservative influence on the Metropolitan's procedure. There is no doubt that he responds to music.

The other members of the Metropolitan Opera management committee are directors who are generous of their counsel and time. They are Cornelius N. Bliss, who was especially active when the change in management took place and when the company was having its toughest sledding; Allen Wardwell, equally devoted; Lucrezia Bori, and John Erskine, who came into his position through his Juilliard connections.

The late Augustus D. Juilliard was one of the sincerest friends of opera. Every one knows of his will and the estate of about $14,000,000 which he bequeathed for the advancement of music in New York. In that will he observed that he wished the Metropolitan Opera to be assisted in whatever ways the trustees saw fit. He suggested aid in financing special productions. He stipulated that no profit must ensue to the company through any help given by the Foundation which was set up with his estate.

At the depths of the depression, when the Metropolitan was obliged to go to the country for aid, the wording of the Juilliard will became a source of contention. There were some who argued that it was the Juilliard Foundation's manifest duty to assist the Metropolitan. The matter came to a head when an interested citizen, William Matheus Sullivan, wrote an open letter which was published in the press, stating the reasons for his belief that the Juilliard Foundation should help and adding that he would take the matter to court. The next day it was announced that the Juilliard

Bigger Boss

Foundation had agreed, quite independently, to contribute $50,000 to the guarantee fund.

The next year the Foundation undertook to underwrite a sum of $150,000, in return for obtaining a voice in the management and for the establishment of a spring season to give young artists an opportunity to sing in opera. Whether the Juilliard influence has been beneficial or detrimental remains for time to show. A case can be made out for either side. I am not interested in entering this controversy. Besides, there are facts about Augustus Juilliard's connection with the Metropolitan which have not been widely known hitherto, and these are worth recounting.

Juilliard was one of those men who always asked questions. He could not seem to obtain enough information about opera. He would frequently chat with Gatti-Casazza and Ziegler. In these talks he was constantly in search of knowledge of the lyric theatre. He attended the opera regularly, and it is believed that he hastened his fatal illness by going to the Metropolitan on a stormy night when suffering from a cold.

One day Juilliard said to one of the officials of the opera: "What can I do for the Metropolitan?"

The official considered and hesitated for a moment. "We have storehouses scattered through the city. We could use one large one. As it is, our sets are not kept in the best way. They are difficult to move, and we must have a larger crew."

"Have you any definite ideas about what you need?" Juilliard asked.

"Yes. We need a building constructed like a shell running straight through from one street to another, with a roadway cutting through under the middle of the building like an enormous arcade. In this building we would have appropriate and clearly marked places for our equipment."

[265]

Opera: Front and Back

"Where would you like it?"

"Near the opera house."

Juilliard nodded. "We'll look into it," he said.

In a short time architects were commissioned to draw up plans for a new storehouse. And the main problem became one of finding a site. Juilliard himself undertook this task. He most painstakingly made a grand tour of the midtown section on the west side of New York. He began on Thirty-first Street at the Hudson River and drove up and down every single street of the West Side, up to the Forties, from the river to Seventh Avenue and back. He examined each of the properties and the sites they stood upon. He settled on a site running from Thirty-eighth through to Thirty-ninth Street near Tenth Avenue.

Juilliard did not stop at investigation. He ordered his real-estate agent to purchase properties with a frontage of 100 feet. He prevailed on H. C. Frick, a close friend, to join in the undertaking. All that remained was to start building.

Before actual construction could start, Juilliard died. The company was in Atlanta on tour when news of the death came through. It was a severe blow to the executives. For the storehouse was never built. Frick was not interested in carrying the project through himself. He had gone into the thing only because of his warm friendship for Juilliard, not because of any love of opera. The estate did not dispose of the property immediately, but the opera company could not find any one willing to go through with the plan.

The Metropolitan had lost a modern storehouse that becomes more of a necessity as the years go by, but it was also bereft of a friend who was ready and willing to spend large sums of money for its advancement.

XVII

DEAR PUBLIC

THE audience at the opera is a show in itself. If you are apathetic to the charms of music-drama but can savor the bearing, dress and behavior of your fellow man, the opera is worth your attention. You may come to scoff or to admire, but you cannot be wholly indifferent to the quality of this gathering. Here, congregated under one roof night after night, is one of the most heterogeneous audiences in the world. Here are the wealthiest people in the land and men and women who earn their daily bread by the sweat of the brow. I do not say that they rub shoulders; usually they do not. The family circle of the Metropolitan Opera House may be reached only through a side entrance and is virtually cut off from the rest of the theatre, while the boxholders who sit in conspicuous glory have even private anterooms.

But if, some time during the performance, you ramble around the opera house and climb up to the family circle, you can observe them all: the rich and the poor and the middle class; persons whose major claim to distinction is the names of their ancestors; men and women of achievement in politics, business, finance, science and the arts; the foreigners who have music in their blood and enough change in their pockets to buy a ticket; the visitors from every part of the land; the ordinary citizen of comfortable means who can afford to subscribe; and the ordinary citizen of microscopic means who can barely scrape together $1.50 for standing room.

The common denominator is that every one wishes to be

within the walls of the opera house. Some come because it is the thing to do and because they wish to circulate among the people who count socially. Others are patrons for the same reason that they vote the straight Republican ticket—because their fathers and forefathers did. Some attend because they like music. Others because they are curious to see in the flesh the gods and goddesses of the operatic stage.

There has been a great deal of talk in recent years regarding the need to make opera more democratic. These observations, which have come from people who should know, have been tantamount to an admission that opera has leaned heavily on limited elements of the public. There is no doubt of it. The initial impulse for the creation of a theatre like the Metropolitan Opera House was not to make the great lyric works available for a nation. The theatre came into being because a coterie of wealthy people wished to establish their rank and prestige as compared to those of another prosperous set at the Academy of Music. And the Academy had been created for reasons in which opera itself played only a part.

For opera has been in the last couple of centuries largely the diversion of the courts of Europe and of the socially elite. In America it has been a badge of culture. It has been, moreover, the province of the rich, like the Horse Show, the America's Cup yacht races and polo. If the opera has basked in a wider limelight than any other theatre in the land, it is because it has had the patronage of the people whose activities are generously chronicled. And if the beneficence of the great lyric theatre has been allowed to filter through to the average man, it is because a large house has galleries and because the galleries must also be filled with paying customers.

Opera, in other words, owes its existence at a theatre like the Metropolitan to the "best people." In recent years, when the depression depleted the treasury, the "best people" invited the little man to help support the Metropolitan. This was described as the first step in the process of democratization. Possibly it is. But the little man continues to sit in the upper reaches of the house or to stand. And once a week he can listen to the opera on the radio in the comfort of his own home.

Nevertheless, there is indisputable tradition and color in the opera audience. Where but at the Metropolitan could you find a parallel to the elderly lady who attended the opera regularly and invariably arrived late? She had to be helped to her seat by the usher, always when the auditorium was in darkness and the show was on. Her neighbors were always disturbed when she was being seated. Then in a high-pitched voice, loud enough for the conductor to hear down front, she would say to the usher: "Now, young man, you may bring me a catalogue!"

2

The opera audience, especially at the Metropolitan, may be divided roughly into three groups: the old guard, the devotees of opera and the transients. We will ignore here the obvious division into rich, poor and middle class, since it is a classification common to all pursuits. There is no strict line of demarcation between divisions of operagoers. A patron may be both a member of the old guard and a devotee of opera just as he may be both a transient and fond of music. It is unlikely, however, that he will be both a transient and a member of the old guard unless he has changed his residence and visits New York on rare occasions.

The old guard embraces most of the subscribers and the boxholders. In their ranks are the leaders of society whose photographs appear in the newspapers the day after the opening night. They are the people who summer in Newport, who winter in the fashionable Southern resorts, who travel abroad, whose names constantly appear in the pages devoted to the entertainments and doings of society. Not all of them, however, are celebrities to the society editors. Some are merely men and women of achievement in various fields of human activity. And some are comparatively unknown, well-to-do citizens who subscribe to the opera year in and year out.

Why do people subscribe? For any number of reasons. A good many, believe it or not, like opera. For some it is a habit. For others it is fashionable, socially correct. Some people go to the opera because it is one of the best resorts for formal dress. The Metropolitan Opera House and the Horse Show rank equally in this respect. The more showy days of the Bradley Martin ball or some other function of the Four Hundred disappeared even before the modern vision of a chicken in every pot and two cars in every garage.

The opera has become the center of new fashions in America. Display and study of fashion is an important by-product of Metropolitan Opera nights. You have but to stand in the Thirty-ninth Street foyer on an opening night and observe the style scouts recording what milady is wearing this year. The style scouts are ranged in a phalanx past which the dignitaries and their ladies—or, to put it more accurately, the ladies and their escorts—march in. The scouts make notes of the new styles, for couturiers have done their best for this occasion. New ideas in evening wear are copied immediately, and presently similar creations may be had at low cost, even at the popular-price emporia on Union Square.

The opera is one of the last remaining places in a city like New York where the foreigner can hear the music of his native land sung in his own language. Provided, that is, that the foreigner has remained a Frenchman, Italian or Prussian. If your foreigner is a Turk or a Scandinavian, he will not hear operas of his native land at all. And if he happens to be a Russian or a Bohemian, he will hear the opera in one of the four languages used—English, French, German or Italian. Nevertheless, it is true that the opera does draw on the foreign-language groups of the communities that would have some difficulty in assimilating a fast-moving Broadway play like "Room Service" with its topical jests.

Another reason adduced for the faithful opera subscriber is the personal touch that prevails in a theatre like the Metropolitan. It is a touch that the subscribers themselves make possible. Everything is done to give the patron the feeling that he is entering a familiar place, like his club. The attendants seldom change. They go on for years; a decade or more is standard for most ushers, box attendants, doormen. Old subscribers are known by name. There is a friendly atmosphere, that never—oh, never—descends to crass familiarity.

A subscriber may depend on his usher to be ready with his coat at the end of the opera. There was one gentleman who regularly delivered his cloakroom check to the man on the aisle before the last act. The usher was expected to have the coat—a heavy, fur-lined garment—ready for his eminence. It was a heavy coat, but the usher was always prepared. The subscriber, it is true, paid in handsome tips for this indulgence.

There are those who leave at a set hour, no matter what is happening on the stage. And the car must be ordered and waiting. An old lady must be helped up the aisle. An elderly gentleman is helped on with his coat. These things have become routine for subscriber and attendant.

To the regulars the operas are like old wine. They know when a sip will be most refreshing. They have a fair acquaintance with the operas which they hear year after year. They know when their favorite arias and concerted numbers turn up. They can go to the lounge for a smoke and a drink. Then they can return for their treasured selections. Some old subscribers seem to have none.

The management, the box-office in particular, must learn to know the whims of the subscribers. Earle R. Lewis, the Metropolitan Opera box-office treasurer, is especially adept at handling the patrons. For all important events he himself allocates the tickets. He and his staff must know the names of those who are nearsighted or hard of hearing and who must, therefore, be seated down front. Some subscribers have gone so far as to install Acousticon apparatus in their regular seats, and the Metropolitan has the mechanism connected to other seats scattered through the house for the benefit of the hard of hearing.

The box-office must know the identity of other subscribers who insist on seats in the front rows because they wish to have the full eighty-five feet of the aisle to walk down wearing their expensive furs and jewels. There are those who believe that the most satisfactory blend of orchestra and voices may be heard from rows T to W and they will take no other seats. Some have decided that the first rows in the balcony and dress circle are the best situated for hearing and will buy nothing else, even though they can afford the highest priced. Others refuse to occupy the front rows in the upper tiers of the theatre because the height makes them dizzy.

Even the private affairs of the old guard must be taken into account in the distribution of seats. If two ladies are feuding, the box-office must learn about it and keep them apart. One genial old soul chatters all through the opera and her neighbors invariably complain. She is a veteran subscriber, and she cannot be turned away. Yet her neighbors must be kept happy. It sometimes happens that the seats around her are not sold at all. There is another woman who is in the market for an upper tier box—and the Metropolitan must think twice before selling her one for the season. She is inclined to be noisy, and no one will occupy the adjoining boxes for long.

The parterre boxes are, of course, not available for sale by the management. The people who have the right to these boxes are the owners of the theatre through their holding of interests in the Metropolitan Opera and Real Estate Company. They may rent or sublet their locations. They may leave them empty or invite their friends to occupy them.

The boxholders are the traditional leaders of society. The semicircle of boxes has become known throughout the world as the Diamond Horseshoe. In former days, when the haut monde was more strictly exclusive, the occupants of the parterre boxes were the whole show. There is still a handful of dowagers who insist on their prerogatives, and some command the spotlight because of the prestige of their names, positions and demeanor. In the old days every one presumably knew the people who sat in the boxes. They even outweighed in importance the people who were behind the footlights.

Society does not seem to be what it was. The descendants of boxholders of other generations are either more informal or do not give a hang for opera. The careful observer can no longer set his watch by the arrival or departure of Mme. Grandedame. Her entrance in the past meant that it was 9 P.M. and the second act was about to begin. She left promptly at 10:30, with the fourth and perhaps the fifth acts unseen. There was an undeviating regularity about her habits. Her sons and daughters and grandchildren, however, often come at the beginning and leave at the end, or they think nothing at all of packing off some poor relations to the opera.

Opera: Front and Back

I knew an old society editor, now called to dwell among the shades of those whom he venerated on this earth, who inveighed in his last years against the shattering of Metropolitan traditions. He would go tramping along the corridors of the parterre floor on opening nights, sniffing at many people who passed for society and smiling benignantly only at the handful who, in his opinion, really belonged. He held forth constantly about the magnificence of the past. He looked down upon the mealiness of the present. He muckraked the genealogy of half the current boxholders, pointing out that this banker's father had been an ordinary miner, that industrialist had been a hayseed in his salad days, this grand lady was the upstart daughter of an immigrant. He was rigid in his rulings. The biggest names fell under his interdiction. And for his colleagues in the business of writing about society —the young whippersnappers who accepted appearances—he had the utmost contempt. He was a severer arbiter than Mrs. William Astor.

The old guard, in the sense that our society editor construed it, is going fast. But in the loose construction I choose to put upon it, meaning the veteran boxholders and subscribers, the old guard comprises a large section of the opera audience. In every city where there is an international opera season the community's leading elements turn out. At the Metropolitan, which is perhaps the oldest permanent theatre in America, this is especially true.

But outside of New York some names still connote the Diamond Horseshoe. When the American Legion was in convention in New York recently and used the Metropolitan Opera House for business meetings, the boys swiped only one memento from the opera—the nameplate from the door of the Vanderbilt box.

[274]

Dear Public

Let us make the acquaintance of some of the most devoted subscribers. There is the physician who takes the same stalls for every subscription in the week. His seats are in the front row because he is not only fond of opera but also because, being a 'cellist himself, he wishes to observe the instrumentalists at work. His tickets are kept in the office of a house official, and if he cannot come himself, he calls up the opera house, notifies the custodian of his tickets that he is sending some one else and his friends are led to his seats.

There is a woman who takes four seats in the middle of the orchestra for every performance during the season, and that includes benefits, Wagner cycles and special events. She has been a steady customer for decades. If she does not put in a bid for her regular seats as soon as subscription or sales are open, the tickets are held for her and she never fails the company. For some special events she takes as many as eight tickets. Naturally, she does not go to every opera herself. But she sees to it that her seats are invariably occupied. When the twentieth century was young, she used to drive up to the Metropolitan in a carriage; now she arrives in a Rolls.

Consider what this woman spends for opera each year at the Metropolitan. Before the depression tickets sold at $8.80 each and the season ran for twenty-four weeks. Her annual bill was almost $6000. Now the season runs for sixteen weeks and the top price is $7. With extras like the Wagner cycle, her bill is about $3500. What is most remarkable about this woman is that she does not arrogate to herself the right to criticize more than any other patron. In fact, she does not criticize at all and she never complains. She has seen her share of poor performances, but she takes the bad with the good philosophically. She may be described as the belle idéale of subscribers.

Opera: Front and Back

There are others like her, who have been faithful through the years. There are at least fifty persons who subscribe for every performance at the Metropolitan. Perhaps two hundred more are on the rolls of half of the subscriptions. And one hundred and fifty more subscribe to more than one performance each week. These people may be classified as the real opera lovers of the old guard. The operas are familiar to them, and the Big House on Broadway is the house of repeats. They do not complain or find fault. They know when a performance is under par, but they have heard so many great interpretations that they can afford to be indulgent. They love the opera house and its traditions. They even treasure their seats. Some families have occupied the same places since the theatre was opened in 1883. This is true in the upper parts of the house as well as in the orchestra. Of course, most of the boxes have been handed down from one generation to the next.

The old guard can take its opera as seriously as the next man. In the days when Toscanini was the leading Metropolitan conductor a lady emerged from a parterre box after a performance of "Tristan" and encountered a musician she knew. She spoke rapturously of Toscanini's "Tristan." The musician listened for a time and then suggested that he considered Anton Seidl's treatment of the Liebestod more accurate and more affecting than the Italian conductor's. The lady was indignant at the irreverence of the musician. She would not speak to him for years thereafter.

Here is a chart that shows the distribution of subscribers to the Metropolitan. The sale of single seats, while it used to be approximately in the same proportion, would now show a larger percentage from distant places. It is manifestly impossible to obtain an accurate checkup on individual purchasers.

Dear Public

The chart:

	Box, Orchestra and Orchestra Circle Per cent	Dress Circle Per cent	Balcony Per cent	Family Circle Per cent	Total Per cent
Manhattan	75.78	48.75	37.15	35.87	52.01
Bronx	0.19	3.33	4.29	7.61	3.73
Brooklyn	2.31	8.75	15.71	16.52	10.20
Westchester	3.46	3.75	5.35	6.30	4.73
Staten Island	.02	2.08	1.79	1.96	1.26
Long Island	3.65	6.67	9.64	7.61	6.47
New Jersey	6.9	17.92	20.0	20.22	15.21
Connecticut	2.88	1.25	2.86	1.30	2.13
Nearby N.Y. State	3.08	5.83	2.14	1.96	3.00
Others	1.73	1.67	1.07	.65	1.26
TOTAL	100	100	100	100	100

3

The greater part of the subscribers in the upper reaches of the house fall into the second group, that of the devotees. Their principal reason for coming to the Metropolitan is to hear the operas. Most of them do not dress, nor do they have their names or pictures printed in the papers. They may be interested in the passing show. Essentially, however, it is only a sideshow for them. They have an appetite for music and for singing. One of the stalwarts of this category was Tom McDermott, an iceman from Jersey City. For fifteen years he had a gallery seat in the center of row A for every performance—an annual cost of $1200. Until illness laid him low he never missed a show. When the company and public celebrated Scotti's twenty-fifth anniversary at the Metropolitan, Tom was invited to represent the gallery gods. A dress suit was hired and a speech was written for him. Tom was to appear on the stage with Mayor Walker and Otto Kahn. He learned that speech as thoroughly as the Lord's Prayer. But when Kahn introduced him, Tom had a severe attack of the jitters. He stepped forward, but his mouth remained shut in terror. Kahn had to read the speech for him.

The heroes of the second classification—some would call them the princes of music lovers—are the standees. Have you ever tried to remain on your feet for three and four hours in close quarters listening and watching intently? It is an ordeal that aboriginal chieftains could have employed in testing the courage and endurance of their young. Yet several hundred persons stand at the Metropolitan almost every night.

Each opera draws its own kind of standee. The Italian works bring out those who like to hear a tenor hit a high C. Some of the standees began attending the opera when Caruso was the great drawing card. They have learned to distinguish between good and bad singing; they can recognize a fine voice instantly. And they do not hesitate to display their enthusiasm. The ringing bravos and the loudest applause emanate from the standees, save when the claque is operating.

The Wagnerian standees are thoroughly informed. Frequently they are students. Just as frequently they are people with slim purses and good taste in music. They are the bravest of all. I have seen squads of them standing on line before the box-office from 6 P.M. to purchase standing room for "Tristan und Isolde." By 7:30 or 8 they enter the theatre to stand through a full four hours of music. Their attention seldom wavers. If there is a disposition in the audience to break in with applause during a scene, it is the standees who hiss the applauders into shame and silence. But when the opera is over, they stay on, throng to the front of the house,

Dear Public

and applaud their heroes and heroines for many minutes until the lights are turned out.

Certain singers have their own followings, and their appearance will bring out the faithful: Caruso, Farrar among the preceding generation; Jeritza in her time; Flagstad today.

The standees have their peculiarities. Some like to lean on the rail that runs around the orchestra circle. They have to appear earliest for these cherished locations. Other standees prefer standing with their backs against the wall. Some like to be at the rear of the auditorium, where they can absorb the entire stage picture. Others do not care about the sets, lighting or acting. They are interested in the music only, and they will crowd the standing space nearest the stage. Some of the standees weaken during a long performance and seat themselves on the floor, hearing but not seeing. Most of them take a siesta during intermissions by sitting on stairways or on the spot where they have been standing.

A person may go to the opera and stand through it once out of curiosity. He does not become a habitual standee unless the opera germ is in his blood.

Among the students, young and old, are the score readers. Especially during performances of the Wagner music-dramas they are to be found seated on the doorsteps, their scores in their hands, the pages illuminated by the faint light of a tiny lamp. But their interest never wavers; and they seldom look at the stage.

One of the most peculiar Wagner enthusiasts is the man who stands at the side of the Metropolitan balcony, beats time, waves his hands, nods—goes through the motions of directing. He must be a frustrated conductor.

4

The transients are the people who go to the opera once a year, once a decade or once in a lifetime. They may have heard the opera on the radio and have come to like it. They may have read about it and its people and wished to see for themselves. They may have social pretensions in their home towns and have come to feel that a visit to the Metropolitan is needful to their position.

The number of persons who come to the opera only occasionally has increased markedly in recent years. The explanation, according to the best guessers, is the radio. Millions have been listening to the Metropolitan every Saturday afternoon for the last five years. They can hear the music, but they feel that they have been privy to but half the experience of opera. They wish to see as well as hear the whole works.

It has been estimated that the solid foundation of operagoers consists of about 10,000 persons, who attend regularly. Another 40,000, it was reckoned several years ago, patronize at least one performance a season. The second figure is probably larger today.

The transients come from all over the world. Visitors to New York from every section of America look in on the Metropolitan, and there are records of Europeans who have visited these shores specifically for the opera which they believe to be on a higher level than it is in the capitals abroad.

5

The audience does not confine its applause or censure to the opera house. There are some who, like the grandstand managers in the sports world, set themselves up as advisers of the director. Edward Johnson and his colleagues receive a host of letters, which curse or approve everything from the repertory to the color of a prima donna's wigs. If "Pelléas et Mélisande" is not presented, some writers squawk. If it is, others do. Some complain because a certain singer has been engaged; others demand why he has not been engaged before. Some complain about too much Wagner; some contend that there is not enough. The manager can do no wrong; by the same token, he can do no right. It all depends on what letters he opens first in the morning mail.

Only one group can be depended upon to approve at all times. That is the claque. They approve for a stated fee. The pickings used to be pretty elegant in former days. But the current management at the Metropolitan has put its foot down on the claque. It announced, in fact, that the professional applauders had been excommunicated. The banishment was effective for a week or so. The claque is back, even if the management has no part in allowing it in.

Claquing used to be a remunerative business. The head of the claque was able to average $100 or more a week; a good deal more if the singers were "co-operative."

Arrangements for professional applauders were never made by the opera management, only by the singers. For young artists who were inexperienced in the ways of the lyric theatre the rates were as much as could be obtained. But veterans were not to be bilked.

Standard rates went something like this: An initial fee of about $25 for a guarantee of two curtain-calls and an additional $5 for every other bow. Thus the bill of an artist who was fond of curtain calls and who sang several times a week could run into money. The tariff was always elastic—whatever the traffic would bear.

Opera: Front and Back

The professional applauders had to gain admittance into the opera house. Leading singers have insisted in the past on receiving a small allotment of complimentary general admissions, good for standing room. For any given performance the leader of the claque sometimes had as many as fifty admissions, and it was whispered about that a nice profit was realized occasionally on a resale of some of these tickets, even at lower than box-office prices.

The first step, therefore, was to forbid the disposal of free general admissions to artists. There is nothing, of course, the management can do if the gentlemen of the callous palms are provided with the money to purchase tickets at the box-office. It is hoped that moral suasion will be effective.

The business of claquing was soundly organized. The leaders had a half-dozen henchmen who could be trusted. They had to be men who had the right equipment to be lieutenants. They were obliged to know the operas. Whether this education was accomplished during a claquer's apprenticeship or in the course of opera-going for pleasure did not matter. The first principle of good claquing was to know when to applaud.

With the free admissions a company of applauders was brought into the theatre. They were divided into squads with a lieutenant at the head of each. Each squad took positions in strategic sections of the house. The lieutenant gave the signal by beginning to applaud and the others did the rest.

Work was less arduous for the claque when the artists involved had large public followings. Then the chief function was to act as the fuse. The paying customers took care of the real outburst of enthusiasm.

The story goes that the late Enrico Caruso was never without a claque, although it was a certainty that the regular patrons would give him all the ovation an artist could want. Being a man of honor, Caruso would never ask for free admissions from the box-office. It was his practice to purchase the tickets for his contingent. It was said that his bill for tickets once ran to several hundred dollars.

On the other hand, there was another tenor, now gone from the Metropolitan, who scorned the use of the claque. He was able to manage without it, although it was rumored that once applause was deliberately generated before an aria was finished and the clinching high C delivered. The singer's difference with the claque was attributed to his native frugality.

"After all," observed one person who has known the claque for many decades, "you can't blame the singers, particularly those from abroad. They are accustomed to more emotional audiences. And to claques. Why, some theatres in Europe have special entrances for the claque."

Wherever the claque had its inception—it has been attributed to Italy, which cradled opera and great vocalists—it has been felt for many years that it had no place at the Metropolitan. Subscribers were frequently irritated by repeated applause that retarded the action of an opera. They resented —when the claquing was inexpert and obtrusive—being told when to applaud.

Veteran claquers, moreover, made bored operagoers. They would congregate in the corridors or on the stairways during stretches of music when their services were not required, as in the Wagner works, and talk loudly. Some of them had bad manners. There was one who never removed his hat, even in the auditorium.

Nor were the duties of these yeomen of the bravo confined to the Metropolitan Opera House. The same crews operated at the Hippodrome during its popular-priced summer opera. Of course, everything at the Hippodrome was on a more modest scale, and income was much smaller. But it was a little something in the off-season.

There are also the inevitable gate-crashers. An old house like the Metropolitan has many hidden passageways, and the shrewd babies know about them. The little-known exits are used for gate-crashing by men. The women storm the main lobbies. According to an old hand at the opera, the majority of crashers are women. It is easier for them. They wear evening clothes, and they have escorts, presumably, who carry the tickets. The trick is to mingle with a party and slip by the doorman before he has had a chance to count the tickets handed to him. One of the most persistent crashers at the Metropolitan is a woman of about sixty. She seems to be comfortably situated. Her clothes are always good and she has an extensive wardrobe. The doormen know her by this time, and she finds the going difficult. Nevertheless, she manages to gain admittance several times a season.

The Metropolitan staff must use caution in its apprehension of suspected gate-crashers. It has ancient subscribers who must be deposited in their seats by their servants. One woman is brought in from her car in a wheel-chair which the Metropolitan has had available for such emergencies for more than twenty years. Obviously, the caretakers of these old and feeble customers must be let into the house. Some gate-crashers know even this practice, and they try to make themselves one of these parties.

6

The audience at the opera—at least, a part of it—comes to regard even inanimate objects with a warmth of feeling that would not be possible in a theatre without a tradition. For example, when the old chairs were removed and luxurious new seats installed throughout the theatre, the company was deluged with requests for one, two or a dozen chairs. In several instances the request was for utility's sake. A church, a city home for aged poor, the headquarters of a mounted division of New York's police, a barn theatre in New Hampshire obtained large consignments for immediate use. But individual subscribers paid the shipping charges for one or two chairs to place in their homes in the country—or even in the city. Recently the floor of the stage at the Metropolitan was torn up and replaced by a new one. Again there were requests from habitués of the Metropolitan for pieces of the old floor to be kept as mementoes. One woman asked for a large chunk which she wished to turn into a picture frame. Her request was accompanied by a check for $50.

Aside from an occasional demonstration, such as the audience put on for the young Tibbett in "Falstaff" or for Jeritza when she sang "Vissi d'Arte" in "Tosca" lying prone, the Metropolitan gatherings observe a general decorum. These audiences are typical of American assemblages in opera houses and theatres. They are typical of the Anglo-Saxon audience. Applause may be prolonged, but it rarely becomes strident. Disapproval is almost never displayed by catcalls or hisses.

Compare the behavior of audiences in other lands, especially the Latin countries. When "Pelléas" was first performed in Milan, the audience groaned in the scene of the subterranean vaults and then gave vent to a collective sigh of relief when the scene changed to the daylight. At the première of "Madama Butterfly" the Italians were displeased and they raised the rafters with their shouts of disapproval.

New York endured for years without much complaint a certain tenor who sounded often as if he were strangling when he was purportedly singing. He sang just once in Barcelona. In the second act he entered in a crucial scene, and as he looked about him on death and destruction with danger staring him in the face, he had to sing twice, "What shall I do?" Some one in the gallery made a suggestion. He shouted, "Kill yourself!" Others took up the cry, and during the ten minutes that remained in the act there was undiminished hooting.

7

For information that may highlight the character of the opera audience let us go to the two concessionnaires at the Metropolitan: the caterer and the libretto vendor. The man who presided over the refreshment foyer used to be Emil Katz, now replaced by Sherry's. Katz knew the operagoers almost as well as did the officials of the company. He was a smiling, friendly, amusing host, but the Prohibition era robbed him of some of his cheerfulness, not to mention a good part of his business. Even in those days, however, he could lead a friend into a rear chamber and provide him with fortification for the ordeal of the lyric drama.

Now that strong liquors and wines and beers are sanctioned by the law of the land, the opera bar finds that Scotch and soda is the most popular drink, accounting for 80 per cent of the liquor trade. Next in order are brandies, cordials, and cocktails. If you can tell something about a man's social environment from what he drinks, the fact that beer trails badly at the opera bar should be instructive.

Monday nights are the best for the bar. The fashionable audience of the week spends most for drinks. Saturday nights, when seats sell at popular prices, are the weakest; obviously the audience has less money for beverages. The night is more important than the opera, but "Tristan und Isolde" means

Dear Public

brisk trade at any time nowadays because it draws smart, capacity audiences. Matinee performances bring a demand for sandwiches, hot dishes and coffee, and a lively sale of soft drinks. Women outnumber the men at the afternoon shows.

Charles Allen, who is in charge of the libretto concession for Fred Rullmann, Inc., reports that sales are weakest on Monday nights. Either the audience knows the operas or does not give a hang. The Saturday matinees, which draw out-of-town persons who are fond of opera, produce the most numerous customers. The standard operas are the best investment. They sell and sell through the years. Occasionally a new opera is a hit and does well, but a novelty or revival that receives two or three performances is a disaster for the libretto seller. Special occasions help. When a train brought 1500 people from Scranton to hear a native boy make his debut, the librettos for "Pagliacci," which usually sell poorly, were in heavy demand.

Salesmen are posted in various parts of the main corridor before the opera and there is a table near the box-office window at all times during the season, even when the show is not on. But most of the sales are made during the intermission. Apparently the operagoer who has calculated that he needs no assistance finds befuddlement creeping upon him, and he rushes for help as soon as the curtain goes down for the first pause.

The opera assemblage may be distinctive in many ways, but it has the failings that all audiences are heir to. People who are habitually reserved will quarrel with their neighbors because an elaborate headdress or tiara obscures the view. Indignant seatholders will complain aloud about towering headgears. Regular patrons will be insulted if the usher asks for their stubs and offers to lead them to their seats.

Opera: Front and Back

No, they can find their own way. When they land in the wrong seats and the rightful owners appear, the intruders will get sore. And when latecomers sail in during the middle of an act and swish down to the front rows, disturbing their neighbors and sometimes the conductor and the singers, neighbors and artists will be wrathful.

American operagoers have innocent ways of making things lively for the artist, even if they are not given to shouting as are Latin audiences. My favorite is the story of the lady who wrote a fan letter to Richard Bonelli, himself a baritone, asking him to use his good offices to obtain for her an autographed photograph of Lawrence Tibbett.

XVIII

BEHIND THE BARS

THE box-office is the clearing house of opinion for the greater part of the paying public. Some people complain or praise directly to the manager by letter, telephone or word of mouth. Most customers choose the box-office attendants as their victims. Here at barred windows are the people to whom good money is paid, and if there is a grievance, the box-office hears about it. I suppose that as much is true for every theatre. It seems to prevail at the opera house in an aggravated form. It may be because tickets come higher or because an opera house is usually an institution doing business at the same spot for decades and not for a season.

The Metropolitan, for example, cannot afford to be snooty when it has a hit like "Tristan und Isolde" with Flagstad, Melchior and the rest. There will be other seasons and other "Tristans" with artists who are not the vogue. There will be, in fact, other operas with lesser figures in the leading roles. You cannot run a season on one smash production. And the good-will of the public must be retained. As in most businesses the customer is never wrong. Well, hardly ever.

Visit the box-office for a day and observe the passing parade. Listen carefully, for the customer's comments are often worthy of being enshrined among the memorable sayings of history.

There are always charges of misrepresentation. When the Manhattan Opera House—which had been Oscar Hammerstein's stamping ground—was no longer used for opera, it was turned at one time into a wrestling arena. During this period a man approached the box-office attendant at the Metropolitan Opera House at the end of the second act of a long Wagner opera. He brandished a long finger and yelled wrathfully,

"I've been sitting in there for two hours," he shouted. "When the hell does the wrestling begin?"

Occasionally operas have to be shifted at the last minute because a number of principals have been stricken with colds or other ailments. At such times large notices are posted at all the entrances and in the main foyers notifying the public of the change. Inserts, moreover, are printed and placed in every program. One night "Norma" was the bill and it had to be replaced at short notice by "Faust." At the end of the first act an irate customer stormed the box-office window.

"You can't put anything over on me!" he cried. "This is not 'Norma'!"

Some patrons resort to violence when their desire to get certain locations is frustrated. A woman was unable to obtain the tickets she wanted for a certain show. She argued with the man at the window and would not take his word that the tickets she wanted were gone. She began to scold the poor fellow. Then, in an access of rage, she stuck her fist through the window and punched the surprised attendant squarely on the nose.

That was not the end of the incident. Behind this woman stood another lady who was an old customer and knew every one in the box-office. She came to the rescue and proceeded to tell the woman with the flying fist what she thought of her. That was a real show.

One customer can tell another where to get off, a thing the box-office would not dare to do. At a special presentation one evening the theatre was sold out. The performance was a benefit and the prices had been jacked up considerably, even for the standing-room tickets. One fellow who seemed determined to obtain admittance kept approaching the box-office and asking what he could buy for $1. The attendant patiently explained that there were no seats available at that price. Each time the prospective purchaser shook his head sorrowfully, went to the end of the line and when his turn came at the head of it, he asked the same question. For the fourth time he inquired, "What can I get for $1?"

Another customer, waiting impatiently behind him, shouted, "Try an Ingersoll!"

It may be that a long siege at the box-office window—any box-office window—tires people and causes them to say things they do not mean. One evening a lady asked eagerly: "Have you got three standing room together?"

People come to the box-office window not only to purchase tickets but to seek information about their favorite artists. When Giovanni Martinelli made his first airplane flight some time ago, the press publicized his fears of the ordeal. The next day several persons appeared at the box-office to find out whether Martinelli had made his flight safely.

The pretensions of the showy element among subscribers are sometimes evinced at the box-office window. A wealthy woman who subscribed for parquet chairs called for her tickets one day. There was a long line of subscribers behind her. She explained that she had lost her receipt and that she could not find the canceled checks for the tickets. The attendant said that he could not hand over the tickets unless she could show proof that they were hers. The woman did not seem perturbed. She snapped her fingers and said, in a tone loud enough for every one in the line to hear her, "Who cares for $500? Thank God, I'm wealthy." And she flounced off.

Opera: Front and Back

The box-office acts as a lost-and-found department, and the usual scarves, gloves, spectacle cases and purses are held for their claimants who call for them in person or telephone about them. A woman phoned one day to report that she had found a glove that fitted her perfectly. She inquired whether the other had been picked up, because she would like to have a pair. Another woman appeared one day to ask whether she could examine the collection of unclaimed eyeglasses. Had she lost a pair? Not at all; she thought she could use an extra.

The most touching claimant—and the happiest when her quest was successful—was a woman who called up and said she had a confidential question to ask and could she trust the person on the other end of the phone. The box-office attendant said she could.

"Well," said the voice, hesitantly, "did you find a set of teeth? Mine hurt me last night, and I took them out and placed them on my lap. I forgot about them until I got home. They must have slipped off."

To the box-office comes a host of appeals and recriminations by mail and by telephone. Some are homely and touching; some are indignant or threatening. The box-office tries to answer them all, except the anonymous missives, and in the course of its duty it performs the function of information clerk, fashion adviser, purveyor of heart balm and instructor in the English language.

A foreign voice, speaking on the telephone one morning, inquired, "What is this family cheerkle? Does it mean you can take your family on one ticket?"

A correspondent is about to fulfil the greatest ambition of his life, going to the opera, and wants to know "the correct attire for a lady and gentleman in orchestra seats." The box-office will advise him to get in touch with a fashion editor or

Behind the Bars

it may take the trouble to outline in detail what the well-dressed man and woman wear at the opera. In any event, the inquirer is not left in the dark.

Another correspondent asks: "Could I have your permission to bring a six-year-old child to the performance of 'Hansel and Gretel'? She would sit on my lap and not inconvenience any one, as I have the aisle seat. It is not possible to send this child alone, and I know the other seats in that row are all occupied." The answer, unhappily, is No. But the box-office cannot be hard-hearted about it and must reply with a careful, sympathetic letter, while insisting on one seat, one listener.

The box-office is often asked to co-operate on sentimental occasions. It has become in recent years a practice to give seats to the opera as presents for Christmas, birthdays and anniversaries. The Metropolitan has met this trend by preparing gift coupons which the givers may purchase and send to the receivers. The coupons permit the holder to obtain tickets for any regular performance.

A lady wrote a letter to the box-office enclosing a dollar bill. She explained that a pair of tickets had been reserved in a certain name. They were $3 each, and she had heard that tickets could be obtained further front for $3.50 apiece. "The tickets," she informed the box-office, "are for my young niece and nephew who will spend the week-end in New York and have never been inside of the Metropolitan Opera House. I trust that you will do the best you can for these young people who are celebrating a wedding anniversary." Then a postscript: "If there are no better seats available leave the money in the envelope; they can use it otherwise."

The letter was ultimately filed away with a notation at its head, indicating that the box-office had followed instructions. The notation read: "Returned $1 in envelope."

Opera: Front and Back

Some prospective patrons justify their request for the best locations by telling the box-office of their acquaintance with the stars of the past or present. One woman once met Geraldine Farrar in a mountain resort. Another writer knows the father of a young American singer. A third lives in the same town as the cousin of the wife of a young American singer.

Among the most touching letters are requests for reservations of low-priced seats from persons who have been hoping to see an opera for years and are, at last, about to realize the dream of a lifetime. Here is one that is typical:

"Years ago—I am now fifty—when I was but five years old, my mother taught me stories of the operas. I can still see her running her hands over the keys and telling me stories of the arias. Years passed and I married. About all we accumulated was babies—babies and books. There was never money for the opera. Nonetheless my love for it was as keen —yet the opportunity never came to give my children the joy of hearing opera. For a short time my daughter and I are in New York. This is all I can spare for opera—so will some of you be nice enough to see that we get two good seats for this money? Remember, it is my daughter's first opera. I don't want her to miss a trick. Will you help to make it as lovely as possible?"

Another woman, writing in the same spirit, informs the box-office that she has heard the opera on the air "to the rhythm of a Dover eggbeater in my hand." Now at last she wants "to see and hear for myself, separated from that culinary implement." She wants the best tickets available "from $2 if you start that low, up to $5, which is my limit, and that a squeeze that would make Culbertson ashamed of himself."

Then there are those who have realized their ambition to visit the opera and report their impressions to the box-office.

Behind the Bars

They write ecstatic letters. Some complain. A group of girls came down from a Connecticut village one night for a performance of "Lakmé." As luck would have it, the performance was poor. It was one of those nights when the soprano cannot sing on pitch, when the tenor seems to be strangling, when even the sure-fire first-act duet of the soprano and mezzo does not come off. Such performances, unhappily, occur. The girls informed the box-office that their illusions were shattered.

Persons who have never been to the Metropolitan and happen to buy the worst side seats frequently have dissatisfied comments to air, to wit, the following note:

"All my life I've wanted to see an opera, so after skimping to get a two-dollar ticket, they give me a seat from which I couldn't even see the stage. This I don't think is fair. Seats such as these should not be sold. After all my anticipation, I left without seeing the one thing I had hoped to see for so long. I had always thought that any one connected with the opera was beyond reproach, but this has shattered my belief. I scarcely expect that the mere desire for money would cause you to sell such seats."

All sorts of explanations come to the box-office with reservations. Two students at Yale want a pair for "Pagliacci" but they must know in a hurry whether they will have them because "this will be our first day of vacation and we are going to hitch-hike to the city." A couple wishes to come down from a Canadian metropolis for the opera's opening night and communicates for reservations, adding "We are traveling light and will have only one day in New York. We will not be able to take seats in which evening dress is obligatory."

There are the cautious purchasers who want to be certain that their reservations will not get into the wrong hands.

Opera: Front and Back

One man sent the box-office half of his calling card, cut in a zigzag line. He explained that he wished the section of the card enclosed with his tickets.

"When calling for them," he observed, "I will present the other half. This may prevent any one else, who possibly may know of my reservation, from calling for them."

Is it germane to add that this letter came from New England?

Some people expect the opera box-office to act as purchasing agents for them. It is not uncommon for requests to arrive, asking the box-office to reserve tickets for another good show in town, if the opera is sold out. Others ask for recommendations for other theatres.

There are the usual quota of letters that seem to come from crackpots. One person, attempting to reserve a single ticket for a matinee, informs the box-office that "I am white, a lady. Also I am a musician—'cello, voice. I am 52." The box-office attendant may well wonder whether this customer is also looking for a match-making bureau.

2

Some letters come in the form of poems, and some are so irate that they exhibit a majestic indifference to the rules of grammar. The most indignant complaints come from customers who have been victimized by the curbstone speculators who in prosperous times congest the sidewalks in front of opera houses. The speculators sometimes have tickets when the box-office has not and sell them at whatever price the traffic will bear. If the production is not popular and there is no large demand for it, the speculators will even undersell the box-office. When the opera is a favorite the speculators reap a harvest. They sell tickets to unsuspecting customers at double the tariff, telling the purchasers that they are center seats when they are actually on the side. And the box-office may be bawled out by these purchasers.

The Metropolitan Opera has always been hounded by a variety of speculators, from the large-scale operator who occupies an office nearby to the sidewalk sharp. Prosperous times bring them out in large numbers. When Caruso was the dominant operatic figure, speculators did a land-office business on the nights—two each week—that the great tenor sang. In the boom days of the late Twenties, also, business was excellent, since going to the opera was the thing to do and money was easy. Now with the resurgence of the German operas because of the advent of Flagstad and her gifted colleagues, the speculators are once more on the increase.

The officials of the Metropolitan box-office, from Earle R. Lewis, the chief, down to his lowliest helper, have occasionally been offered tidy sums as bribes to give the speculator a little hand. One operator offered the box-office staff a rake-off of $1.50 for every ticket that would be delivered to him for the world première of Puccini's opera, "The Girl of the Golden West," which had Caruso and Emmy Destinn in the leading roles. He would have sold them from $3 to $25 above the marked price and would have made perhaps $5000 from the transaction.

Since bribes were turned down indignantly, the speculators resorted to other methods of obtaining a sufficient supply of tickets. They knew that they themselves were known to the box-office and their job was to find some persons to act as bona-fide purchasers. The box-office cannot stop every customer and ask for his credentials. It must sell its tickets to those who ask for them. It can draw the line only when the offender is known beyond a possible, probable shadow of doubt.

Opera: Front and Back

A favorite practice of the speculators was to go down to the Mills Hotel on the Bowery and bring up a dozen of its residents. The boys were given $20 bills and were told to stand in line and to purchase as many tickets as they could for the money—two in the orchestra, four in the dress circle, six in the balcony or eight in the family circle. For their troubles they received an average of 50 cents for every ticket they succeeded in purchasing. It was a satisfactory scheme for every one but the Metropolitan Opera Company and its genuine customers. It worked nicely until one day Lewis devised a trick to counteract it.

A large line had formed in the lobby before the box-office window, and the attendants thought they recognized a platoon of Mills Hotel worthies. They barred the doors that opened on Broadway, where the speculators waited for their fronts. An attendant announced that all tickets were sold and requested the persons on line to follow him. He led them into the opera house, down the corridors and allowed them to leave through a Fortieth Street door. This was a glorious opportunity for the gentlemen from the Mills Hotel. They clutched $20 bills in their mitts and their bosses were waiting on the Broadway side. Most of them skipped with the $20. A half-hour later the speculators discovered what had happened. There was nothing they could do but rage at the duplicity of the box-office.

A frequent gag was to have the same purchasers get on line several times during a morning and depend on the box-office attendant to be too busy to recognize them. Sometimes the speculators would ask a chauffeur who was waiting beside a limousine while the owner was shopping or on business nearby to approach the box-office and purchase a couple of tickets. The chauffeur made a couple of dollars easily and he readily assented. The box-office could not turn down such purchasers because they had no way of knowing which were authentic. If you turn down a bona-fide customer on suspicion, he is apt to create more trouble than a dozen speculators.

The speculator evil caused the Metropolitan to make a rule that no seats may be reserved by telephone, except by customers of long standing. The box-office learned that some people who had reserved the tickets in good faith did not call for them. What was worse, speculators used the reservation method, giving phony names. If the opera was in demand, the speculator would make a deal with some one outside the theatre and then enter and call for them. Thus the speculator could obtain double the price of the ticket without risking even the initial price of the seat. His only cost would be a nickel—for the telephone call.

Speculators are able to continue their operations because they can buy tickets from some subscribers for resale. In recent seasons, for example, there has always been a scarcity of tickets for "Tristan und Isolde" with Flagstad, Melchior, et al. The speculator may be able to obtain as much as $50 a seat for "Tristan" from a person who is in town for a day, who is desperately eager to attend this music-drama and who does not care what the cost will be. The speculator gets to know some subscribers. He telephones them and offers them double the marked price of their tickets, and for some subscribers the offer is difficult to turn down. They have seen this "Tristan," they will have further opportunities to hear Flagstad. If they are persons of modest means, why not take a little profit on their tickets? Some subscribers find that other engagements prevent them from going to the opera that evening and they gladly dispose of their tickets at a profit. It would require co-operation from every subscriber to root out the speculator evil. It would need also a severe campaign by the police.

The Metropolitan recently decided to increase its vigilance against speculators, since it knew that their operations developed ill-will in the long run. Notices were posted announcing that the management reserved the right to refuse admittance to persons who obtained their tickets from sidewalk speculators. The company also hired special policemen. The hope is that the purchasers will beware. But the danger always remains that a bona-fide purchaser will be stopped by mistake.

It is likely that the cleverest and most comprehensive plans in the world will not eradicate the speculator evil. The parasites will find ways for their depredations so long as there is easy money to be made. And some of the victims will continue to berate the box-office and to accuse its officials of every conceivable perfidy.

But they will not be any more irate than was an out-of-town customer years ago who appeared at the box-office at the end of the first act of "Siegfried" and demanded to know, "Where are the girls?"

"What girls?"

"The girls on the stage!" the customer exclaimed.

It appears that he had asked some one to reserve tickets, not for "Siegfried," but for Ziegfeld!

XIX

WHAT AUDIENCES PAY FOR

OPERA, like books, perfumes or girdles, has its best sellers. They may be artists; they may be the works themselves; and they may be a combination of both. The test is simple, like Verdi's admonition to the young opera manager. When the theatre is full, not empty, you have, as any schoolboy will tell you, a sell-out. When you have a sell-out every time you give an opera, you have a hit show. Allowing for all those who go to the opera out of curiosity or the desire to mingle with the "best people," there is still a large residue of operagoers who are customers because they wish to see and hear certain operas with certain singers. The records show what works and what artists have the largest followings.

In the last quarter of a century there has been a group of phenomenal draws among the singers. At the top of the list are Enrico Caruso, Geraldine Farrar and Mary Garden. Other singers have been or still are potent box-office figures and belong in the top flight, but Caruso, Farrar and Garden earned the right to their laurels because they drew superbly over an extended period of time. In the history of the Metropolitan Opera there has been no other artist who attracted the public as consistently as Caruso for a decade and a half or more. What Caruso was to New York, Mary Garden was to the rest of the country. The Chicago Opera toured the length and breadth of the land when Mary Garden was the queen of the troupe. She became America's first glamour girl. Year after year she pulled them in. Her audiences came from distant places to see and hear her. Farmers drove 250 miles in

carriages and paid $5 and $6 for a Mary Garden performance
—not once, but annually.

Caruso drew because he had a magnificent voice and used
it with consummate art. There was universal agreement that
he was the world's greatest tenor. And there is no doubt
that his enormous audiences were seldom disappointed. The
tenor voice of the century did things to people. Its great
pealing organ-like tones were breath-taking in their brilliance, and the fine-spun legatos and pianissimos were equally
enchanting. People went to hear Caruso sing. If he acted a
role with masterly effect as he did the old Eleazar in "La
Juive," that was an unexpected beneficence. The public would
not have cared if Caruso had not acted at all. There were
more thrills in his voice than in a well-constructed Hollywood shocker.

Mary Garden packed them in for the opposite reason. She
was a magnificent singing-actress. She was also one of the
best-publicized women of the time. That, too, was due in
part to the genius of the woman. She had a flair for saying
or doing the things that caused people to talk. Press-agents
who worked with her relate that she was marvellously quick
on the uptake. A suggestion from them would be translated
into a wonderful improvisation. She could make newspapermen feel that they were her confidants. She talked with be-
guiling frankness and would end an interview with the dis-
arming comment: "I have never told such a pack of lies."

Perhaps not. But Mary was always good for a story.

If people flocked to see Mary Garden because of extraneous things, she conquered them and captured them as her
followers through the power and magnetism of her impersonations. She could play the seductress Thaïs with devastat-
ing realism, and several nights later she could do a bewildered, simple, pathetic, innocent Mélisande magnificently.

Nor was it all acting. Her voice, though it was constantly criticized, was sufficient to her needs. James Huneker, who was Mary Garden's most eloquent rhapsodist, spoke of her voice as "a sonorous mirage." When she was on the stage, the average operagoer was not conscious of its limitations. He was too absorbed by the characterization as a whole.

Caruso drew consistently. Yet he had his flops. His appearance in a new opera by Mascagni, "Lodoletta," was one of these. It was a miserable failure at the box-office. At the other extreme was "Pagliacci." As Canio, Caruso literally panicked them. Seats were at a premium and speculators reaped a harvest.

Just behind Caruso came Geraldine Farrar. For almost twenty years she was an outstanding drawing card. Her "Madama Butterfly" was always good for a sold-out house, and it did not matter who else was in the cast. When she joined with Caruso in an opera, the public's joy overflowed. Farrar and Caruso in "Carmen" constituted one of opera's best sellers of all time.

Among the other leading attractions have been Feodor Chaliapin, whose impersonation of the title role of "Boris Godunoff" ranks at the top with the best sellers; Maria Jeritza, especially in "Tosca"; Rosa Ponselle, in "Norma"; Lily Pons, in "Lakmé" and "Lucia di Lammermoor," especially during her first few years at the Metropolitan; Lucrezia Bori, in "Traviata," and Lawrence Tibbett, in "The Emperor Jones."

We must not forget Kirsten Flagstad. If she remains at the Metropolitan long enough, she may take rank as the peer of Caruso and Farrar. Today she is the biggest draw in the land so far as opera is concerned. When she appears in "Tristan und Isolde" with Lauritz Melchior, a sell-out is a certainty. In eight performances of this music-drama during the season of 1936–37 the receipts were about $120,000, which is more than some successful Broadway plays gross in eight weeks of eight performances each.

Although not a singer, Arturo Toscanini proved to be a potent figure at the box-office. During his years at the Metropolitan his name as the conductor brought people into the theatre regardless of the identity of the prima donna. But he was not then the attraction that he has become. Today he is the dominating personage at Salzburg. When he conducts, the house is sold out months before the event. When he was at Bayreuth, he had the same effect on the box-office. His ministrations at the head of various symphony orchestras in guest appearances fill their halls. It is not given to most conductors to attain such prestige with the customer.

In the last analysis it is not the singer or conductor that the audience comes to see exclusively. The opera has more than a little to do with it. Some works have been as consistent at the box-office as Caruso and Mary Garden. "Carmen" and "Aïda" are the best examples. In bad times or good, with poor singers or great ones, these two masterpieces of the lyric theatre have always done first-rate business. They have everything for the audience; absorbing stories, an endless flow of good tunes, the panoply of grand opera, irresistible ballets, stunning choruses. With big names in the leading roles, "Carmen" and "Aïda" are unbeatable. But they are dependable even with "cats and dogs."

Some time ago a study was made of the Metropolitan's best draws among the operas over a ten-year period. The records covering the seasons of 1924–25 through 1933–34 were analyzed, and the most popular operas were charted. The list is worth an examination, although it must be borne in mind that some operas attained success because certain singers were available at the time, while others languished only because the best artists were not on hand. We will come back to these considerations.

Popularity was estimated on a basis of individual ticket sales. Subscriptions are purchased before the programs are announced, and the subscriber does not know what operas he will see. The only possible basis is the single-seat sale. The analysis worked out a certain average demand for single seats and called it 100. The best sellers were charted on their standing in relation to this average.

Here is the chart of the twenty most popular operas presented ten times or more during the regular seasons of these ten years:

Operas	Total Number of Times Given	Per cent of Single-Ticket Sale to Average of Each Year
Norma	14	167.6
Peter Ibbetson	13	159.4
Mignon	15	152.3
Rigoletto	25	146.5
Carmen	17	143.6
Tosca	16	142.5
Cav. & Pag.	13	131.0
Aïda	40	128.8
Lucia	23	123.8
Traviata	32	123.8
Turandot	14	121.6
Barber of Seville	16	119.2
Faust	29	118.5
Manon	17	113.4
King's Henchman	12	109.7
Don Giovanni	13	108.4
Tannhäuser	29	105.8
Tristan	33	103.5
Gioconda	31	103.
Trovatore	14	99.6
Average of list		126.1

Opera: Front and Back

Three operas were more popular than some of those listed above, but they were given less than ten times. The figures for them:

Boccaccio	5	123.8
Forza del Destino	9	112.9
Louise	4	102.3

And here is the record for all the others, performed more than ten times:

La Juive	17	98.1
Sadko	11	96.6
Africana	22	93.1
Bohème	32	92.3
Lohengrin	35	90.6
Butterfly	30	88.6
Götterdämmerung	17	86.9
Tales of Hoffmann	14	85.2
Rondine	10	83.1
Pelléas	27	82.5
Rosenkavalier	14	78.5
Meistersinger	31	76.8
Walküre	35	73.6
Romeo	24	72.8
Falstaff	13	65.7
Siegfried	16	64.9
Andrea Chenier	24	59.2
Elisir d'Amore	11	58.4
Bartered Bride	10	55.9
	Average	79.1

It will be seen, in a study of the leading twenty operas, that the first two were performed a good deal less than "Aïda." The chances are that, had they been done as often as the Verdi mainstay of the repertory, their averages would be lower than they were. It may be that Rosa Ponselle in

"Norma" could have packed them in five, six and seven times a season had she chosen to appear in the opera that often. Be that as it may, the position of "Norma" at the top is deceptive. Although it is a work of rare genius, it has not attracted the public unreservedly through the years, as have "Carmen" and "Aïda."

By the same token. "Peter Ibbetson" would not lead in an all-time compilation. Its place as runner-up in this ten-year stretch was owing to the fact that it was the best American opera that had been done at the Metropolitan up to that time. It had three favorite artists in leading roles—Bori, Johnson and Tibbett. It told a good story well, and it was splendidly produced. Would it continue to draw the public? The answer has already been indicated. When "Peter Ibbetson" was presented two years after the première, the curiosity had abated and the audience had dwindled alarmingly.

Consider the case of "Tristan und Isolde." In this chart it is eighteenth. Today it is far and away in the van. The explanation is, obviously, Flagstad.

Scan the list and you will find no mention of "Lakmé." It was revived for Lily Pons in 1933–34, and in that season it was the biggest box-office attraction of all. That was because a new and popular coloratura soprano had appeared and there was curiosity to hear her sing the Bell Song.

What about the "Ring"? The three great music-dramas, "Walküre," "Siegfried" and "Götterdämmerung," are near the bottom. Today they would certainly take precedence over a good many other operas. The Metropolitan not only has Flagstad but a well-rounded company of Wagnerian singers. The result has been a resurgence of interest in these works, bringing them into the repertory more frequently and with gratifying returns at the box-office.

Louis Gruenberg's setting of "The Emperor Jones" is

another work not in the record. Yet in the season when it was produced it had seven performances which took in about $100,000. It was a best-seller that one season. The next year it did not draw as well. Again, it was the excitement that came with a première of a native work plus a coruscating interpretation of the title role by Lawrence Tibbett that lifted it, at least temporarily, into the best-selling class.

The best sellers, it is clear, vary with the years, and with special conditions. It is said that modern audiences prefer short works, but look at the current success of the long Wagner music-dramas. The singer, the conductor, the production, the fact that the work is by an American may all have something to do with bringing the public into the theatre. Sometimes it is the composer. When Puccini was the best known of living writers, a new work, such as "The Girl of the Golden West," was an event. It could run successfully for a season or two on the strength of this fact alone. On the other hand, the composer's fame may have no influence. Take the case of Montemezzi. His "L'Amore dei Tre Re" was a considerable draw when it was first revealed in America at the Metropolitan. Obviously here was a composer of parts who should be represented by other works. The Metropolitan obtained the rights to "Giovanni Gallurese," another Montemezzi opus. It failed dismally.

Perhaps the real gauge of what an audience pays for should be the long-time view. Find the operas that have been performed the greatest number of times over the decades and the centuries and you will find the real attractions —always with the condition that great artists will make some more popular than the others temporarily.

In the twenty-seven years that Gatti-Casazza was the general manager, the Metropolitan presented the following

operas one hundred times or more, including performances
in New York and on tour:

Opera	Number of Times
Aïda	264
Bohème	243
Pagliacci	239
Butterfly	214
Tosca	185
Cavalleria Rusticana	171
Lohengrin	161
Die Walküre	151
Faust	147
Rigoletto	145
Traviata	140
Tristan und Isolde	137
Carmen	130
Tannhäuser	130
Trovatore	123
Meistersinger	112
Gioconda	107
Lucia di Lammermoor	102
Manon (Massenet)	100

We have here a total of nineteen operas, not enough for
one season's repertory. Let us look at the operas that were
presented more than fifty times during this twenty-seven-
year epoch:

Opera	Number of Times
Hänsel und Gretel	98
Parsifal	86
Boris Godunoff	86
Barber of Seville	85
Siegfried	73
Romeo et Juliette	66
Götterdämmerung	62
Andrea Chenier	57

Opera: Front and Back

Opera	Number of Times
Amore dei Tre Re	56
Rosenkavalier	56
L'Oracolo	54
Marta	52
Manon Lescaut (Puccini)	52
Les Contes d'Hoffmann	52
Samson et Dalila	52
Coq d'Or	50

An addition of sixteen operas. Some in the second list would not draw more than a corporal's guard at the box-office today. They were able to rank as high as they did because of special circumstances. The presence of Antonio Scotti in the role of Chim-Fen—one of his notable impersonations—made "L'Oracolo" one of the better attended works. "Marta" did well because it had a revival with Caruso and the public was eager to hear the tenor sing the bittersweet air, "M'appari."

Let us concede, for the sake of argument, that the operas in these two lists represent the general public's taste. What about art? Many of the popular operas are works of undisputed genius. But there are others, some greater, much greater, than those that the public has consistently patronized. Obviously the public is not interested. If it is, it is too small a public. Or it may be a fickle public.

Here, at any rate, is a group of operas which the public was not over-eager to hear:

Opera	Number of Times
Norma	29
Mefistofele	32
Orfeo	25
Africana	47
Huguenots	10

What Audiences Pay For

Opera	Number of Times
Cosi fan tutte	12
Don Giovanni	18
Marriage of Figaro	15
Magic Flute	42
Girl of the Golden West	40
Rondine	15
William Tell	17
Eugene Onegin	8
Ballo in Maschera	13
Falstaff	27
Otello	28
Pelléas et Mélisande	32
Louise	23
Ariane et Barbe-Bleu	7
La Juive	40
Armide	7
Thaïs	39
Le Rossignol	8
Mignon	32
Fidelio	19
The Bartered Bride	38
Elektra	6
Salome	8
The Flying Dutchman	12
Rheingold	27
Der Freischütz	18
Skyscrapers (ballet)	11
Dance in Place Congo	5

Not all masterpieces. But some of these works are pinnacles in the history of opera. Some are the most memorable works of their composers. Note that Mozart is not represented in the first two lists. Note that "Falstaff" and "Otello," the two operas in which Verdi reached the summit of his achievement, are among the infrequently heard operas.

Opera: Front and Back

Observe that Gluck and Weber, Beethoven and Tchaikovsky, Bellini and Meyerbeer, Debussy and Stravinsky—names known by any one with the slightest knowledge of the history of music—are all represented only in the last list.

There is no moral in the contrast. I am not even deprecating the taste of the public or the unwillingness of the management to jam the masterworks down the listener's ears. These are the simple facts. Let who will make the most of them. One thing should be said for the public: It has turned thumbs down on a host of unlamented operas that were trivial, pretentious or uninspired. Its average is remarkably high. In this best of all possible worlds, where the blundering in politics and economics attains to monumental proportions, that is something.

XX

BUILDING THE AUDIENCE

UNTIL the advent of radio, opera was for the few in America. Companies were supported by several major cities, and only a small fraction of the population had opportunity for contact with the art. The radio has remedied the difficulty only in part. You can hear opera during the season, but there are still limited chances to see it. There are several hardy impresarios, notably Fortune Gallo, who runs the San Carlo Grand Opera Company, who keep a company on the road each year. They do make opera available in places where no other troupe penetrates. But these smaller organizations added to the major companies do not begin to compare with the development in some European countries where as many as fifty companies are maintained in one nation. The wide diffusion of opera in such countries has brought it close to the life of the average man and woman. They know the operas; they gravitate to the lyric theatre; the audience is virtually the entire population.

The major opera companies in America are aware of the need to attract a new audience into the opera house. The march of technology has brought some help from an unexpected source. The radio has whetted the curiosity of hundreds of thousands. And the screen, which has used opera singers increasingly and presented them in scenes and arias from the best-known works, has reached millions. The principal job is to capitalize on this new curiosity. How to do it? That is a question that has perplexed managements throughout the country.

[313]

Opera: Front and Back

Years ago the Metropolitan decided that benefit performances under the auspices of various charitable and educational institutions was one way of tapping new audience sources. The committees that ran the benefits could sell only a small fraction of their tickets to subscribers and regular operagoers who had their fill of opera. They had to seek individuals and groups who went to the opera infrequently or not at all. Since they were working for a cause, they had no hesitation in bringing social, moral, even business pressure on the individuals they cornered. People will buy tickets for benefits that they do not want. But opera tickets come high, and once purchased they are almost always used. The result was that persons who came to the opera to scoff remained to pray, and better still, to come a second time without the bludgeoning of some pertinacious committee woman.

To encourage the benefit sponsors, the Metropolitan provides them with the most attractive shows. If a revival with a famous star is planned for the season, the première is often allotted to a benefit. If "Tristan und Isolde" with Flagstad and Melchior is the biggest draw, a couple of charities will get the opera as their show. The first appearance of a major artist in a new role may be assigned to a sponsoring group.

The organization that runs the benefit pays a flat sum for a performance. Its profit is the difference between the gross receipts and the amount it pays for the show. The customary price is $9000 which is less than the cost of the production. This fee assures the usual quota of big-name principals. If the sponsor wishes additional stars, the price is increased.

Profits for one benefit performance have run as high as $10,000. The committee can sell the parterre boxes which are not available for sale at regular subscription performances. It can also increase the price scale of tickets. Front row seats in the orchestra have gone for as much as $25. It all depends on the connections, the selling powers and the sheer nerve of the committee.

A dozen or more benefits are presented at the Metropolitan during a season. Two or three times that many could be sold to committees and institutions which have been clamoring for the privilege to act as sponsors. But the company can allot only a limited number. Currently, when the seasons are short, the number is smaller than it used to be when a season ran for twenty-four weeks.

Organized audience groups are another development. It is not new, although it has taken novel directions in recent years. At least two of the older groups are the Metropolitan Opera Club and the National Opera Club. The latter is made up of women. It meets at regular intervals, hears lecturers and artists and tries, in a modest way, to disseminate the gospel of opera. Every Saturday evening it takes a block of seventy seats for its members who attend en masse.

The Metropolitan Opera Club has closer relations with the opera house. It has a club room on the Thirty-ninth Street side of the grand-tier floor. And it purchases exclusive rights to the omnibus box, which is near the stage in the grand-tier row of boxes on the Thirty-ninth Street side, for Monday, Wednesday, Friday nights and Saturday afternoons. This box seats sixty-one persons and on any subscription night you will find it populated by a group of elderly men, always punctiliously garbed in starched shirts, white ties and tails. The club pays $137.50 a night for use of the box and club room.

The Metropolitan Opera Club is restricted to men. Its membership is exclusive and its aim, presumably, is to bring together, congenially, men who are interested in opera and the Metropolitan. It may be compared with the Jockey Club at the Paris Opéra, although its prerogatives backstage, as

Opera: Front and Back

Edward Johnson said recently, are not like those of the Paris unit. While it tries to stimulate an interest in opera, the Metropolitan Opera Club is not a ponderable force in attracting newcomers to the theatre. It may bring in a few new listeners. But not many. Its membership rolls are too small for that.

The newest and most potent audience builder is the Metropolitan Opera Guild. Mrs. August Belmont, its guiding spirit, conceived the plan and began to carry it out just before Edward Johnson took over as general manager. What seemed like a pink-tea idea has developed into a permanent and valuable organization. It has had a phenomenal growth, achieving an active membership of more than 3000 in recent months. If it continues to be channeled as shrewdly as it has in its brief existence, it may assume a position of prime importance in the American operatic scheme. For the idea is susceptible of imitation in other cities. Some cities—Philadelphia, Chicago, St. Louis and Toronto—have written to the New York office for information and have received it together with a blessing.

The Metropolitan Opera Guild is open to any one who is interested in opera or the Metropolitan. Like the theatre itself, it has probably drawn into its ranks people who care more about social prestige than art. No matter. Motives in most human pursuits are mixed. The significant fact is that both opera and the Metropolitan have benefited from the guild's ministrations.

The guild's principal aims are to widen the audience for opera and to effect a closer contact between the opera house and its audience. For the price of membership, those who belong to the guild receive various items that are worth, even on a pecuniary basis, more than the annual fee. The guild brings its members into the opera house on informal occasions.

[316]

Building the Audience

It enables its members to see a dress rehearsal. It arranges to have them taken backstage. It conducts courses on intelligent listening. It publishes a little magazine called *Opera News* which is lively and informative. It runs a ticket service division which simplifies the business of making reservations long in advance—a problem the box-office is not equipped to handle—and which purchases tickets for members who live out of town and who would find it too troublesome to buy their own directly.

The sum total of these activities is to produce a better informed, a more satisfied and a more interested public. People who have sat through a dress rehearsal and seen the conductor telling a famous star to repeat a passage several times feel that they are on the inside of things. Persons who are permitted to view the backstage area may realize the deficiencies of the theatre and its equipment and may appreciate the handicaps and the achievements.

As it grows the guild broadens its scope. It has undertaken to stimulate the circulation of opera tickets among students in the music and public schools. It has interested some of its members in contributing to this work and has made tickets available to youngsters who have never heard an opera in their lives.

When it has a surplus, the guild uses a large part of its funds to proffer some concrete aid to the Metropolitan. One year it was a gift of a cyclorama and a new sound-proof curtain to replace the outworn one for "The Ring." The next year it was the setting up of an endowment fund with an initial gift of $10,000 and the refurbishing of the room in which the instrumentalists rest before the performance and during the intermissions.

There is much that can be done and that the guild hopes to do. The endowment fund is a small beginning for an institution like the Metropolitan. If rich men bequeath generous sums to organizations like the Metropolitan Museum of Art, universities and dog hospitals, why not to the Metropolitan Opera? There has been no precedent, and the guild has set one up and proposes to preach the idea of enlarging the endowment. To this end a trustee's committee has been organized to advise on ways and means.

Another idea for the future is the development of an opera museum in which will be placed on view costumes of the past and present, rare manuscripts and other operatic memorabilia, including such items as the crocheting that Sembrich, who did not fake these things, did as Rosina in "The Barber of Seville." Reaching the radio public is another matter that commands attention. The guild, the opera house and the broadcaster receive repeated calls from groups throughout the land for help toward more intelligent listening. The guild knows that much can be done to stimulate the listener. Literature can be provided, and some day perhaps a squadron of touring lecturers.

To Mrs. Belmont belongs much of the credit for the guild's accomplishments. Through her personal influence she brought the first members into the guild. She is fond of opera and has communicated her enthusiasm to those with whom she has worked. What is more, she has ideas about opera and its development, and the path the guild has taken reflects her principles and her capacity for leadership. Hers was the signal honor of being the first woman ever to be elected to the board of the Metropolitan Opera Association, and she was followed into the board by Lucrezia Bori and Mrs. Vincent Astor.

There is no doubt that the guild has brought new people into the opera audience. It has brought them from the ranks of those who can afford to pay for the better seats. The guild's achievement need not be exaggerated. Its influence has been largely on people of comfortable means. The operagoer who sits in the family circle or stands has not the funds for guild membership. Nor does he require external stimulation. His zeal for opera is so great that he will spend what little money he can spare for the worst seats in the house. The problem would seem to be to provide him and his fellows who would go to the opera and do many of the other "nice, cultural things," if they could, with the requisite purchasing power. And this is a problem for a nation, not an opera guild.

XXI

ON WHEELS

THE road, whether it be for the spoken drama or opera, is not what it used to be. There was a time, three decades ago, when the Metropolitan Opera made a jaunt as far west as the Pacific Coast. The presence of the company in San Francisco at the time of the earthquake discouraged some of its eminent members, including Caruso, from ever wishing to have any part or parcel of the West Coast again.

On the night of April 17, 1906, the company headed by Fremstad and Caruso had sung a brilliant "Carmen." On the morning of the 18th the earthquake shook the city and then came the fire. The singers lost their clothes and costumes; the orchestral players, their instruments; the company, its music and scenery. When the bedraggled troupe got back to New York, Sembrich postponed her European trip to give a benefit concert for chorus and orchestra, and $10,000 was netted to aid particularly in replacing destroyed instruments. Of course, there was no Hollywood in those days to serve as a counter-attraction to temblors.

The Chicago Opera debouched on long tours as recently as in the late Twenties. The depression put a stop to that; in fact, it put a stop to the company entirely for several seasons. The depression even withered the hardiest of perennials among the touring opera companies—the small troupe led by an indomitable impresario.

There has been a recrudescence of touring activity in the past two or three years. The Metropolitan has stepped up its post-season tour to as much as three weeks and is considering further expansion. The smaller troupes have dared to brave the road again, and at least one is making money. But touring remains a shadow of what it was in the uncomplicated past when motion pictures were just experiments and modern radio entertainment was a dream.

A Metropolitan tour nowadays is distinguished from most other road trips in that the company does not travel at its own risk. All out-of-town engagements are guaranteed by local committees. If a city such as Boston, Cleveland or Baltimore wishes a visit from the Metropolitan, a group of citizens underwrites the possible deficit. If the visit proves to be successful, there may not be any call on the guarantors for funds. If the audiences do not turn out, the guarantors must contribute the difference between the box-office receipts and the cost of the visit.

It was not always thus. Thirty years ago tours were undertaken at the management's risk, much as individual impresarios run their companies. There were one- and two-night stands. There were long railroad jumps between stops. There were, in short, all the accoutrements of barnstorming on a big scale. The Chicago Opera toured extensively as recently as ten years ago, making a grand circle through the south, west and east, stopping in various cities from one night up to two weeks.

A tour of such dimensions was an undertaking fraught with all manner of dangers. It was a lucky company that hobbled back to New York intact, with tempers unruffled and health untouched. It is one thing to have a collection of prima donnas in one center with separate residences and different circles of acquaintance. It is quite another problem to have them all together on one train.

The mere deficiencies of local theatres were a continuous

Opera: Front and Back

hazard. The town op'ry house was entitled to that name only
by virtue of diplomatic courtesy. Stages were too small for
sets. Dressing rooms were inadequate. Orchestra pits were
always too small, and it was no rarity to have a couple of bull
fiddlers lodged in a box on one side and the master of the
kettledrums in another box on the opposite side. Acoustics
were like a grab-bag; if you were lucky, you landed in a
theatre in which the voices and orchestra blended reasonably.
It was no rarity to play in an op'ry house where even the ponderous voice of the bass tuba could not be heard by half
the audience.

The Chicago Opera paid a visit once to a Texas town. Because of illness in the company, a last-minute change in program was required, and it was decided to do "Salome" with
Mary Garden, even at the risk of outraging the respectable
citizenry with this tale of a gory psychopathic gal. It developed that there was no space under the stage floor. How
could you play "Salome" without a cistern in midstage from
which Jokanaan must emerge? The stage director and his
crew considered the problem and decided that the only solution was to take up a small section of the floor and to dig a
hole in the ground at that spot to make room for Jokanaan.
They proceeded to dig and discovered why no basement had
been constructed under the stage. The ground underneath was
marshy. Several inches of water seeped into the enclosure. It
was hardly the place to ask a singer to camp for the greater
part of an hour.

It was too late to make a change, and the question of going
through with the performance was put up to Georges Baklanoff, the baritone, who played the role of Jokanaan. He was
a hearty Russian and he agreed on one condition: that he
could fortify himself with a bottle of spirits. Before the performance he descended into the cistern carrying an earthen

jug of strong liquor. From time to time the voice of Jokanaan thunders from below in imprecation against the sinfulness of Herod and his court. Baklanoff's voice became increasingly raucous. Mary Garden as Salome ran to the edge of the cistern much more often than the drama required. Each time Baklanoff muttered that the water and mud were rising to his knees. After every complaint he took another swig, tilting the jug until it could almost be seen from the balcony. Salome had a difficult time keeping a straight face, and Jokanaan was becoming so boisterous that his admonitions could be heard in the next county.

The thing that worried the company most was that Jokanaan, in the fullness of his stimulation, would continue to sing after he had been beheaded. Somehow he remembered that he was dead. At the end of the opera he climbed slowly out of the improvised cavern, clutching his earthen jug. Its capacity had been about a gallon and it had been full when Baklanoff began the performance. At the end it was completely dry.

The shortcomings of a local theatre were never better exemplified than by a famous one-day stand that the Metropolitan made in a Nebraska town. The equipment in this house was antediluvian. There were not enough dressing rooms, and the chorus had to use the flies. The women of the chorus were perched aloft on one side, and the men on the other. The curtain was raised and lowered by manipulating a heavy wheel. It was a strenuous task to move the curtain once. Nellie Melba sang a matinee performance and she took so many curtain calls that the stage hands working the curtain labored like stevedores. There would have been rebellion in the ranks before the performance was over had not Melba tipped the boys generously. Curtain calls, after all, are fundamental to the prima donna.

Opera: Front and Back

It was the evening performance, however, that was most memorable. The opera was "Faust," which needs special lighting effects. The electricians discovered that the theatre did not have sufficient voltage. "Faust" was out of the question without more juice. The chief electrician made a hasty survey and decided that the only solution was to connect a line to the overhead trolley cable that ran along the street in front of the theatre. He prevailed on the traction company to let him make the temporary connection, and the added power was channeled for the exclusive use of the stage.

Early in the performance all the lights on the stage were suddenly extinguished. For several moments there was darkness, while the singers continued to sing. Then the lights went on with equal suddenness. Some time passed, and the same thing happened again. The electricians conducted a frantic investigation. They discovered, midway in the performance, that when the trolley stopped in front of the house, it disconnected the circuit for itself and the theatre. Nothing could be done to save the situation. The company managers were in a sweat as to what the audience would think and do.

The audience gave the performance a tremendous send-off. And the next day's press commended the Metropolitan's "Faust," singling out for special approval the originality and ingenuity of the lighting effects.

Sometimes there are extraneous difficulties on tour with unforeseen factors impinging on the performance. The Metropolitan once stopped in Cleveland in a theatre where the circus had just completed a visit. The circus had gone to a nearby community for a short trip and had left two elephants in the basement of the Cleveland theatre, to be collected when the company passed through again. The elephants did not seem to be in the opera's way. They were in the animal room in the basement, behaving with exemplary decorum.

On Wheels

The opening opera of that visit was "Hänsel und Gretel," with Alfred Hertz conducting. The orchestra began the opening bars of the work and it had not progressed over a dozen measures when there was a terrific detonation. The building seemed to shake. It felt like an earthquake. Alfred Hertz was not easily ruffled. Picture him with his shining bald head and dark flowing beard, continuing his vigorous beat despite the shock of the crash. The music went on, but not for long. Again there was a thunderous eruption. This time Hertz stopped. The stage hands and company directors scurried about to find the cause. Everything seemed in order. Some one went down to the basement and the elephants stood in their accustomed places calmly and innocently. Word was sent to Hertz that nothing seemed to be wrong. He poised his baton, and began conducting with stolid determination. Again there was a crash that shook the stage and the orchestra floor. This time the cause was discovered. The culprits were the elephants.

A stage hand, who had remained in the basement, observed that the animals seemed to be irritated by the music overhead. They indicated their displeasure by unfurling their trunks and slamming them with tremendous force against a huge boiler. Two elephants bombarding a boiler were able to make a hell of a racket.

The performance was halted and was not resumed for almost half an hour. Peace was restored only when a bale of hay was procured and the elephants were kept occupied with food throughout the performance.

When an opera company goes on tour replacements are carried along for all the major roles. You never know when a singer will come down with germs in the throat or a cold in the nose. In Louisville the Metropolitan once found itself in a jam because it had taken a chance on making this step without a substitute for Amato. The opera was "Rigoletto" in which the baritone, Amato, played the principal dramatic role. Amato had developed a throat ailment and could not sing. He was absolutely voiceless. There were no planes in those days to fly a singer to Louisville within a few hours. The only thing to do, short of canceling the performance, and the local authorities would not hear of that, was to give the performance as best it could be done. "Rigoletto" runs normally over three hours. On this occasion every passage for Rigoletto himself was eliminated. The performance took an hour and a half.

A near disaster because of a lack of a substitute occurred in Rochester some years ago. The Metropolitan had scheduled one performance, "Faust," in that town. José Mardones, hitherto an irreproachable artist, was scheduled to sing Mephistopheles. He seldom missed a performance and he never created difficulties. The company arrived in town and put up at a hotel across the street from the auditorium. Mardones unpacked and decided to take a stroll. He walked around the theatre and glanced at the billboard announcing the performance. He saw that the names of the other principals were in type twice the size of his name. The local sponsors were responsible for this slight. Mardones did not stop to inquire who was guilty. He did not speak a word to any one in authority. He returned to his hotel, packed his bag and went to the railroad station.

The officials of the company were apprised of the trouble by a telephone from the depot.

"There is a fellow here," said a voice from the station, "who wants a ticket back to New York. He says you'll pay for it."

"Who is it?"

"I don't know," said the voice, "and I don't give a damn.

On Wheels

He insists he has a right to a ticket and he won't pay for it."

"Don't give it to him!" the opera official screamed.

He hurried into a taxi and down to the station. At first Mardones would not explain why he wanted to leave. Nor would he agree to return to the hotel. Then suddenly he burst into a tantrum that would have done credit to any prima donna. It was the only time that he had given any indication of such a bent.

The opera official listened and suffered. He tried to point out that the matter would be rectified immediately. He pleaded with Mardones that the performance depended on him, that there was no other Mephistopheles available. Mardones cooled off after a spell and allowed himself to be led back to the hotel. The only reason the Metropolitan did not have a catastrophe in Rochester that trip was because Mardones was too frugal to pay for his own railroad ticket.

The personnel of an opera company, with rare exceptions, relaxes on the train trips between out-of-town appearances. When the Metropolitan goes on tour it has a special train of about ten cars, with the sets shipped ahead on a freight train the day before. If you stroll down the length of these cars, you may have a view of a company of three hundred persons of every occupation in the opera house. They are at rest and at play. In the principals' car there are several groups in animated conversation. Some persons read. A group or two play bridge. Flagstad tries her hand at this game, but her companions at the table will observe later that she is a far better Isolde than bridge player. Artur Bodanzky, Lauritz Melchior and Friedrich Schorr play skat, and play it with serious concentration. They remain absorbed in a game for hours.

In the orchestra car there are readers and conversationalists, but the emphasis is on poker and pinochle, with perhaps a bridge game. In the chorus car the men play cards. The women chat and knit. You observe that the sportive figures of the stage are sedate adults. The women remove their high-heeled shoes; this is perfect repose. In the ballet car there is a little more liveliness. The young men and women seem to grow restive on a long journey and move about. And in the stage crew's car there are additional serious card games, and some richly colloquial observations regarding Tammany, the Administration and other aspects of the political scene.

One of the most playful persons on tour was Michael Bohnen, the German bass-baritone. He was a powerful man, an amateur heavyweight wrestling champion with an abiding interest in sports. He would go off to watch wrestling matches at every opportunity, and he took a liking in this country to what he called "ees hukkey." In New York once he lifted a telephone booth in which sat the rather massive Leon Rothier and set it down several feet away. On tour once, an artist—a small man of ample girth—began to tease Bohnen. Whereupon the basso lifted him bodily and placed him on a baggage rack. The small man squealed like a stuck pig until Bohnen relented and set him on the ground again.

Once on a trip to Atlanta there was a stop at a junction for a change of engines. It was a hot day and a good many persons in the company got off the train to walk on the platform. One chap, trying to be funny, announced dramatically that he did not want to go any farther. He was fed up with life, etc., etc. He lay down and placed his head on the rail underneath the carriage. The jest was taken seriously by some spectators and they looked on alarmed. One or two even made as if to drag him off. As the weary one lay on the track, speaking his final words, some one in the car flushed a drain. The weary one was in the line of fire.

The most prodigious entertainer of opera folk on tour was S. Davies Warfield, president of the Seaboard Air Line. He invariably made the trip with the Metropolitan Opera from Baltimore to Atlanta. His private car was added to the opera special, and on the train and in Atlanta he was a prodigal host. During the week in the Georgia city he gave dinner parties every evening, and whoever was free that night was welcome. On the way down or en route back, every one would stop at his home in Manor Glen, Md., for a day, where there would be milking contests, lavish dinners and general gaiety. For once the opera company was really a big happy family.

Some productions must be altered on tour. An elaborate set designed for the Metropolitan Opera stage may be too large for a small theatre elsewhere, and new sets must be improvised or sections of the original décor left behind. There is also the question of the tender sensibilities of some cities. In a recent visit to Boston the ballet girls, who did a vigorous can-can in a dance production known as "The Bat," were told not to flip their skirts up as high as they had in New York.

Supers are not taken along on tour and they must be recruited in each city. It is easy enough to find willing candidates; it is not so simple to keep them under control once you have them on the stage. When not too many supers are required, individuals associated with the company are asked to serve. Wives of artists who have accompanied their husbands on the road have taken on bits as supers.

The audiences in the road towns are an amalgam of about the same personalities that make up the New York assemblages. There are the town's social elements. Cities like Boston take society perhaps more seriously than even New York. There are the individuals who are curious about opera and its people. And there are people who love music. In Boston one year a lame girl came with a campstool and waited the whole day for the privilege of purchasing one of ninety standing-room tickets. Another girl traveled by night bus from a town in Maine, and reached Boston in the morning, when she immediately took her place on line. She stood the whole day waiting for the box-office to open. For what? For the privilege of standing through the evening.

An organization like the Metropolitan Opera House can manage, because of the size of the company, to make out-of-town visits even in the midst of the season. Cities that are more than a few hours' ride must be played after the season. But communities like Philadelphia, Hartford, Newark, Westchester and Brooklyn can be visited on Tuesday nights when the home house is closed. In more prosperous days the Metropolitan played in Philadelphia every Tuesday night of the season and sent out a second division of the company to one of the other opera houses simultaneously. Now the schedule is more staid.

The cost of a performance of opera out-of-town is somewhat higher than a benefit at home. It may be estimated at about $10,000, with variations up or down depending on the distance from New York. The Metropolitan must calculate the cost of the fares and the transportation of sets, properties and costumes. It is desirous of putting its best foot forward on tour. A full quota of first-line singers is always provided. For they are the best publicized element of the Metropolitan's productions, and communities afield pay to hear them.

Some towns must scale their tickets higher than the Metropolitan to break even. Some can afford to ask less, since their theatres have enormous seating capacities. For example, in Cleveland the Metropolitan has had audiences of about 10,000 persons for each performance. Philadelphia with a house that seats less than 3000 must ask for much higher prices than Cleveland.

Why does the Metropolitan tour so little? Three weeks,

after all, is a drop in the bucket, considering the size of the country. The answer is that a longer tour is difficult to arrange. There are demands from many cities for visits from the Metropolitan. Places as distant as Texas and California have shown interest. But a tour without the leading stars would be unsatisfactory. The public out of New York knows who the big names are and will not pay to hear any one else. The big names, unfortunately, have commitments to sing in opera in London, Vienna, Paris, Salzburg; they are not available for tour after the end of April. Some of them, because of their concert engagements, are not even available for tours that late.

For the smaller, individually promoted opera companies, it is a boon that the Metropolitan does not travel extensively. The field is left wide open to them. In good years a profit may be had from a carefully run opera company. Look at the record of Fortune Gallo and his San Carlo Grand Opera Company. He provides employment for artists who are competent but who have not the requirements for the top; for instrumentalists, choristers and stage crew.

Recent seasons of the San Carlo have run as high as thirty-five to forty weeks. The total audience that sees this company is larger and more diversified than that which watches the Metropolitan at work. The repertory is devoted to the standard French and Italian works—"Carmen," "Aïda," "Rigoletto," "Traviata," "Bohème," "Faust." Three German operas, "Tannhäuser," "Lohengrin" and "Hänsel und Gretel," are added to give the repertory class.

Companies of this kind are the American substitute for the many opera houses that dot the European landscape. They familiarize thousands of persons with some of the operas. If they do not perform them with consummate art, they have a professional touch. They do not stand and wait; they serve.

Indeed they serve remarkably well considering that their rates are seldom higher than $1.50 to $3 for the best seats, with a $1 top not infrequent.

Not all the small companies have standards as high as the San Carlo. There are some impresarios whose chief stock in trade is the providing of opportunities for operatic debuts to persons with money or angels. One woman paid a small company $2000 for a performance, and a larger one as much as $10,000. Another woman received a debut because she was the wife of a city official. For the most part women with money or with husbands who have money are the good providers in this racket. The urge to sing in public is a strong one. Some impresarios will take these women whether they can go through a role or not. A few will insist that the prospect be able, at the least, to sing a part from beginning to end, no matter what the quality of the voice or the musicianship.

A woman whose husband was wealthy inveigled a manager into casting her as Micaëla in "Carmen" in a performance of a small company in the midwest. She had little to commend her as a singer save her husband's money. In the third act Micaëla sings an air, "I try not to own that I tremble," that is the expression of her sweetness and purity. When she has finished, Don José, standing guard unseen by her, fires a shot that almost hits Escamillo. At this performance, one indignant operagoer, who knew more about singing than the story of the opera, arose to go. He thought that Don José had aimed at Micaëla. As he walked out, he yelled so that every one in the audience could hear him, "Too bad he missed her!"

There are elderly women whose admiration for certain young artists—mostly young men—leads them to provide payment for debuts for their protégés. The angels of opera are

On Wheels

a godsend to the shoestring impresarios who would flounder without them. In the years that followed 1929 one such impresario went out of business temporarily because, as he phrased it, "there was a depression in suckers."

The fly-by-night companies do a great deal of harm. They put on unrehearsed opera. One wealthy woman who was to make a debut with such a company hired an orchestra and a cast and rehearsed her role with this troupe several times a week. But most performances are not prepared in this fashion. They are hit and miss. The audience obtains a distorted picture of opera. And the poor singers are too often swindled of their promised earnings, which are, in all conscience, little enough.

It is in companies such as these that graft is most rampant. The cutback, that vicious invention of gentlemen with business ethics of the lowest racketeers, is frequently practiced among the orchestra players. The device is known in higher places. The union fights against it. But the books are kept straight, and the poor players must return a large share—as much as 50 per cent—of their promised pay to some intermediary.

Shady dealings have been known to occur even in the major opera houses of the world. They are beyond the province of this book. Some day there will be an end to extortionate commissions, to cuts that were not earned, to payments for services that were not rendered. It will be a pleasant day for the victim.

XXII

ON THE AIR

I N A brief span of ten years radio has done more to spread a nationwide familiarity with the lyric theatre than the opera houses of America had accomplished in a century and a half. If music is, as Emerson has said, the poor man's Parnassus, then radio has provided the best graded trail up. And if opera ever becomes truly democratized, if it ever achieves an integrated synthesis with our culture, a tremendous share of the credit will belong to the radio. Broadcasting has made the finest productions of the Metropolitan, the Chicago, the San Francisco and the European opera houses audible to millions of Americans. Television will some day make opera visible.

The forces that radio has released are, in the exact sense of the word, incalculable. There is no way of knowing precisely how many people listen to a broadcast of a full-length opera. It will probably never be charted how they listen; with intense concentration, with fluctuating interest, or with indifference. Thousands probably use opera as they do other radio programs, as a background to conversation, cards, housework. One of the most vicious aspects of radio is its employment as a wall of sound, when the ears have other business to attend to. Senses already bruised, especially in the cities, by ubiquitous noises, have become even duller. Listening to broadcasts in this fashion may be heavily discounted.

There must be, however, hundreds of thousands of persons who give all their attention to opera on the air. Saturday afternoons when the Metropolitan is broadcast are set aside religiously.

On the Air

And here is a straw in the wind. A woman writes to the Metropolitan from Gilmer, Texas, that she would like to be informed as early as possible the choice of operas to be broadcast. "A group of women in this small Texas town is planning to have several programs this fall based on opera. We will examine the myths or legends from which the inspiration for the libretto came and trace other literary developments of the theme. The only practical manner in which we can manage to have the music—the opera itself—as part of our study is to plan our work so that our programs will coincide with the dates on which you broadcast."

How much each auditor gets from the radio depends on his power of concentration. Good listening, whether it be in the concert hall, opera house or the home, is developed by experience. It is no mean feat to be able to follow a full opera effectively by the ear alone. Consider how the attention of persons in the opera house wanders. They have stage pictures to follow. When the eye is co-operating, it provides sensory compensations that are not possible to one who must use only the ear.

All estimates of the numbers and quality of the radio audience are sheer guesswork. It is better to tackle the problem from the sender's rather than the receiver's end. Here figures are available. Opera constitutes one of the biggest shows on the air. A cogent case can be made out that the Metropolitan broadcast is the biggest show of all. It has a network of more than eighty stations in the United States and Canada, besides short-wave transmission that sends the broadcast to the corners of the earth. There is no other regular broadcast that receives as much time as the Metropolitan. Three hours are normal. When Wagner works are performed, the broadcasts run four hours or longer.

It may be presumed that the men who are in the business

of broadcasting know what they are about. Evidence, of course, is submitted frequently to the contrary, and a great deal of it is persuasive. By and large, radio chains and individual stations are run on a profitable basis. The owners and executives, whatever their shortcomings in other directions, know how to make money. And when they assign to opera as large a chunk of their time as they do, the reasons are practical. They have found that there is an enormous response to opera. They assume that the audience is vast and that it cuts across every section of the population.

There is, of course, a certain type of American business man who is a sucker for Culture. He is seduced by the blandishments of the Culture promoters. He feels that he is serving the nobler side of his nature by helping Art. There are such men in the radio game, and the constant propaganda that is leveled by critics, women's clubs and artists in favor of Art hits the mark. It may therefore be argued that the business sense is not responsible for all the broadcasts of opera, symphonies and chamber music. For a time practical considerations might be ignored. But not for long. Good music would be reduced to a minimum if it did not pay, in cold cash as well as in prestige.

The most important factor of the Metropolitan broadcasts is that the opera is put on the air in its entirety. There are no short cuts to the appreciation of lyric works. It is enormously desirable that the design of the composer be represented honestly. Condensations, makeshift or skillful, do not give the listener a just idea of an opera. Some works possibly are the better for judicious cuts, but the masterpieces of opera are injured. So is the listener. How many times have you tuned off in disgust after listening to a one-hour program that sought to appeal to every taste—light, heavy, whimsical, romantic—and achieved a miserable hash?

On the Air

From the radio audience's point of view, the skill with which the opera is transmitted is virtually as important as that it should be broadcast at all. Technical equipment and knowledge have improved so rapidly that they are taken for granted. Artistic sensibilities are required in equal measure. For the microphone has neither judgment nor discrimination. It is not enough to place it in the footlights or above the stage and expect it to do the rest. The human head and heart and hand must bridge the gaps of the physical world.

There is not space here to dilate on the acoustical problems, but several examples are worth consideration. A famous tenor at the Metropolitan builds up crescendos with impressive effect. The audience in the opera house is always deeply stirred, so large is the voice, so vibrant its quality. On the air this same crescendo sung by the same tenor must be doctored, or the radio audience will hear a distorted version. It happens that the dissonant harmonic content of the voice increases as it grows in volume, while the fundamental harmonic content does not increase correspondingly. The average ear combines or mixes these refinements of tone. The microphone does not. What is more, the microphone transmits what it hears. At the receiving end the radio listener would become conscious of the deficiency in tone quality where he would seldom be aware of it in the opera house. The engineer at the controls increases the power at the crescendo by three or four decibels, and the deficiency in the tone becomes inaudible.

There is a tendency among some prima donnas to employ too much voice on the upper notes. Nothing conquers an audience more decisively than a show of power on the top tones, and many sopranos turn on the juice at strategic points. But this tactic of the opera house produces disastrous results on the air. The unpleasant qualities of the voice—rare is the

Opera: Front and Back

vocal organ that does not lose its purity and smoothness when it is forced—are accentuated on the air. The engineer subdues the voice and helps to eliminate unpleasant quality.

The man at the controls plays a tremendous role in the broadcasting of music, especially opera. He is the ears of millions of listeners. He should be an artist in his own right. He is as important to the radio audience as the conductor in the pit. Leopold Stokowski is one of the few maestros who has discerned this need and has concerned himself with the work at the controls. And even he has found that the problem is difficult. On one occasion he undertook to operate the controls for a symphony broadcast. In a span of fifteen minutes he managed to tune the concert off the air several times. Nevertheless, he undertook to master radio's difficulties and he is now able to make valuable contributions to a broadcast. The problems of broadcasting will never be solved wholly and rewardingly until great musicians join with leading physicists in a common solution.

Let us examine the technique of broadcasting opera, with a view to discovering how the art of the composer and the interpreter may be affected by the methods of the engineer.

Eight microphones are employed in a broadcast from the Metropolitan Opera House. Four are in the footlights and four are suspended from aloft over the orchestra. The footlight mikes are placed in pairs, about a quarter of the length of the stage's rim from the sides. Each pair consists of a close perspective and a long perspective mike. The names indicate the functions of the mikes. The close perspective is used to pick up tone from a singer nearby; the long perspective is best for singers at a distance. The footlight mikes are designed principally to pick up the tone from the stage. The music of the orchestra is transmitted through the overhead mikes. These are placed at two levels. Two close perspective mikes are hung closer to the orchestra; the two long perspective mikes are much higher and farther above the instrumentalists. A thin tone will come in on the close perspective mikes; a blaring fortissimo on the others.

The eight mikes are connected to the control board, known also as the mixer. A special control board has been designed by Charles C. Grey, who is the engineer in charge of Metropolitan Opera broadcasts. He himself operates this mixer. His is the most important job in the scheme of broadcasting the opera. The mixer is, in effect, his keyboard. On it he plays his version of the opera. Fortunately, he is a sensitive, intelligent individual. He spends all his spare time experimenting. He is fascinated by the problems of broadcasting opera. He realizes that it is a new craft and that he has much to learn. His humility and his curiosity are the qualities that commend him as much as his undoubted accomplishments.

Observe what the man who operates this mixer can do. He can tune out any or all of the microphones. He can increase the tone that is transmitted through any one to an ear-shattering intensity. He can blend several of them. He can give an aria delicacy where the singer is ranting simply by tuning in a mike that is farthest away. He can give a bleating soprano the fullness of voice of a Flagstad by tuning in the closest mike and stepping up the juice.

The control engineer works in semi-darkness. He knows the dials of his control board as a virtuoso knows the piano keyboard. He must work rapidly to keep pace with the interplay of orchestral, choral and solo passages. Where a singer has a big aria and delivers it standing or sitting in one spot, the task of the engineer is comparatively simple. But when the artist sings his aria while acting all over the stage, the mixer must follow him with sureness and adroitness. He must shift the singer from one mike to another without losing the continuity of the music. One slip of the hand, and the work of the singer is distorted.

You can't fool the microphone. It is kindest to a naturally beautiful voice, smooth and equal throughout its scale. The voice of Flagstad, for example, is gratefully transmitted by the radio. The man at the controls does not have to resort to tricks to aid or abet her singing. He does not even have to chase her around the stage. She knows the value of economy of movement and gesture. When she sings, the radio engineers are not required to make many adjustments.

The microphones are placed in the footlights instead of the rear of the stage because the broadcasters wish to pick up the tone as it comes off the wooden apron, the last reflecting place before it enters the auditorium. This location also helps to eliminate all backstage noises. Yet they intrude from time to time, and the man at the controls must be vigilant to erase them instantly. The voice of the prompter, situated at the footlights midway between the two sets of mikes, gives the engineers the most trouble. There was a time when the radio audience could hear the prompter's admonitions, despite the engineer's care. Now the prompter is warned to be especially careful on Saturday afternoons.

The footlight mikes can pick up any sound on the stage, and they are sufficient for all the singing. There was one scene, however, where they did not prove effective. In "Mignon" the soprano enters on a balcony at a side and sings while a large crowd fills the stage. The mass of humanity acted like a tone absorber, and the mike in the footlights transmitted only a thin wisp of tone. Live and learn. When "Mignon" was broadcast again, the engineers had a special mike set up somewhere near the balcony so that this passage could be picked up easily.

The man at the controls sits in a darkened box on the

grand tier floor. His job is to watch the stage and the conductor while his hands manipulate the mixer. In the rear of this box is a score reader who follows the music and who gives the engineer the signal of important climaxes, decrescendos and the like. The score reader has marked his copy of the opera carefully, so that he can give the engineer at the controls ample warning. Usually four measures before is enough. Behind the glass door in the anteroom of the box the announcer is located, as well as an assistant engineer who keeps amplifiers and other equipment in order. The adjoining box is employed during intermissions for commentators, interviews and additional announcements.

The preparation for the broadcast is not extended. On Saturday morning the technicians arrive early at the Metropolitan Opera House and set up their equipment. Then, as they put it, they go in and do the show. There are few rehearsals, no excitement, no temperament. The results in the first years of opera broadcasting may not have been completely satisfying. But the experience gained each Saturday afternoon has helped to improve the technique. New microphones have been developed that give better definition of the orchestral choirs. New receiving equipment has been created that permits more comprehensive reception. And the engineers have learned how to use their equipment artistically.

Several years ago the National Broadcasting Company began to make recordings of the opera as it came through on a loud-speaker, and examination and criticism of the previous broadcast became possible.

Many criticisms have been directed at the men who preside over the broadcast. Some are justified; others are unfair. It is charged that the singer is accorded greater emphasis than the orchestra, which may be acceptable in an opera where the voice is predominant, but which is a distortion in music such as Wagner's. Bad balance, the engineers reply, is attributable in large part to receiving sets that have an insufficient frequency band. Their limited range precludes the hearing of the full scope of the broadcast as it is being transmitted.

The censure is sometimes fantastic. People write letters complaining that the engineers change eighth-notes into half notes, that they alter the rhythm, the phrasing and the intonation. But these are matters depending on the musicianship of the artist. Neither the technical equipment nor the technicians can alter by one jot or tittle the artist's interpretation. Their field of operations is limited to such matters as balance, tone quality and dynamics.

The engineers can be helpful to an artist in trouble, or they can be downright harmful. Some seasons ago a young debutante launched on a difficult aria and her voice bogged down in a series of florid, brilliant measures. There was no aiding the girl in the opera house. More than 3000 persons were witnesses to her misery, some suffering with her. But the radio audience knew little of her disaster. The man at the controls pulled up the orchestra so that its tone covered and obscured the cracking voice of the debutante. In a similar instance the engineer could easily let the soprano do her worst, and permit an audience of millions to hear her tribulations. If he wished to be malevolent, he could even increase the power at the juncture where the voice began to break. He could, in other words, aggravate or ameliorate the singer's dereliction; he could not, with the aid of all the king's horses and all the king's men, put her back on pitch. A device that would achieve such a miracle would be worth its weight in radium.

On the Air

Radio practices have resulted in some peculiar inquiries at the Metropolitan Opera. There was the occasion when "Tristan und Isolde" was being performed on a Saturday afternoon and, naturally, was being broadcast. The house had been sold out for a week. A woman called up several days before the performance and asked for three tickets; one for herself, she explained, and two for her daughters. She was told that the tickets were all gone.

"That's what they always say," she said, laughing.

"You can't buy them," she was informed.

"I didn't want to buy them," the woman replied. Then she added impatiently, "I wanted to help you out. Don't you need a studio audience?"

The quality of opera broadcasts would probably be enhanced if the stage directors of the Saturday matinee shows at the Metropolitan were to confer with the radio engineers. The singers in a large concerted number sometimes stand in the wrong positions for the purposes of the radio. Suppose that the quartet from "Rigoletto" is being sung. If Lawrence Tibbett, singing the title role, does not stand behind Lily Pons, the Gilda, the microphone will naturally give greater prominence to his voice. It would be easier to blend his baritone with Miss Pons's delicate coloratura soprano if he were placed behind her.

In an elaborate scene when a principal is mingling with a large chorus and ballet, the man at the controls must be able to single out the principal and to focus the most desirable microphone on him. If he loses sight of the principal and tunes in the wrong mike, the radio audience will hear a distorted version. Singers who choose to do a piece of effective acting by singing a passage with their backs to the audience give the engineers acute headaches, because the voice becomes difficult to pick up. Stage settings that are designed for artistic effect on a living audience may provide the wrong acoustics for the microphones.

It should be clear from these observations that the conditions required for a broadcast are different from those that are right for an audience in the flesh. It is probable that the requirements of both audiences could be satisfied by judicious study and co-operation. But remember how rushed the opera house is to put on its shows under prevailing conditions. Remember how hard-pressed the management is for rehearsal time. Perhaps we should not complain, considering that the broadcasts are more than reasonably satisfactory. Perfection would probably be attainable only in performances that were designed exclusively for the air.

The time when this consummation will be achieved may not be far off. The radio companies have indicated a disposition to arrange opera broadcasts from their studios. As long as television is not in common use, there is no need for an opera broadcast to have sets, costumes or action. The singers, orchestra, chorus and conductor are sufficient. The enormous cost of gathering a troupe like the Metropolitan is the major obstacle. On the creative side the radio has started another significant procedure. The National Broadcasting Company, for example, has commissioned young Gian-Carlo Menotti, skillful composer of the witty, spirited and delightful "Amelia Goes to the Ball," to write operas specially for the radio, even as the Columbia Broadcasting System has requested a group of composers to write for the air, including a radio opera by Louis Gruenberg, based on W. H. Hudson's "Green Mansions," and another by Vittorio Giannini.

One of the problems radio must continue to wrestle with, especially in broadcasts from the opera house, is what to do during intermissions. Various schemes have been tried, and each has had its element of ineffectiveness. There have been breezy and dignified, gossipy and learned, male and female commentators. There have been interviews with the stars, one or two informative and original, most of them platitudinous or in bad taste. There have been talks by officials and backstage folk. A host of letter writers always approves of one approach; a large number excoriates the same thing. Even silence was once tried during an intermission. That brought a holocaust of censorious letters.

Whatever the broadcasters do, they hear from the public. The letter writers to the management of the opera house are a corporal's guard compared to the enormous number of persons who take the trouble to tell the radio executives what they think about the opera. The correspondents are on every conceivable side of an issue, and when the issues seem exhausted they create new ones. You cannot stop a radio fan from writing. The broadcasting companies probably would not try to if they could. For the letters are still among the principal indications by which they steer their course. It has been observed that the intelligent radio listeners write an inconsiderable fraction of the letters in proportion to their numbers. Probably they are less inclined to praise or to blame. You can always turn a dial and be done with an irritating broadcast. But there is merit to the broadcaster's contention that you cannot alter the body politic without an exercise of your franchise. If you have ideas about opera broadcasts, write, phone or telegraph; don't just brood.

The radio, whether we like it or not, will probably increase in influence. It has already made itself enormously felt in the realm of the opera house. The Metropolitan has evidence to prove that hundreds of persons who have heard the operas on the air have come to the opera house to complete their experience by seeing as well as hearing. The potential audience has been multiplied on a gargantuan scale. The effects have been beneficial on the career of the individual artist, for stars have found that their concert hall audiences have increased throughout the world.

On the debit side there are the problems that the radio has tossed into the lap of the management—the dovetailing of broadcasting engagements for singers with appearances at the opera house, and the competition of the tremendous fees that radio pays compared with opera salaries. The consoling factor is that the opera company receives a large lump sum for broadcasting rights to bolster a weak exchequer.

The Metropolitan sells the radio rights to the National Broadcasting Company. The latter organization tries to dispose of the broadcast to a commercial sponsor. It has succeeded in the past—too well. There seemed to be a charming rightness in keeping with the spirit of some of our commercial mores that the Metropolitan broadcasts should be used to advertise a cigarette that is allegedly kind to the throat, or, again—better still—a mouth wash.

XXIII

PAYING THE PIPER

OPERA was cradled in wealth and bred in opulence. It has depended for its existence on the largesse of princes and potentates, states and municipalities, bankers and captains of industry. The traditions of opera are rooted in munificence. It could not be otherwise. A first-rate opera company ranks among the most expensive theatres in the world. That may be one of the secrets of its fascination. The world has rarely failed to be awed by grandiose costs. The courtesans who were kept in the finest style are best known to history.

Until the movies and the radio came along with their fabulous budgets, opera was the most expensive theatre so far as cost of production was concerned. Opera is still sui generis, for the admission price comes higher than in any other amusement. The movies and radio, despite huge expenditures, are modern industries with a rationale of mass production, and their product is to be had at low or nominal cost. Opera continues to traffic as a luxury. A single performance can play to a limited paying audience. Since that performance is put on at a mountainous cost, the price of admission is correspondingly high.

Although the top prices in the opera house are higher than in any other theatre, the income obtained from the sale of seats has never been sufficient to meet all the obligations. Not even at the Metropolitan, which balanced its budget for two decades and managed to establish a reserve fund of more than $1,000,000. The final accounting was in black ink instead of the customary red because the Metropolitan had additional sources of income—the sale of recording rights and the profits made from managing its own concert bureau which booked artists already under contract, to cite but two.

The Metropolitan, even today, is a million-dollar enterprise. It has had to tighten its belt, reduce salaries, cut expenses in order to survive. It has decreased the length of the season and lowered the price of tickets, thus diminishing its income. Nevertheless, the total cash turnover in a season is somewhere between $1,000,000 and $2,000,000 a year. And in the days before 1929 it did an annual business of about $3,000,000. The Chicago Opera in this period showed figures that were not far apart.

How is the money spent? Here is a chart for the Metropolitan season of 1936–37 that gives you an idea. Every dollar can be broken up in this fashion, to show what part of it is defrayed for the various elements of a Metropolitan season:

Artists, conductors, assistant conductors, stage managers...	$.30
Orchestra, including stage band, chorus and ballet	.29
Administrative staff	.05
Stage department, including sets, stage crew and wardrobe..	.15
Ushers, doormen, carriagemen	.02
Superintendent's department, including porters, cleaners, etc.	.03
Engineering department	.02
Rental of storehouses	.01
Taxes	.005
Gas and electricity	.01
Insurance	.01
Advertising	.0175
Supernumeraries	.005
Hauling and trucking scenery and baggage............	.025
Tickets, printing and stationery	.01
Miscellaneous, including royalties, music, railroad and steamship fares, postage, telephone, telegraph and cable tolls	.0475
	$1.00

Paying the Piper

The largest item, as you might have guessed, is the salary of the principal singers. What the total outlay may be in an American opera house of front rank it is impossible to say. Opera managements are secretive about these figures. They do not have to file corporate reports with the Securities and Exchange Commission, and they are thankful that they do not have to make individual salaries public. The heartburnings that would be created for artists who are paid less than others whom they look upon as their inferiors would be poignant beyond description. The recriminations, however, would not be beyond utterance.

The highest fee for a performance ever paid by the Metropolitan Opera went to Feodor Chaliapin, who received $3000 every time he sang. His was a contract for a limited number of performances a season, so that his total earnings at the opera house in any one year were not equal to those of some of the leading singers who worked twenty weeks or more.

The largest amounts, year in and year out, were collected by Enrico Caruso. He was paid a peak salary of $2500 a performance. He averaged two operas a week, and more than twenty weeks a season. His Metropolitan pay totaled more than $100,000 a year. In the days when Oscar Hammerstein was making things uncomfortable for the Metropolitan with his vigorous opposition at the Manhattan Opera House, he tried to tempt Caruso away from the Broadway house. He offered the tenor $5000 a performance. Caruso went to Gatti-Casazza and told him of Hammerstein's offer.

"Very well," said Gatti, apparently unruffled. "We shall meet the competition. We'll give you $5000. Only . . ." here his impassive countenance took on a rueful expression, "we shall have to save the money elsewhere. We shall put

[349]

nonentities in the cast with you. We shall have a smaller ensemble for your operas. But . . ." Gatti permitted a slight smile to cross his face. "We shall not let you go."

Caruso was indignant. "I did not say that I was taking Hammerstein's offer," he cried. "I am not! I stay here, at the old salary."

The Metropolitan did not pay the highest fees in this country, nor did it pay higher fees than the European opera houses, despite the popular belief that the New York opera house gave the highest salaries in the world. Caruso was offered $10,000 a performance in Mexico City, and in Buenos Aires he sang for $6600 a night. Chaliapin, when he sang in Chicago, worked for $4000 a performance. In the days of Insull, Chicago paid higher fees generally than New York. Contemporary stars can obtain from European theatres as much as, sometimes more than, they do in New York. And the farther west or south they travel in the Western Hemisphere the higher their earnings in comparison with New York's opera.

The Metropolitan has been able to trade on the prestige of its name. It has had to do so in the depression years. Artists will gladly sing at the Metropolitan for less than they can earn in other fields because it pleases their vanity to be known as members of the Metropolitan Opera Company. Some realize that the association with the Metropolitan will bring contracts for radio, concert, record and movie work at fat fees. As for the European artists, most of them are glad to come to America to work where the economic and political situation is not as chaotic as on the Continent and whence they can take away their earnings, which they cannot do in half the countries of Europe.

There are many singers who love opera, and who sing in it even though they can earn much more money in other fields.

Paying the Piper

The tenor, Richard Tauber, for example, sets aside two months each year to appear at the Vienna Opera, and he will not forego this period for tempting movie, radio or concert offers. And there are artists of the same mind at the Metropolitan—Tibbett, Crooks and Flagstad, to name but three.

Before the depression, there were a handful of tenors and prima donnas who earned as much as $2000 a performance, and another batch who averaged $1200, $1500 and $1800. Rosa Ponselle, Maria Jeritza, Lucrezia Bori, Beniamino Gigli, Lauritz Melchior, Lauri-Volpi were among the select group. But when the bottom fell out of the market, the days of these salaries were ended. Some fees were cut in half, with no sustained squawks, save from Gigli. He engaged in a public quarrel with Gatti-Casazza. At a time when thousands of American families were going on short, if any, rations, Gigli asserted that he would not endure the indignity of a cut from about $100,000 a year to a paltry $70,000. It was, he contended, the principle of the thing.

Leading sopranos and tenors are always better paid than singers whose voices happen to have lower ranges. Chaliapin was the only exception. Titta Ruffo and Michael Bohnen received the highest figures ever paid baritones by the Metropolitan, $1000 a performance. That was in the prosperous era. Their salaries would be measurably lower today.

A new scale has become effective since the depredations of the lean years. The Metropolitan now pays a top price of $1000 a performance. This sum is paid to a charmed circle: Kirsten Flagstad, Rosa Ponselle, Lauritz Melchior. A group of others—Martinelli, Tibbett, Schorr, Pons, Lehmann, Maison, Crooks, Rethberg, Pinza—earn between $500 and $1000. The salary scale drops to less than $100 a week for some of the lesser singers, and for this sum they may be requested to sing four times a week. Lawrence Tibbett has told me that in his first year at the Metropolitan—he was, of course, unknown and inexperienced—he received $60 a week. The next year he was raised to $75. He did not move into the higher salaried division until he leaped into prominence.

The fee for each performance is not the complete index of what the artist earns at the Metropolitan. Some singers in the higher brackets appear three or four times a season. Their total earnings are small. Artists like Kirsten Flagstad, Melchior, Tibbett are engaged for most of the season. Flagstad's contract, for example, calls for at least two, possibly three, performances a week. Melchior's requires two. If the season is sixteen weeks long and it is followed by a tour of three weeks, Flagstad may receive about $40,000 for her efforts. Which is considerably less than she would have earned, in view of her rank and drawing power, ten years ago.

Compare these figures with the salaries that are paid singers in the small opera companies, if you wish to discover why the Metropolitan charges a top price of $7 and the inferior company $1.50 or $1. The best paid principals in the San Carlo Company receive $200 for singing several times a week. Others are paid as little as $50 a week. I like best, as a comment on singers' salaries and, if you like, human achievement as well, the figures in a certain popular-priced performance of "Pagliacci" in New York. The Canio was to be paid $10, and the Nedda was promised $5, if she sang well, while for the donkey required in the opening scene of the opera the impresario had to pay $15 in advance.

Leading artists at the Metropolitan, who are paid on a performance basis, receive their fee only when they work. Illness is no excuse. The management, however, will try to provide a singer with an opportunity to make up lost performances if he can be maneuvered into the casts conveniently. The contract with the artist also gives the Metropolitan the right to send him out on concert. Twenty-five years ago this was a regular practice, but this contractual clause is now virtually ignored. The contract gives the management another concession in this clause: "The artist agrees to sing and perform without any compensation, whatsoever, in one or two performances or concerts during each season, at the Association's option, for the benefit of the Association or any similar purpose. Such performances or concerts shall not be counted in computing the number of guaranteed performances or concerts herein provided for." The management asks the artist to sing only at the Sunday night concerts under this stipulation.

If the Sunday night concerts do not entail payments to the principals, the exchequer is affected by the agreement to transport the artists to and from Europe each season. A little less than half the company are Europeans, and transportation costs for a group of this size adds up to a considerable sum.

The fees of singers are scaled according to drawing power and artistic prestige. Flagstad brings in more than she earns. Other artists do not attract any perceptible patronage, but they are needed for certain roles. There may be a shortage of first-class tenors, and the management must enter the open market and bid for the best that are available. The result may be that the company is paying a higher fee than the services of a given tenor warrant. There are always several such contracts in operation.

If the Metropolitan uncovers a new, shining star, it may benefit temporarily from a favorable agreement. When Flagstad made her unanticipated success, the Metropolitan had a tremendous bargain in her first season. Her $500 a week covered two or three performances. Lily Pons, in her first season, had a similar contract, and she, too, was a source of comfort to the treasury. She drew so many customers into the theatre during that season that the Metropolitan, I understand, presented her with a bonus.

3

As for the others, the first-line conductor may be paid nowadays about $25,000 or $30,000 a season, a figure that represents more than 50 per cent reduction from the highs of a few years ago. In refuting a charge that he left the Metropolitan because of salary cuts, Tullio Serafin let the cat out of the bag some time ago. His salary arrangements with the Metropolitan, he said, were as follows: Up to the season of 1932 he received a total of $58,000 a year—$50,000 for twenty-four weeks of the season; $6000 for the tour; and $2000 for pre-season rehearsal work. When he left the Metropolitan, he had taken three cuts which had reduced his salary to $34,000.

The manager may receive about $25,000 a year, and his assistant about $20,000. These are not, as American corporation stipends go, enormous figures. The Metropolitan is, after all, a sizable enterprise, and the men who head it work the year round. Their business cannot be neatly routined by efficiency experts. The human element—and an erratic element it is in the opera house!—is predominant.

The wages of the unionized help—orchestra, chorus, stage crew and wardrobe staff—are considerably higher today than they were three decades ago. When Grau was the manager the orchestra could be asked to rehearse without pay. The other groups worked for salaries that were much smaller than today's. It is unquestionably an advance that the men and women who do not take bows before the footlights should be well paid. The facts are stated only to show why the best tickets to the Metropolitan sell for $7 apiece.

The depression has caused the opera to trim its sails in many directions. In the prosperous era several productions were made—and they ran only for a limited number of performances—that cost about $75,000 each. Such operas were "Turandot," "Jonny Spielt Auf" and "Rondine." A large portion of the amount went for the sets, whereas recently an appropriation of $4000 was set aside for the décors for "Samson et Dalila." It was almost a miracle that any set was produced. The canvas for a drop 70 feet by 42 feet cost $150; cutting it cost another $100, and carting it, $50; the initial cost for one drop, then, was $300. There are a number of drops in "Samson" and they are only a part of the entire set.

4

You would think that royalties would not concern the opera house, since its chief stock in trade is music written many years ago. The works of many composers are in the public domain, of course: Gounod, Verdi (with the exception of "Otello" and "Falstaff"), Donizetti, Rossini and Wagner. In Germany, however, during the inflation of the Twenties, the opera houses were asked to pay a small percentage on their intake for Wagner performances to help out the Master's family, which had been hard hit economically. It may not be generally known that Maurice Grau, during his tenure as general manager at the Metropolitan, tried to make a deal with Cosima Wagner whereby he would pay a lump sum for the rights to all the Wagner works, but he was turned down.

Some operas are in the public domain, but since it is impossible to obtain copies of the scores, rental fees must be paid the publisher that are tantamount to royalties. Massenet belongs in this category. So do the Russians—Mussorgsky, Rimsky-Korsakoff, Tchaikovsky and the others. Russia did not join in the Berne convention on copyrights, and there is no obligation to pay royalties. But the scores are scarce, and their publishers must be paid rentals.

Among the composers whose works command royalties are Debussy, Charpentier, Offenbach, Humperdinck, Puccini and Richard Strauss. The last two draw the highest rates. For a performance of a Puccini opera in the winter season the Metropolitan must pay about $400 and about $200 for one in the spring season. Strauss leads them all. His reputation as the most exigent business man among living conductors is not unwarranted. The Metropolitan pays $500 and more a performance for his operas.

It may now be told that Edward Johnson considered the plan of giving a Strauss cycle at the Metropolitan several years ago, but he held off because of the royalty requirements.

The Metropolitan pays a flat sum in royalties, in contrast to the percentages of the receipts that foreign theatres must deliver. The reason is obvious. The Metropolitan has a large subscription audience that pays for its seats long before the repertory is selected and that subscribes no matter what the operas are. Payment of a percentage on this portion of the receipts would manifestly be unfair.

For a world première there is a special fee. The Metropolitan has paid as much as $1200 and $1800 for first-performance rights. Puccini's "Girl of the Golden West" and Humperdinck's "Königskinder" commanded high première rates.

5

The principal source of income is the money received from the sale of tickets. And what a fluctuating source that is! Every little wind that blows may affect the purchaser of opera tickets. When the stock market went for a downward ride in the fall of 1937, many persons who had subscribed for seats to the opera did not take them up. They had not been wiped out financially, as some were in 1929, 1930 and those gloomy years. They were perfectly able to pay. But opera was a luxury to them. It was one of the first items to be eliminated in a hasty plan of retrenchment. And when the stock market reversed its course, many of the timorous returned to the subscription fold.

A second important source of income is the payment made for the broadcasting rights. They are purchased by the National Broadcasting Company for a sum in the neighborhood of $100,000. If the broadcasting company manages to sell the Metropolitan to a sponsor, there is no increase in the sum received by the opera. The arrangement with the Metropolitan permits the broadcaster to sell its rights to a commercial sponsor.

A third and wholly unpredictable source of aid comes in gifts from individuals, groups or organizations. This form of support is much smaller than one might expect. Considering that the Metropolitan is the foremost institution of its kind in the land, it receives almost no large gifts or bequests, as do museums, universities and research organizations. The endowment fund started several years ago by the Metropolitan Opera Guild with a gift of $10,000 is an inconsiderable amount. Such a fund would have to be at least $1,000,000 before its income would mean anything to the company.

Personal gifts that represent the affection of a man or a woman for the lyric theatre there always are. A friend of the Metropolitan offered recently to pay for a new swan in "Lohengrin." Mr. Johnson informed the prospective donor that a swan had just been purchased, but suggested that a new cherry tree for "Madama Butterfly" would be equally welcome. The giver accepted the hint. Another friend purchased a new set of bells for "Parsifal."

Mr. Johnson is delighted with these offerings. He feels

that the giver derives a sense of personal identification with the gift. When he hears the bells in "Parsifal," he may feel that he has a part in the performance. The management prefers a concrete gift to a donation of the several hundred dollars that it represents, because the money disappears into the bottomless pit of the opera's expenditures and the donor has no recurrence of satisfaction.

Not that the Metropolitan sniffs these days at any sum of money, no matter how small. Since the depression it has worked on a narrow margin, and it has counted its pennies with the care of the small entrepreneur. Gone are the days when an extra rehearsal could be scheduled at will, when a new costume could be purchased without a second thought, when a set could be replaced without cautious consideration. The deficit must be watched with unending vigilance.

6

The inevitable deficit! After you have enumerated all the sources of income, there is a deficit to contend with. What is its size and who pays it?

From 1910 to 1930 there were no deficits. When the debacle came, the deficits were enormous, and the reserve fund of more than $1,000,000 was speedily wiped out. The deficit mounted to as much as $300,000. Finally, when the reserves were eaten up, the opera went to the country for help. And now a guarantee fund is underwritten in part by the Juilliard Musical Foundation and the remainder through the efforts of the board of directors.

The recovery from the financial nadir of 1932 reduced the size of the deficit. When Gatti-Casazza finished his final season, he did not leave the company stone broke. Thanks to his discovery of Flagstad that year, he left behind him a sum of about $50,000. In Edward Johnson's first year as man-

Paying the Piper

ager the deficit was a little less than $100,000, and in his second it was down to about $50,000.

The truth is that the Metropolitan cannot hope to break even in a fourteen- or sixteen-week season. It must run for at least twenty weeks at capacity or near capacity to achieve this happy state. Overhead expenses, such as taxes, rentals, administrative salaries and maintenance of the theatre, go on the year round, and they cannot be balanced unless they are distributed over a longer period.

Where do the boxholders come into the picture? They are, of course, the owners of the theatre and the site. There are thirty-five boxes in the lower tier and each boxholder owns one-thirty-fifth of the Metropolitan Opera House. They are assessed $4500 each year, and this sum, a total of $157,500, is used for the maintenance of the building and the payment of taxes, as well as the administration of the owning company, the Metropolitan Opera and Real Estate Company. In return for this assessment the boxholder has the right to the use of the box for every regular performance. Figure out what this is worth in admissions. A box seats at least eight persons. Calculating on the basis of $7 a seat—which is low, considering that the parquet chairs are $7—each performance is worth $56. For the week's five major subscriptions the box is worth $280, and for a season of sixteen weeks, $4480. These estimates do not take into account the boxholder's right to the use of his box for Saturday night subscription performances and for the spring season. On the cost of seats the boxholder more than breaks even.

It is true that the boxholder's investment represents a frozen asset. He receives no interest from his share in the property, and his stake in it is estimated at about $200,000. It is also true that a man would not normally purchase tickets for so many performances of opera in a season. But being a boxholder connotes a certain social aura, and for some people that is more valuable than the money involved. Before 1929, and it may be true again, the boxholder could sublet his box for certain nights or for the major part of the season and get back a large part of his assessment. Finally, the assessment can always be listed as an income tax deduction.

It has been pointed out that twelve of the boxholders are now estates. The trustees, whose prime duty it is to liquidate the assets of an estate, seek to protect the investment for future realization. They vote against most ideas of expenditures. They form an initial conservative bloc. There are the second and third generation inheritors of boxes who do not give a hang for opera and who prefer to spend their money on yachts, polo, a string of race horses, a flier into the movies.

The questions are posed: What will happen when the rich men and the estates that make up the boxholders become fed up? Will they not put the house on sale at the first favorable opportunity, and will not that bring an end to the Metropolitan?

Suppose, for the sake of discussion, that they should bail out. The present arrangement is not all love and kisses. If opera has any vitality, it would survive. It would tie up with the radio, the movies or even the government. In any event, the rigmarole of society, which is of no importance to art, would disappear. Art would stand or fall on its own merits.

I wish that a certain daring project that was secretly discussed in the season of 1934–35 had come to fruition. It is a story, not told publicly before, that has elements of excitement.

When Gatti-Casazza had announced his resignation as general manager before that season began, the board of directors considered ways and means of going on. One plan that was proposed and finally turned down was an amalgamation with the Philharmonic-Symphony Society. Then the board confessed that there seemed to be no apparent solution. In a grave statement, the chairman of the board, Paul D. Cravath, announced that there was imminent peril that the Metropolitan would have to close its doors.

At this juncture the men and women who *are* the Metropolitan in the truest sense—the singers, conductors, et al.— undertook to act. They met in secret conclave. There were about sixty prominent members of the company at the meeting: the stars from Bori, Tibbett, Johnson down and the conductors from Bodanzky down. The conferees agreed that they would carry on the Metropolitan, come what may. They assumed that they could obtain from the board the use of the theatre and its sets and costumes, but they were willing, if that permission were not forthcoming, to go into another theatre. Some even had decided on Edward Johnson as the general manager of the co-operative enterprise.

When the board heard of this movement in the ranks it went speedily into action. A meeting of the full membership was called, and several days later came the announcement of the agreement with the Juilliard Foundation to underwrite the 1935–36 season to the extent of $250,000.

It is exciting to know that the artists were ready to take action on their own. It is perhaps a pity that they did not. Most astonishing of all is the fact that this story has never leaked out before.

XXIV

MAKING THE NATION'S OPERAS

YOU cannot run an opera house without operas. A lyric theatre can survive caterwauling sopranos, whining tenors, unmusical conductors, inept décors, insensitive audiences and even a dearth of angels, provided it does not have to put up with all of them at the same time. An absence of operas that have the power to charm and to stir the emotions would be fatal. An axiomatic proposition? No doubt. But the composer seems to be taken for granted; the interpreters receive the most attention from the public and, with honorable exceptions, the press.

The explanation is easy to perceive. The interpreters are among the living. There is a greater urgency in the problems of our contemporaries, especially if they are to be heard or seen and if they are constantly discussed in print. Most of the composers represented on our opera stages have been dead anywhere from twenty to two hundred years. Students, antiquarians, critics and some laymen may be fascinated by the psychology of Wagner, the reasons for Beethoven's deafness, or the effect of Mozart's poverty on his greatest works. They are, indeed, absorbing problems. They have their place and their value.

But what of the present? Shall we always be venerating the past to the exclusion of our own time? We shall be told that contemporary composers are a dull, pretentious, noisy lot, and that if we would contemplate the eternal verities, we must concern ourselves with the Masters. This is especially true in the United States, which has not yet produced an opera able to stand on its feet in the repertory.

Making the Nation's Operas

What is to blame for America's backwardness in developing an operatic culture of its own? We have no widespread diffusion of opera in the flesh, with small permanent companies in all the major centers. On the other hand, we have no native operas which would attract our people and with which we could fill the repertory of scores of local theatres. Which is the cause, which the effect? It is like determining the priority of the chicken or the egg.

One thing it is important to remember: if America is lagging in the production of works of creative genius in the lyric theatre today, the countries of the Old World are no better off. Where are new significant works being produced? The state of the world, in transition from one form of society to another, may have something to do with it.

The Metropolitan Opera House has the reputation of having tried to give the native composer a hearing. Gatti-Casazza was convinced from the moment of his arrival in 1908 that the Metropolitan, America's ranking lyric theatre, owed a duty to the home-bred composer. He instituted a prize contest with a first award of $10,000 and a Metropolitan première. He traveled out of town to hear new compositions. He welcomed the submission of scores. He had, as one of his colleagues said recently, a fixation about the need to give American operas. For this reason he accepted and mounted patently mediocre works, knowing in his heart that they had no chance. In his twenty-seven years here he produced sixteen American operas and ballets, giving them 126 performances in and out of New York.

Edward Johnson has declared that he is equally eager to give the American composer a hearing. In two years he has put on two works: Richard Hagemann's "Caponsacchi," and Walter Damrosch's "The Man Without a Country." The first had a total of two performances; the second, four thus far.

[363]

Opera: Front and Back

The most successful native works performed at the Metropolitan, from the financial or artistic point of view, were Henry F. Gilbert's "Dance in the Place Congo," John Alden Carpenter's "Skyscrapers," both ballets, and Deems Taylor's "Peter Ibbetson" and Louis Gruenberg's "The Emperor Jones," both operas. Gilbert's music, on the word of credible authorities, was distinguished by integrity and a feeling for one corner of the American scene. It was not a popular success, achieving a total of five performances. The other three works were good theatre. They were smoothly staged and they had the benefit of excellent interpreters.

The remaining fourteen were well-meaning gestures from the Metropolitan management, but they missed fire. One or two of them may have had a glimmer of good music, a scene that caught fire momentarily or a story that had some vitality. In the aggregate, they were stillborn. The public knew it, and the management was compelled to recognize the dolorous facts. But the composers were not always persuaded that they had failed. Horatio Parker, who wrote the opera that won the $10,000 prize—"Mona," with a libretto by Brian Hooker—insisted that he had created something of merit and was convinced that the public and the critics had been wrong in their judgment.

Another American composer, whose opera finished a poor also-ran in the Metropolitan stakes, never shifted from the optimistic view he had of his work while he was writing it. His librettist inquired one day how long the opera would run.

"Four hours or so," was the reply.

"But that is a long stretch," the librettist said. "Modern audiences will not sit for four hours in any theatre."

The composer was not disturbed. Without a trace of self-consciousness he said: "What about 'Meistersinger'?"

[364]

Making the Nation's Operas

Occasionally a composer is honest enough to admit the shortcomings of his work. Deems Taylor, who was working recently on his third opera, was asked by a friend why his new work was taking so long to complete.

"I did not realize," he replied, "how difficult it is to write a good tune."

When a new American opera is being mounted the composer naturally is on hand to observe and advise. He can be a burden to the conductor and the performers, for the practical problems of the stage and the visions that the composer tried to capture on paper may not jibe.

Henry F. Gilbert, who was American to the core in his bluntness, vigor and essential democratic nature, made himself unforgettable to people connected with the Metropolitan. When his ballet was in rehearsal, Gilbert was constantly on the stage. Ottokar Bartik, the ballet master, tried to induce him to go elsewhere and finally ordered him off the stage. But Gilbert was not gone for long.

When the score was suggested to Otto Kahn and the Metropolitan, Gilbert was asked to take it to Bodanzky for an examination. Bodanzky recommended the ballet for performance. Did that make Gilbert any the more pleased with Bodanzky? Not at all. He described his visit with Bodanzky to a friend in the following words:

"You ride up in an elevator with gold leaf." Gilbert's voice became gloomier and he sniffed. "Then Bodanzky hands me a long cigarette with his name printed on it. He's a dude. He played my music as if it were a Viennese polka. I won't have him conducting it."

Gilbert told the Metropolitan authorities much the same thing. In the end, Pierre Monteux conducted the ballet. Gilbert was not satisfied with the production. A year later he contributed his comments to Philip Hale's Boston Symphony program notes and excoriated the Metropolitan, from Otto Kahn down.

But Kahn recognized Gilbert's talent. He spoke of him as a composer who had the inner necessity to write music. And out of his admiration for the man's gifts he sent him each year at Christmas time—despite Gilbert's criticism—a check for $500.

How does the Metropolitan obtain its American operas for production? Most of them are submitted by the composers. Several of them have been commissioned. The latter method has not been oftener used because it is both dangerous and expensive. The Metropolitan cannot pay large sums for a new American work. It would be a poor investment because the rights would bring nothing from other parts of the country. In Europe—until four or five years ago—a publisher or theatre that commissioned a first-rank composer knew that there would be ample returns. For example, when Paul Hindemith was writing "Cardillac," bids for its performance, even before it was finished, arrived from thirty-four—count 'em, thirty-four!—theatres. After the première, about a dozen of these opera houses reneged, paying a forfeit. The others went through with their agreements. This was, of course, in the old Germany. The Nazis have tried to discourage curiosity in anything but their own depravities.

In France the outstanding composers are encouraged to write for the lyric theatre because they know that their works will be done. The government makes it a condition of its subsidy to the Opéra and the Opéra-Comique that they will do a certain number of new native works. In recent years the Opéra has been required to mount five, and the Opéra-Comique three annually.

But in America there is no endowment to provide composers with funds so that they will be able to give all their time to turning out an opera. The Metropolitan cannot offer much in cash. It will make a reasonable payment, as it did to Deems Taylor. It will copy the parts, saving an enormous labor or expenditure for the composer. It will mount the work. It will pay the royalties. But it has not the resources— so it claims—to do more.

The Metropolitan management once invited a distinguished composer to write a new opera. He was successful in other fields of music, not excluding the popular. He also taught. He managed to make a comfortable living. After considering the Metropolitan request, the composer said that he would undertake to do an opera only if he had a year, clear of all other obligations, in which to write it. He estimated that he would need $30,000 in advance. Another eminent composer put an even higher price on his services. He requested $20,000 for six months.

If the Metropolitan did not feel it could spend a great deal of money to commission new operas, Otto Kahn was not hesitant in assuming the initiative. When Ernest Bloch came to this country, almost two decades ago, it was suggested to him that he write an opera for the Metropolitan. Artur Bodanzky took him to meet Mr. Kahn to discuss the project. The latter was eager to promote it. He gave Bloch an advance payment of $1000. But Bloch never did write the opera. Possibly he was persuaded that his one and only opera, "Macbeth," written when he was a young man, was enough and that his gifts were not for the stage. And it may be that Kahn was not troubled over Bloch's failure to write the opera. Kahn was perhaps pleased that this opportunity had been offered him to help a man of genius.

There are always some composers or their relatives and friends who are willing to pay for a performance of their operas. I know that one leading Metropolitan conductor was offered $10,000 to put on an American work. Even if the conductor or the opera officials cared to be paid for a première—which they do not—the operas that carry such premiums are unhappily of no account.

The Metropolitan management sees to it that every opera submitted is examined thoroughly. Even if a score is offered a second time years later, it is looked over once more. Considering the size of the country, not many operas are being written. Certainly not many are sent to the Metropolitan. Here are the figures for new operas submitted in seven years:

```
1930 ..............................  21
1931 ..............................  16
1932 ..............................  12
1933 ..............................  11
1934 ..............................  12
1935 ..............................  60
1936 ..............................  42
```

The figures jumped in 1935 and 1936 because a new manager was named at the Metropolitan, and a good many disappointed composers took fresh hope and sent their old scores to Edward Johnson.

Two or three refusals do not discourage some composers. One man has submitted his opera half a dozen times. For the last fifteen years he has refused to take the score back. He says that he wants the Metropolitan to have it in the safe—just in case . . .

Another composer once submitted his brain child to the Metropolitan, and while the opera was being examined one page of the libretto was lost. The composer sued the Metropolitan for $20,000. Of course he did not collect. But the Metropolitan learned to take no chances. It now demands that its liability be limited.

Making the Nation's Operas

The Metropolitan begins by examining the libretto of every new opera submitted. Most plots deal with spacious biblical themes requiring the kind of staging and expense that were lavished on Max Reinhardt's sumptuous half-million-dollar production, "The Eternal Road." Or they have secular themes in which the convolutions of the plot are too deep even for the opera house, which is used to complicated plots. The majority of operas have to be rejected without further ado because of the weaknesses of the story. Nevertheless, the Metropolitan studies the score. Members of the conductors' staff are asked to look it over and to report. If there is any hint of talent for composition, the management will re-examine the libretto, to see whether it can be saved by revision.

The operas that show promise but that have not the qualities worthy of immediate performance are returned with suggestions to the composer. Those that look as if they could be staged are played by a member of the opera association staff, and the executives of the company sit in. Occasionally revisions are necessary in the story, often in the music. When they are made, the Metropolitan may undertake to produce the opera.

Once a new American opera is under way, it undergoes further changes. Wise is the composer who knows where, when and from whom to accept advice. It is no secret that Deems Taylor willingly listened to recommendations. If a singer thought that the vocal line was ungrateful or difficult of production, Taylor was prepared to make reasonable changes. If the conductor advised a shift in the instrumentation, he gladly followed his counsel.

The Metropolitan Opera will cheerfully accept recommendations regarding the existence of new operas. It was a music critic, Olin Downes, who spoke of "The Emperor

[369]

Opera: Front and Back

Jones" to Gatti-Casazza. Mr. Downes did not recommend the opera, he merely suggested that the Metropolitan examine it. The rest is history.

The Metropolitan has learned that it cannot seek out a story with fine, operatic possibilities and then farm it out to a composer. There is always the danger that the musical setting will not be right. The metabolism of "Merry Mount" was an excellent lesson. Richard L. Stokes wrote the libretto and took it, at the suggestion of another music critic, Lawrence Gilman, to Howard Hanson, who agreed to prepare a score. The Metropolitan was advised of the parturition of this opera and somehow it was committed to it. The setting turned out to be ordinary. It should be added, in fairness to the composer, that the libretto missed the opportunities of its magnificent theme, New England in the first years of its colonization.

Assuming that a limited number of operas are being written by Americans because there is little likelihood of a hearing, what is wrong with those that are being composed? Even if he is born with a gift for opera, the composer cannot master his business anywhere but in the theatre. Donizetti wrote sixty or more operas. Verdi turned out thirty. Who remembers his earliest efforts, "Oberto Conte di S. Bonifacio" or "Un giorno di regno"?

It was Verdi who once summed up the composer's task. A young composer, Franchetti, who was considering the libretto of "Tosca," later set by Puccini, of course, had asked the great maestro whether the verse, "E lucevan le stelle," should be set to a romanza, a canzonetta or an arioso. Verdi made a classic reply.

"Write," he said, "a little music, just a little music."

Is no one in America writing "a little music"? Are we, as

a nation, really barren of creative possibilities in the field of opera?

A full discussion of these questions might fill a separate volume. They pose the problem of our entire esthetic. Each man's answers will depend on his criteria. Certainly the opera houses of America are acting on the basis of the standards held by their leading figures.

While the Metropolitan has searched for worthy American operas, it has, judging entirely by the works it has produced, tried to find lyric works that followed the general pattern laid down by the composers of Europe. It has awarded the accolade of a première to works that, with one or two exceptions, followed a well-known formula. Even the Metropolitan has recognized, however, that the European approach will not fit an American theme. For this reason it turned down Vittorio Giannini's "The Scarlet Letter." Here was a composer who wrote with a prodigal outpouring of melody. But his gifts were Italian in spirit. His style, it was clear, was not suited to an austere Puritan theme.

But opera, as I pointed out in an opening chapter, need be nothing more nor less than a combination of music and drama. I have seen and heard, in theatres outside the opera house, scenes that were more truly American opera than many of the native compositions produced at the Metropolitan. There was a production called "Run, Little Chillun" produced on Broadway some years ago, with the Hall Johnson Negro Choir. The conception was Mr. Johnson's. The story was banal. But the last scene had an unforgettable impact. It was built around a church meeting in which the Negro spirituals were employed with stunning dramatic effect. There was counterpoint of singing and of action. It was dynamic and superlatively American.

[371]

Opera: Front and Back

The late George Gershwin gave a hint of another truly indigenous conception. Not in his abortive and pretentious "folk opera," "Porgy and Bess," but in the opening scene of "Of Thee I Sing." The setting was a typical American political parade, and the music, "Wintergreen for President," matched the staging, in its humor, raucousness and rich American flavor. And there were moments in "Show Boat" that suggested a feel and a grasp of the American spirit.

But these are, admittedly, only beginnings. Neither Gershwin nor Jerome Kern possessed the technical equipment and the sheer genius needed to realize a large American conception. But composers will appear who will utilize the ideas and the ferment of social movement and aspiration that is America. They will create in our own spirit and out of our own time. The opera companies perhaps will not recognize them. And those whose eyes and ears are forever turned to the past may be preoccupied grubbing in the archives and inditing for the nth time rewarmed rhapsodies to some departed genius. But the new, the authentic American expression will be heard. Possibly not in the opera house nor in the concert halls. It may emerge full-throated from some remote corner of the land and its notes may sound in the moving picture theatre, through the radio, or even in the night club. For a healthy, vigorous people must sing.

ANOTHER PERFORMANCE

The second act of "Coq d'Or" with Pons and Pinza

THE REHEARSAL
Isolde (Flagstad) and Brangäne (Thorborg)
Samson (Maison) with a beret and Dalila (Wettergren)

THE CONDUCTOR
Toscanini gives a cue, and he means it
Bodanzky ponders the next move

THE CONDUCTOR AGAIN

upper left, Pelletier leads the orchestra; *upper right*, de Abravanel works with
Tibbett; *below*, Panizza asks for pianissimo

MORE REHEARSALS
Assistant conductors synchronize offstage voices; *below*, Wotan (Schorr) in spats faces the Valkyries

THE ORCHESTRA NEEDS REHEARSALS TOO

upper left, 'cellos; ***upper right***, bassoons; ***lower left***, trombones;
lower right, harps

STAGE EXECUTIVES

Chorusmaster, régisseur, Johnson, conductor, and assistant; *below*, Another régisseur and chorus, also prop men

THE STARS LEARN HOW

upper left, Martinelli with cane; *upper right*, Lehmann and Crooks
in "Tosca"; *below*, Tibbett as the rogue Gianni Schicchi

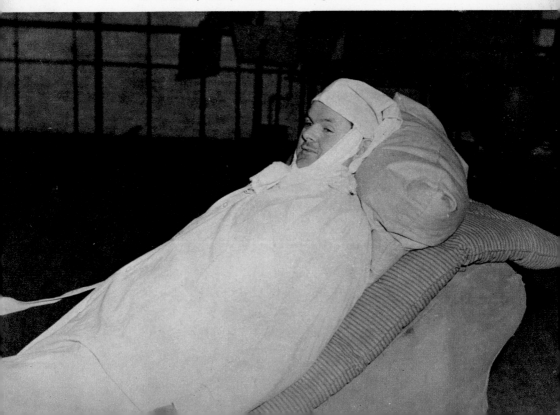

SIEGFRIED (HARTMANN) IN GALLUSES
OCTAVIAN (THORBORG) AND BARON OCHS (LIST)

REHEARSAL FOR TWO
Bovy and Martini, with Panizza beating time

REHEARSAL FOR ONE
Erda (Thorborg) uses a lift to emerge from the bowels of the earth

TIME OUT
A pause in a rehearsal; *below*, When Gatti was boss and Bori and Johnson were just singers

MANAGER, PAST AND PRESENT

Gatti looks things over on stage
Johnson tackles a problem in his office, with secretary Villa

THE BALLET, LARGE AND SMALL

The regular corps rehearses; *below,* The diminutive auxiliary being aided by their mothers

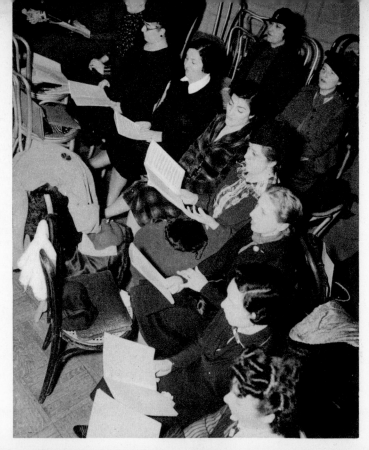

THE CHORUS
Ladies of the
ensemble rehearse

Gentlemen as
boyars

THE SUPERS
The distaff side; *below*, Card players and kibitzers await their cue

AND STILL THE ORCHESTRA REHEARSES
upper left, violins; *upper right*, trumpets; *lower left*, tuba;
lower right, tympani

FEROCIOUS BEAST—
The dragon in "Siegfried" rehearses

CHORUSMASTER CLEVA GIVES HIS CHARGES THE PITCH

CONTROLS FOR
MACHINES AND
HUMAN BEINGS

**Electricians check
the lights**

**The prompter gives
the singer some
help**

THE STAGE CREW
Rigging a set; *below*, Fixing a bedroom scene

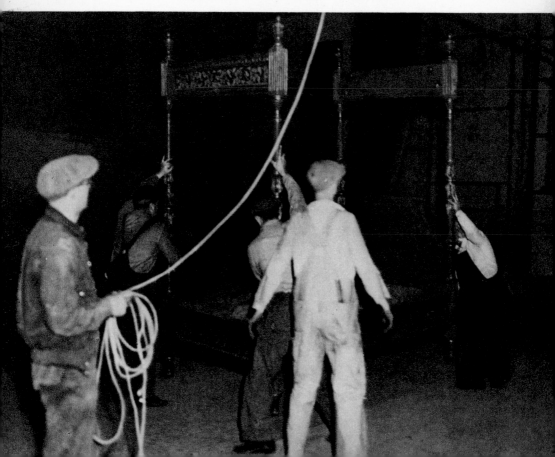

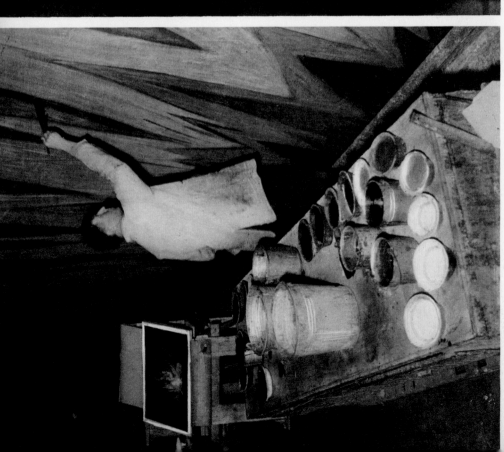

Adjusting lights

COLOR AND LIGHT

On the paint bridge

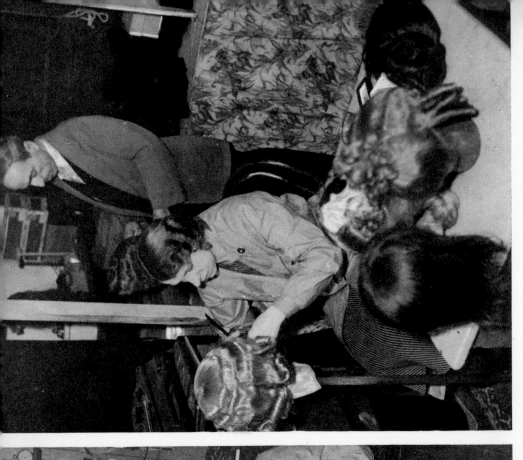

FRILLS AND CURLS

Seamstresses and wigmakers preparing their share in the opera

Bori turned into Violetta

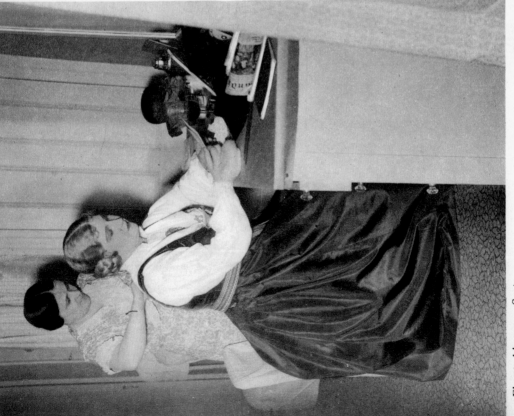

Flagstad becomes Senta

IN THE DRESSING ROOM

MOVIE STARS BACK IN THE OPERA HOUSE
Lily Pons (*above*) and Gladys Swarthout

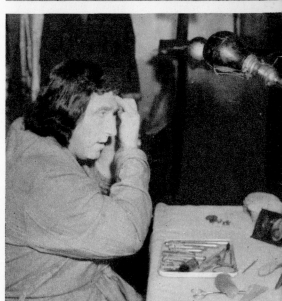

THREE TENORS AND A BARITONE

upper left, Crooks with a hairdresser; *upper right*, Huehn vocalizes; *lower left*,
Maison through the looking-glass; *lower right*, Martinelli grows long hair

LIBRARIAN: The late Lionel Mapleson, at Met from 1889 to 1937
MUSICAL SECRETARY: Giuseppe Sturani fixes rehearsal schedule

CONFERENCE: Johnson and assistant managers Ziegler and Lewis
FAREWELL PARTY: Gatti, Toscanini, Farrar, Galli and Ponselle entering

THE CUSTOMER
In the lobby and from the box-office window

Taking a nip at the bar

Following the score

THE AUDIENCE

INDEX

INDEX

[375]

Index

Index

Index

Index

Dutchman," that her husband might hear her, 131; 197, 215, 229, 231, 246, 279, 289, 297, 299, 303, 307, 314, 327, 340, 351–3, 358

Fleischer, Editha, 92, 134

Floor cloths to guide setting of scenery, 37, 38

"Flying Dutchman, The," 130; sung for the benefit of Mme. Flagstad's husband, 131

Flying machines for Rhine-maidens, 39

Fokine, Michel, teaches Lily Pons a "Coq d'Or" dance, 193

Food in opera sometimes real, 40

Forsell, John, 241

"Forza del Destino, La," 6, 86

Franchetti, Alberto, 370

Fremstad, Olive, 56, 80, 87, 320

Frick, Henry C., 266

Furtwängler, Wilhelm, 162

Gadski, Johanna, tries for a come-back, 92

Galli, Rosina, ballet mistress, quarrels over stage temperatures, 106; 186–8; cuts up ballet costumes, 192; her personal interest in her corps, 193

Galli-Curci, Amelita, her discovery by the Chicago Opera Co., 89; an ordinary drawing card at the Metropolitan, 90; her intelligence and a goat, in Gatti's judgment, 252, 253

Gallo, Fortune, 313, 331

Garden, Mary, 9, 81, 87, 93; endures wandering hand of a baritone while reclining on a couch in "Tosca," 116; 150, 247; general manager of Chicago Opera Co., 260; 301–3, 322, 323

Garlichs, Frank, 238

Gate-crashers, their wiles, 284

Gatti-Casazza, Giulio, frequent visitor backstage during performances, 34; insists on Toscanini rehearsing without score, 48; reply to musicians who complained of Toscanini's calling them names, 49; abandoned an opera only once, 58; waits fifteen years to produce "Pelléas et Mélisande," 64; sought new work by American composer, 66; 68; preparation of opening the season, 70; arranged subscription nights with

scientific precision, 77; 79; preparing for his last season, 82; faith in Konetzni misplaced, 83; takes chance on Tibbett in "Falstaff," 84; 87, 89, 90; keeps secret the engagement of Lily Pons, 90; his early engagement of Jeritza, 92; 95, 98, 106, 117, 118; a moment of congratulation, 123, 124; 129, 131; soothes Caruso's ire over criticism, 138; 142–4, 148; reconciled with Toscanini, 149; 150; instituted chorus school at the Metropolitan, 181; 182, 183, 189; breaks supers' strike in "Aïda," 199; 218, 221, 238, 240–3; Verdi's advice to him, 244; his eclecticism, 245; 246–50; his methods of appeasement, 251–3; 255–8, 262, 263, 265; list of operas he presented 100 times or more, those more than 50 times, 308–10; counters Hammerstein's offer to Caruso, 349, 350; 351, 358; his resignation, 360; instituted prize contest for an American opera, 363; 370

Geese in "Königskinder," sequel in Christmas dinners, 14, 15

German Opera Co., 92

Gershwin, George, 372

Giannini, Vittorio, 344; his "Scarlet Letter" turned down, 371

Gigli, Beniamino, 81; hopes for Caruso's laurels, 99; slaps Jeritza's face over curtain call, 101, 102; carries on Christmas giving, 111; his departure from the Metropolitan, 117; his intelligence and a goat, in Gatti's judgment, 252, 253; 351

Gilbert, Henry F., his ballet "Dance in the Place Congo," 364–6

Gilbert, W. S., on unintelligible patter, 7, 8

Gilman, Lawrence, 370

"Gioconda, La," 6, 28, 106; Scotti carries an egg through a scene, 121, 122; its music as a test for clarinetists, 170; 183

"Giorno di Regno, Un," early opera by Verdi, 370

"Giovanni Gallurese," 308

"Girl of the Golden West, The," 46, 225, 297, 308, 356

Index

Index

lying prone, 61, 285; 72; her rise in European opera, and engagement by Gatti, 92, 93; in fight with Gigli over curtain call, 101, 102; clever at managing stage effects, 209; 227, 279, 303, 351

"Jewels of the Madonna," 55

Jockey Club (Paris) creates uproar over ballet in "Tannhäuser," 186; 315

Johnson, Edward, his caution to a singer, 9; likes to visit backstage, 34; as Pelléas, 64; seeks new work by American, 66; 69, 73; search for singers, 87, 93; 168, 211, 238, 241, 243; his methods with the company, 253–5; 281, 307, 316, 356–8, 361, 363, 368

Johnson, Dr. Samuel, opinion of music, 5

Jones, Robert Edmond, scene designer, 51; driven to tears by opposition, 52

"Jonny Spielt Auf," 355

Jorgulesco, Jonel, scene designer, 51

Judels, Jules, in charge of supers, 199, 203, 220–2

Judels, Maurice, 199

Juilliard, Augustus D., his friendship for opera, 264, 265; his death, 266

Juilliard Musical Foundation, 264, 265, 358, 361

"Juive, La," Caruso's last opera appearance, 19; 26, 132, 233, 302

"Julien," 248

Kahn, Otto, recommends Mme. Flagstad, 82; his opinion of Gatti-Casazza, 242; his plans for new opera house, 255; the Abou ben Adhem of directors, 256–60; his death, 258; 262, 278; his recognition of Henry F. Gilbert's talent, 365, 366; 367

Katz, Emil, catered at the Metropolitan, 286

Kern, Jerome, 372

Kiesler, Frederick, scene designer, 51

"Kill yourself!" advice to a tenor with a strangling voice, 286

"King's Henchman, The," 211

Kipnis, Alexander, 92

"Königskinder," 14, 15, 245, 356

Konetzni, Anna, 82; Gatti's faith in her unfulfilled, 83

Kullmann, Charles, 9

"Lakmé," its music as test for oboists, 170; 197, 209; poor performance shatters some illusions, 295; 303, 307

Lanzilotti, Nicholas, in charge of costumes at the Metropolitan, 226, 228, 230

Latecomers at the opera, 6

Laubenthal, Rudolf, his good and bad qualities, 57, 58

Lauri-Volpi, Giacomo, 14; his claims as Caruso's successor, 99; 351

Lawrence, Marjorie, 9

"Legend of Tristan, The," 248

Lehmann, Lilli, 80, 128, 129, 133, 203, 223

Lehmann, Lotte, 92, 93, 351

Leider, Frida, misses cue in "Walküre" by attack of dizziness, 11; 82, 83, 92

"Leonore" overture No. 3 as a test for violinists and bassoons, 170

Leporte, Rita de, prima ballerina, 193

Lewis, Earle R., 71, 73, 272, 297

Lewisohn Stadium, 193

Lighting controlled from call board, 37

List, Emanuel, 133

"Lodoletta," a miserable failure, 303

"Lohengrin," 18, 29, 130, 159; its music as a test for violinists, 170; 183, 209, 331, 357

Longone, Paul, director of the Chicago Opera Co., 241, 261

"Louise," singer who forgot her line, 11; 81, 151, 247

Love-making among singers, and its complications, 102–5

"Lucia di Lammermoor," singer interpolates role from "Trovatore," 10; 303

Lully, Jean Baptiste, 3

"Macbeth," Ernest Bloch's only opera, 367

McCormack, John, his engagement at the Metropolitan turns out a fizzle, 88

McCormick, Edith Rockefeller, dominant in Chicago Opera, 262

McCormick, Harold, contributor to Chicago Opera, 260, 261

McDermott, Tom, a galleryite for fifteen

Index

Index

"Mona," wins $10,000 Metropolitan prize, 364

Montemezzi, Italo, his "L'Amore dei tre Re" an early success, his "Giovanni Gallurese" a failure, 308

Monteux, Pierre, conducts Gilbert's ballet, "Dance in the Place Congo," 365

Moore, Grace, 9, 96, 226

Morgan, J. P., the elder, responsible for dual management at the Metropolitan, 263

Mozart, Wolfgang Amadeus, 80, 151, 217, 311, 362

Muck, Karl, 44

Mugnone, Leopoldo, tells Russian régisseur how "Pique Dame" should be done, 161

Musicians complain of Toscanini's calling of names, 49

Musicians' union regulates rate of pay, 172

Mussolini, Benito, 162, 163

Mussorgsky, Modest Petrovich, 355

Muzio, Claudia, finds Musetta singing her Mimi, but does her own dying, 36

National Broadcasting Co., 341, 344, 346, 357

National Opera Club, 315

Negro singers limited to minor opera companies, 96

Neuger, Konrad, chorus master, 184

New Theatre, an added burden to the Metropolitan, 168

New York Post, The, 82

Nikisch, Arthur, his fondness for poker, 152

Nissen, Hermann, 92

Nordica, Lillian, her indifference to physique, 9; 80; tribute of student supers, 198

"Norma," 3, 64; revived for Rosa Ponselle and Gina Cigna, 65; Toscanini's refusal to go on with a performance, 58; 129; its effect on a patron when replaced by "Faust," 290; 303, 307

Novak, Joseph, in charge of Metropolitan's scenery, 232, 233

"Oberto Conte di S. Bonifacio," early opera by Verdi, 370

Oenslager, Donald, scenic artist, 51

"Of Thee I Sing," 372

Offenbach, Jacques, 356

Old guard of the opera, 269, 270, 276

Olszewska, Maria, 92

Opéra (Paris), 315; conditions of government's subsidy, 366

Opéra-Comique (Paris), conditions of government's subsidy, 366

Opera News, Metropolitan Opera Guild's magazine, 317

Operas most popular in a ten-year period, 305; those not so often performed, 306; list of those not so popular, 310, 311; number of new works submitted to the Metropolitan management in seven years, 368

"Oracolo, L'," 126, 310

Orchestra players, their trials and tribulations, 164-7

Organ on wheels, 41

"Orpheus," 194

"Otello," 3, 111; its music as test for trombonists and double bass players, 170; 311, 355

Page, Ruth, ballet mistress, 186

"Pagliacci," 25, 34, 197, 209, 215, 287, 295, 303; Canio gets $10, the donkey $15, 352

Papi, Gennaro, 25

Parker, Horatio, wins $10,000 Metropolitan prize with "Mona," 364

"Parsifal," exceeds time limit in performance, 37; 41, 44, 56; put on during the holy days, 63, 155, 165; its music as a test for trombone and trumpet players, 170; 171, 178, 184, 187, 203, 209; its scenic and light effects, 212, 213; 214, 225, 233, 358

Patti, Adelina, 223, 260

Pauly, Rosa, her success in "Elektra," 254

Pay of opera musicians, 172

"Pelléas et Mélisande," 64, 81, 151, 178, 205, 244, 247, 281, 285

"Peter Ibbetson," 68, 183, 307, 364

Petri, Edoardo, director of chorus school, 181

Philadelphia Orchestra, 172

[383]

Index